Voices from Alabama

The University of Alabama Press

Tuscaloosa and London

Voices from Alabama

A Twentieth-Century Mosaic

J. Mack Lofton, Jr.

Photographs selected by
Michael Thomason

Copyright © 1993
The University of Alabama Press
Tuscaloosa, Alabama 35487–0380
All rights reserved
Manufactured in the United States of America

designed by Paula C. Dennis

∞

The paper on which this book is printed meets the minimum
requirements of American National Standard for Information
Science–Permanence of Paper for Printed Library Materials,

Second Printing 1995

Library of Congress Cataloging-in-Publication Data

Lofton, J. Mack, 1928–
    Voices from Alabama : a twentieth-century mosaic / J. Mack Lofton,
Jr. ; photographs selected by Michael Thomason.
        p.   cm.
    ISBN 0-8173-0684-6 (alk. paper)
    1. Alabama—Social life and customs.   2. Alabama—Biography.
3. Interviews—Alabama.   I. Title.
    F326.L63   1993
976.1—dc20   92-36110

British Library Cataloguing-in-Publication Data available

for
Ashley and Tyler,
Rachel and Brooke

Contents

Ole-Time Religion   115

Getting There   125

Preface

It seemed relatively simple at first, sitting in the office of the publisher, planning to write the story of the first half of the twentieth century as told by a cross section of Alabamians. But, as I drove back to Birmingham from Tuscaloosa, I began to wonder about such a vast undertaking and began making some tentative plans on the best way to proceed. I had some experience in finding storytellers across the South and telling their tales in a series of magazine articles. I believed that I would have no problem discovering an army of men and women who would sit down and tell me how they grew up—their triumphs and disasters, how they lived, what they ate, and what they did for entertainment.

The project began in earnest when on a sunny morning in Key Largo, Florida, I walked into the post office with letters to the directors of every library in the state of Alabama. I simply asked each librarian to give me a couple of names of people in the community who could tell a good tale or two about the 1920s, '30s, or '40s. If all the librarians responded, I would have a list of about three hundred names. I returned to Alabama expecting a huge number of letters, but I received correspondence from only about twenty librarians. Incredibly, I received a letter from the director of the library in a major city telling me that nobody in that town was suitable for such an interview.

On a large Alabama map, I stuck colored pins in the names of towns I had heard from and put "plan two" into action. At the locations not covered by colored pins I mailed a similar letter to the manager of the chamber of commerce, again asking for some good storytellers. More pins went up, and a representative pattern began to emerge. I put up more pins after contacting several historical societies.

The next phase of the project involved contacting the people whose names were on my list, telling them about my research, and asking for their help. I was not surprised when all but a few graciously consented to see and talk with me. At this point I had more than a hundred people to talk to, and the matter of geography had to be addressed. I began making appointments close to Birmingham, going out on one-day trips, talking to two people in Sylacauga, for example, and driving to Talladega for two more in the afternoon. My circle widened and I made appointments in a certain area when an overnight trip was required. In this manner I traveled the entire state over a period of five months, talked to more than one hundred men and women, and logged more than two hundred hours of stories on tape.

Some of my plans did not work out as expected and I would find myself in some distant town without anybody to interview. This was no problem. I found that every town has one place, usually a local restaurant, where the "coffee gang" hangs out in the morning, retirees more than likely. I would walk into one of these places, make myself at home, and ask where the storytellers were. In Demopolis, somebody asked, "Why don't you go talk to Hardenia Johnson?" I visited Mrs. Johnson in her home, the walls full of civic awards; she is a black woman who with her husband has put all eight of her children through college. At the Corner Cafe in Demopolis, somebody introduced a subject to me, and fourteen or so patrons commented, making up the story I attribute here to the "Corner Cafe Gang." In another town, I was an hour early for an appointment and walked through the courthouse next door. In the sheriff's office, a colorful individual in cowboy boots and hat was berating a deputy about excessive noise made by pulpwood trucks in front of his house. While waiting to talk to the sheriff, he gave me some good stories about his early life on the edge of the coalfields. At some interviews, my contact would bring a friend eager to tell about his or her early life, and sometimes a person would tell me, "You've just got to talk to my friend who has better stories than I have."

Prior to World War II, Alabama existed as an agrarian state, the people and their activities closely tied to the land. With the exception of small pockets of industrialization such as the steel mills in Birmingham and Gadsden and the cotton mills scattered along the Georgia border, business was related to the raising of cotton and peanuts and the cutting of timber. The merchants and bankers in the small, county-seat towns were affected by the cyclical temperament of crops as they loaned money, extended credit, and sold goods, betting on the ability of the farmer to bring in a profitable harvest.

For the most part, living was hard. Outdoor plumbing, light from kerosene lamps, a dearth of reading material, and the absence of radio, television, telephones, electricity, automobiles, and most (if not all) appliances constituted the norm out in the country and even in some of the towns. Lack of transportation kept most people close to home; many never strayed more than a few miles from where they were born. One person remembers that her community was so isolated that neighbors married neighbors and "if you were a stranger moving in and if you weren't kin when you came down here, you were before you left."

The pattern for the first half of the century was almost the same over the state even though the topography was varied. Farmers in the hilly north scratched their rocky hillside patches with a mule and plow, moving on to new ground when the soil wore out. In the west, they either agonized over the thin topsoil or gloried in the rick, dark dirt along the rivers. Farmers in the southern counties planted cotton and later peanuts, pecan trees, and even citrus and clean-cut thousands of acres of virgin pine forests. In the east, they sometimes came off the farm to work in the cotton mills but their ties to the earth were close and they kept some of the land if they could. And in the middle of the state, they sometimes moved to the coal-mining camps and the company houses of the steel mills, thinking regular wages would be better than the uncertainty of making a cotton crop. But the script was the same, the historical scenario one of haves and have-nots. Strangely enough, conditions were accepted for the most part, because what could people do? Where could they go? Their horizons were limited by what they could see and by their lack of understanding of the world in general.

It might be simplistic to observe that everybody has a story to tell, but I found in moving around the state that each person did have at least one priceless nugget to contribute, and from these nuggets the material was developed. During my odyssey, I found myself on back roads and crossroads, in small and large towns, talking to college presidents and pulpwood workers, ministers, lawyers, bankers, and housewives. I enjoyed the changing scenery—the mountains in the north, the lush farmland of the Black Belt, the flatland below Montgomery down toward the coast.

The first four parts of the book have rough geographical designations as upper and lower Alabama but do not pretend to divide the state exactly in half. Some of the people who were interviewed appear in several sections of the book and county identifications for all who shared remembrances are based on where most of the story took place. In some instances, however, several locations are mentioned in the same piece and the county identifications are the locations where the persons were interviewed.

Alabama provides a rich human landscape, and my goal was to convey a portrait of the times, as told to me by people from across the length and breadth of this wonderful land. I did not consciously seek out representatives of every group, for that would have been a different project altogether—one more suited for the skills of a social scientist than for a collector of tales about human triumph and human persistence.

This, then, is not a history of Alabama in the first part of the twentieth century but a memory book containing personal remembrances of Alabamians from the Tennessee River Valley to Gulf Shores and every place in between. They have some humor, some tragedy, some triumphs, but most of all they give us a feeling of where we came from and a sense of the bedrock foundation of our past.

Acknowledgments

I am indebted to the men and women across the state of Alabama who shared their time and experiences with me while I researched this book. Their stories weave a rich fabric of human experience, and they graciously received me into their homes and offices, remembering other times and other generations. Malcolm M. MacDonald, director of The University of Alabama Press, gave me free rein to develop the material as I found it, letting me work under very liberal guidelines. I also thank Beverly Denbow, copy editor, for her questions, suggestions, and magnificent work in correcting my many mistakes, and Clarke Stallworth, writer, editor, and teacher, for his encouragement before and during the compilation of this book. The *Clarke County Democrat* and *Hometown Magazine* in Huntsville provided valuable research material.

Finally, I could not have finished this book without the patience and understanding of my wife, Rose, whose support and encouragement helped me through the months of its preparation.

Country Life, Upper Alabama

*Hoeing greens, Coffee County, 1941
(John Collier/Farm Security
Administration photo, Library of Congress,
Washington, D.C.)*

The Fields

Willie David Jenkins, Hale County

I was born in Hale County, in Greensboro, Alabama, and my parents farmed, yeah, that's all we ever did was farm. In them days, all the black chillun had to go to the fields, you see. You didn't see nothing black around the house unless it was a chicken or a cow or something 'nother like that. But all us chillun had to go to the fields. I been going to the fields since before I been big enough to walk 'cause they carried us to the fields 'cause everybody went, and if they was a baby, he had to go 'cause they wasn't nobody to take care of that baby at home. Ever since I know myself, I was working. I had five sisters and three brothers. I started picking cotton when I was seven years old. I wasn't big enough to pull a sack so I had to pick and put the cotton in my mama's sack.

The two chillun what was younger than me, why we had to take them to the field in a basket and set them under a shade tree, and if they wasn't no shade tree, we had to find a sassafras bush and put that basket down under that sassafras bush for shade for them chillun. And then we would come by and see about the babies and stuff like that, and Mama nursed the child and go right back to work. I ain't had nothing easy, but I enjoyed it 'cause I didn't know nothing else. So, I work, I work, I work, and when I got a little bigger, I be up about eight or nine years old, Daddy got the pneumonia and I had to do all the plowing and stuff like that. I was so little I couldn't turn the plow around and the mule had to drag it around. I had the line around my neck but the mule had to drag the plow around.

Yeah, we went to school a little bit, but mostly we were in the fields. When we did go to school, we had five miles to walk. Well, see, when you working for somebody else, to get along, you had to do what they wanted you to do. Now, all the winter, we was cleaning up new ground and stuff like that, all around the edge of the pasture, sawing wood. I was the oldest one and I had to saw wood for myself and saw wood for Mr. James Clay, too. He was Route 1, Box 17, Akron, Alabama. That's where we got our mail at and he was our next-door neighbor. So, him and I was about the same age. I had to get wood for them and I had to milk cows for them and I had to feed their mules and stuff like that. When I was doing that, why they gave me three meals a day and fifty cents a day, and I was making some money then. Yes, sir. I guess I was about twelve. This was along about 1932.

Miss Mattie Clay learnt me how to drink milk. It's bad to say that, but they did. I didn't even know how to drink milk. What I would do is suck it up, you see, and they stopped me from sucking up that milk and coffee. They feed me in the kitchen and all the white folks they eat in the dining room and stuff like that, see. And so, I be back there in the kitchen just sucking up that milk and Miss Mattie Clay come back there and taught me how to drink that milk. Then, sometimes I work all month and didn't get nary a dime 'cause when they didn't pay no fifty cents a day, they paid eight dollars a month. Then when the end of the month come, he don't have the money and he say, "I ain't got none and if I get ahold of some, we'll pay you." Well, you had to keep on working 'cause you couldn't leave 'cause where you going? You go to 'nother one and he want to know why you comin' to him. I stayed there working around with Mr. James Clay 'til I got grown.

My mama learned me how to count. Mr. James Clay and all of them were going to school 'cause they had a school bus, but we played together anyhow. The only time we rode the school bus was to play ball. It sho' was. When Miss Mattie Clay would go out, she leave Mr. James over there with us, and when we couldn't go with my mama and 'em, we went over and played with the white chillun. But we couldn't go to school with 'em 'cause we had to work. We worked all the time, even when it was raining we had to work. We had to shell corn. We had to shuck corn. We had to kill rats out of the crib. We had to pick off peanuts and stuff like that. That's what we did all wintertime. Now, in the summertime, it didn't get too bad to work. You know these gloves people have now? We didn't have none of that. We plowed out there bare-hand. We had one pair of shoes in the wintertime. Got one pair of shoes in the summertime, and that's all. They would give us a pair of overalls, a new pair of slipover underwear—you know what they was—one jumper, and a cap with the ears on them and them big glasses on them.

We played ball, though. That's all we did was work and play ball and I could play ball. We were good on playing ball 'cause we didn't have nothing else to do. And I could pitch a ball and we would ride over to Eutaw on that school bus to play ball. And down there in Sipsey to play them boys over there and they come over here to play us. Yeah, I'm talking about baseball, 'cause there wasn't no football for us, 'cause we could play baseball down in them big pastures. That's the reason we grow so. We just run and played and work. One time we were playing across the Sipsey River and we were winning and The Man from the other team come up to me—I was pitching, see—and he say to me, "Goddam, you let my man hit that ball." We had to do it, we had to lose. And Mr. James Clay, he say to me, "David"—he called me David—he say, ah, "David, let 'em win." I kind of lightened up on my pitching, kind of lobbing up there. We get away from here, we won't be coming back. And then we let 'em win, but it didn't do no bit of good. Most times, you do something bad enough, they kill you and throw you in the Sipsey River and you never be found. We come along on that bus and they all down there on the side of the road shooting those shotguns at that school bus, and Mr. James Clay say, "You-all hit the floor! Hit the floor!" Well, they ain't going to shoot Mr. James Clay. They want to shoot us, even though we let them win.

On the Mountain

Houston Cole, DeKalb County

I was born on Lookout Mountain out from Fort Payne on the twenty-fourth of November, 1899, in a little community called Coon Rock. Old doctor Killian got up about two o'clock in the morning and rode a horse two miles to our house, delivered me, and had breakfast in our home before leaving, and that's how I came into the world.

My father was a farmer in part. He had twelve children by his first wife, of which I was the eleventh, and three children by his second wife, and now, I'm leading up to this. He had all that responsibility of feeding all those children, and you know there was no government to help then, and he grew all kinds of vegetables, watermelons and other vegetables during the crop season, and after, when the crops were laid by. He would get up at two o'clock in the morning three times a week, hitch up the mules, make his own breakfast, and head toward Fort Payne. The day before, we would have loaded up the wagon with vegetables that he would take to town to sell. It would take my father three hours to reach Fort Payne and it would take him about two hours to sell out. He didn't have any trouble selling his produce because he had good stuff and people would buy it. He would come home with ten or fifteen dollars in his pocket, and that was a lot of money at that time, and that was how we lived. If we had just depended on the so-called cash crops, we would have been in bad shape. Our cash supply back then came from cotton and corn and peddling the produce.

There were so many of us that four children would sleep in one room. My father and mother and two younger kids would sleep in another room, but the rest of us slept about four to a room, you see. As for relieving ourselves, we would go out behind the woodpile or out in the woods, or in the barn if we wanted to be secret, and that was true everywhere about the turn of the century. There were no indoor facilities or a "little house out back" even. Our house had a big porch with a big rocking chair on it. My dad would get up about four o'clock on the mornings he didn't go to town and we would have breakfast about five. We never did sleep much later than five because we had to get out and go to work. During the farming season, we would go out and work until about 11:30 in the morning, come in and take off an hour and a half to eat dinner, lie down on the porch to take a little nap, and then take the mule out and start back to work.

Back at that time, I chopped cotton and plowed, and the girls worked in the fields, too. My mother and stepmother never worked in the fields because they were too busy cooking for our big bunch. We never suffered for food because my dad was active, always looking to the future. Not all the farmers around there looked ahead and some of them about starved. In the wintertime, we would feed the farm animals and prepare for spring planting. By that I mean there were a lot of woods up there on that mountain and we would clear away some of those woods and put that land under cultivation the next spring.

Discipline problems? You can imagine my dad had some discipline problems with fifteen children. He would use a switch if necessary. You see, my grandfather was killed in the Civil War and my father came up under his grandparents and he was one generation removed from the philosophy of raising children. If a kid didn't behave, he got punished, and that's all there was to it.

Our mail came out from Collinsville in a buggy. Mr. Cunningham was the carrier at the time. The mail came out every day except holidays.

At Christmastime, we boys got together enough money to buy some firecrackers. You would get about fifty for ten cents, so at night we would celebrate by pulling them off one at a time and let them go. This was about nineteen and four and nineteen and five. My mother always had something a little special on the table on Christmas Day but there never were any presents. None of that at all. The closest store was about a quarter of a mile away and it was operated by Will Jackson. Now, his daughter was married to one of my brothers so we always got a little concession at the store.

While we were kids, my dad put about eight of us and my mother on a train there in Collbran and we went all the way out below Fort Worth, Texas, to a farm that my uncle had. Somebody had told my dad that if you go out to Texas you'll get rich. That train ride to Texas was an awful experience. I remember that my younger brother cried all the way from Collbran to New Orleans. My dad was awfully unhappy in Texas, so at the end of about nine months, after one crop, we all took the train back to Lookout Mountain.

Gunters Mountain

Burton Troup, Marshall County

I was born in 1909 in Grant community, a crossroads settlement up on the mountain. My granddaddy's house was on one corner of the crossroads, a big general store and a post office was on another corner, and across the way on another corner was a wood house. About 1911 or 1912, Tommy Stewart was taking some pictures of my family one day and he came out from under the hood and walked across the road and gathered up a bunch of bushes and brought them back and put them down in front of Papa's feet. I wondered about why he did that, and about two years later, another baby was added and we had another picture made. Now, Papa was quite dressed up but it looked like he had on his cow shoes and Tommy was looking for some excuse to cover up those shoes so he broke off another bunch of branches and put them in front of Papa's feet.

Papa was a farmer. He had one little patch of new ground and it produced a lot more than the old, worn-out land because that was before we started using fertilizer. Well, if they had known about fertilizer, they couldn't have hauled it up there on that mountain. Papa thought if he could find some more new ground he would have it made. He found two hundred acres of virgin timber and bought it. When he bought it, he sold our old farm and started building a new house. He found out pretty soon that the new place wasn't worth one-fourth of what it would cost to clear off the timber. Two men with a crosscut saw cutting those big old trees that had never been cut—why, it would take them years to clear a patch. But it was too late then because he had already put his money in it. He was down there in Willis Hollow one day with a neighbor trying to decide the land lines and he looked up and an idea came to him. There was a steep, crooked road coming up that mountain and he had the idea of cutting a new road, a straight road up the mountain. They took drills and hammers and dynamite and he and some neighbors built that new road, three-quarters of a mile. Papa got that road built just in time for the DAR folks to come up on that mountain and decide to build a school there.

The main thing on that mountain was Sears, Roebuck and Company. How that mail carrier carried all of that and got it delivered in a buggy, I don't know. Sometimes we would order coats and caps and things for four or five kids and get the orders all mixed up and have to reorder. When we got up to about the fifth grade, we were getting highly educated and thought we would help some of those people fill out orders for Sears and Roebuck. We thought we were real big when somebody would ask us to help them because they couldn't write, you see. This was about 1917. What we would do is get together later and compare notes about what different people had ordered. One I remember was this lady told me to order a pair of shoes and such and such catalog number and she said to tell Sears to send them in time for Decoration Day because Mary wanted to wear them to Decoration. One woman ordered a dress and she said to be sure to get it here because Sue wanted to wear it to the picnic in Will Campbell's pasture . . . if it don't rain. We wrote it down just like they said. Stanley, the boy who thought he was a horse, he ordered one of the first disc records. When it came, the heat had got to it and it had kind of melted down, you know. Stanley wrote them back and said, "Dear Sears and Roebuck, that record I ordered, when it come it was cupped up like a frying pan. I'm not asking you for another one but I just wanted you to know it wudn't no good."

My uncle Oscar had a little gristmill and he powered it with a little gasoline engine and so he ordered a real high-priced battery from Sears Roebuck. It worked for a time or two, but Uncle Oscar was out there and he turned and turned and turned but it wouldn't start. Uncle Oscar looked down at the ground and said he was going to write Sears Roebuck and Company a letter. We always said "Sears Roebuck and Company" because we thought Sears was his first name. Uncle Oscar said he was going to start it off like this: "Dear Sears Roebuck and Company . . . Dear son of a bitch."

One thing I looked forward to was the triweekly *Constitution* from Atlanta. The *Constitution* had continued stories. We lived a quarter of a mile from the mailbox and I would run over there to get the paper because I just couldn't wait to catch up on the stories. My favorite story ever was "Girl of the Golden West" and lots of times I would run that quarter of a mile and find an empty box and I would have to wait two or three more days. I learned to read real early, but the only thing we had in the house was a Holy Bible. Well, Mr. Riley Ledbetter, the principal of our two-teacher school, had a little cabinet with about three hundred books in it and he filled that cabinet with books ranging from the first grade up to *Robinson Crusoe* and *Gulliver's Travels*. In time, I read every book in that library and some of them twice. When school was out, he made arrangements with our cousin Grace Bryan to give me the key to that cabinet. The school was never locked, but the cabinet was and I had the key to many hours of enjoyment.

Of course we all went to church. We would be down at the church and they would sing "Give Me That Ole-Time Religion," it will save us when we are dying, and it was good for Paul and Silas, but I didn't know any Paul and Silas. I would ask Mama who Paul and Silas were and she would try to tell me about heaven and hell, and hell stayed with me. I never did think about heaven much for worrying so much about hell. That liked to have scared me to death.

The roads were always in real bad shape up on that mountain and you would see bad mud-holes all over the place. One day, I was out playing and my aunt Liza who had twins called my mama on the telephone. They had telephones up on the mountain almost before they had roads. Aunt Liza asked Mama to meet here down at the mud-hole between our houses. That mud-hole was so big that you couldn't get the baby buggy around the hole on the high side and I walked the buggy around on the low side while Mama and Aunt Liza carried the babies. When they got home, they took the babies in the house and I would push that carriage around, up the road and down to the barn. I was having the best time I had ever had in my life, I think, and about then, a man came along down the road on a bicycle. I can still see that man sitting there and it looked like he was just floating along, and those bright wire spokes in those wheels were flashing. That just about set me on fire. I pushed that baby carriage up to the porch and never did pick it up anymore. I had done got beyond pushing a baby carriage. The next bicycle I ever saw was when I came to town when I was ten years old, and it was the first time I had ever been to town.

Nineteen nineteen was the first time I came to town. I knew two or three days before that I was coming, and I was so excited that I couldn't sleep. I had visualized all sorts of things that a town would look like. We lived out there with woods all around and Daddy didn't smoke and when we got down to the ferry and crossed the river, I could start smelling that cigar smoke and the coal smoke and the rest of the town odors. I've heard that there were some of those people up there on Gunters Mountain that never did go to town. They had dances and all.

My daddy had a string band. My aunt Ada beat the strings of the fiddle and my uncle Lon played something and I had some cousins that were real fiddlers. My brother, the last boy, came along about fifteen years later right at about the time when menopause was supposed to set in, and Papa got him a fiddle and you ought to hear that boy play. I remember my daddy coming in at night and playing on his fiddle, Casey Jones and whatnot. They would have the dances over there at Grandpa's house over in Honeycomb Valley and the house had a big wide hallway and they would come over there.

Old man Stewart bought his daughters an organ and the people in the community would come there at night and play and sing. Old man Stewart got to fussing at his daughters and they said, "Daddy, we can't tell them not to come." One night, he told his wife that he knew how to fix them. Now, old man Stewart slept with just his old shirt on, and one night he just went in there with just this old shirt on and ran round and round just in his shirt. They really did scatter and his daughters just cried and cried about it.

Both Mama and Daddy could sing real good and my mama would sing tearjerkers, boy. She would sit there at that sewing machine and sew and sing. She would sing that "Dying Cowboy" and when she would get down a few lines, man, I would just cry, and I would get up and slip out so the other kids wouldn't see me crying. I would sit out there and my heart would be just broken and then I would compose myself and go back in the house and the kids would be wham-banging and they hadn't heard one word about why I was crying. And Mama would sing "as I walked out in the streets of Laredo," and I was the only child who was affected this way.

I remember about the time that World War I was over, we got the wrong signal out on Gunters Mountain one night and people celebrated, but it was too soon. On November eleventh, the war was over, but the word didn't get out there 'til hours after they knew in town, and Daddy went in the house and got his old shotgun and he would stand out there and shoot. Boy, they were happy.

When I got out of high school in 1929, I came home and my daddy had seven acres in strawberries and he had me out there. Now, I hadn't been out there in the hot sun, going to school and all, and it was about nine o'clock in the morning and I knew my mother wasn't at home. I was standing in that strawberry patch with a six-quart handy about half-filled and I carried that handy up to the packing shed, set it down, and went home, got my few duds in a suitcase, and walked about a mile and a half to the bus line and borrowed fifty cents from my cousin to get to New Hope. I had an uncle over there and I knew he would let me have some money. While I was waiting on the bus, a man came along and said I could ride with him, and I gave my cousin that fifty cents back. I got forty dollars from my uncle and I ended up in Detroit and that was in 1929.

Ice and Eggs

Betty Crawford Ferguson, Hale County

I lived out in the country about ten miles from Greensboro, and in the thirties we didn't even have an icebox at our house. We would come into town on Saturday and my daddy had a car, but most of our neighbors didn't have a car, and we would haul ice in our car for our neighbors. When we got home from town, we would wrap our ice up in a blanket and bury it in a sawdust pile. Every morning about 11:30, our job was to go out to the sawdust pile and get a chunk of ice, wash it, and put it in the glasses for dinner. I was about ten years old when we got electricity. We had a lot of hands out there on the farm and my mother would have to fix dinner for the cotton pickers and cotton choppers, and as long as the ice lasted, we would put ice in their glasses, too. Another job we had was to ring the dinner bell at 11:30 and all the hands would come in. We fed all the hands in the kitchen. Everybody had wood stoves back then for cooking and we used that wood stove for heating water and for washing dishes and taking baths.

The only day we came into town was on Saturday. Everybody came into town then and the stores would stay open way late, sometimes until midnight waiting on the trade. Our family always got home before dark, though. And we would go to the picture show on Saturday. We got in with two eggs. We would wait for the hens to lay, and if they didn't lay, we were in trouble. We put the eggs in a sack and carefully brought them into town. Down at the picture show, they had a tester to see if the eggs were rotten or not before we could get in. Instead of giving them a dime at the box office, we gave them two eggs. The children would go to the picture show while Mama and Daddy did their shopping. My daddy also brought produce and eggs into town on Saturday and sold them.

Coming Off the Farm

Tom Roberson, Talladega County

The Robersons I came from migrated to North Carolina from England. They went by wagon train to Rome, Georgia, built barges, and floated down the Coosa River to Cedar Creek where they settled. They built a dam there on Cedar Creek and built a mill and crushed meal for the Indians and traded with the Indians. That's in Talladega Springs, a little due west of Sylacauga.

My daddy was one-eyed, so World War I wouldn't take him as a soldier, but they took him and taught him how to run a sawmill and to be a carpenter. When the war was over, he went to Sylacauga and was very successful as a contractor until the depression hit. Then, he lost his business and had to move back to the farm. Now, I was young but I was big. All Robersons were early bloomers, so consequently, I was forced to do a man's work while I was still a child because I was as big as most men. I had finished the second grade and had just started the third grade—that makes me nine years old— and I'm working as a man. Daddy pulled out of that pretty quick though, and we moved back to town after five years on the farm. I surely was glad to get off that farm because it was sheer agony the kind of work I had to do.

All our entertainment was at the church. On Sunday, you went home with somebody or they went home with you. The older people would sit out there on the porch and rock and talk and the young people would play. Well, they were sitting out there on the porch one day, talking, and I was lying down out there under a cottonwood tree close by because I was too tired to play. Up there on the porch, they were talking about Mr. Victor Russell, that he owned a lot of land and stayed dressed up all the time. I heard them saying that Mr. Russell was a college graduate. I didn't know what a college graduate was, never heard that term, but it stuck in my mind that if that was what he is and he owned all that land and stayed dressed up all the time that that was what I ought to be. So, on Monday at school when we went out for recess, I hung back and I asked my teacher, I said, "What is a college graduate?" and she was kind of taken back, but she explained it to me. She told me that I was capable of doing it if I wanted to, so from that day on, I knew I was going to be a college graduate.

After we moved back to Sylacauga, I pretty well had it made after that. I played ball all year long: baseball, tennis, track, football, and whatever was in season. We just had one coach and if we had a baseball game that afternoon, we played baseball, and if we had a track meet, we went to the track, and if it was tennis, we went to the tennis court. I played everything. When I graduated from Sylacauga High School in 1941, colleges didn't give basketball scholarships back in those days. Football players played on the basketball team and the other boys played just because they liked basketball.

I went to Alabama on a football scholarship and they put me at tackle. I played end in high school and I was just as big when I was fourteen as I was at twenty and that was about 210 pounds. When I got to Alabama, the big surprise to me was that the other players were as big and strong as I was. The team went to the Cotton Bowl that year, but freshmen couldn't go. Freshmen were just tackling dummies. I had been to the campus before I enrolled. After my freshman year in high school, we used to go down to Tuscaloosa to coaching clinics and a lot of the regular football players would be on campus working out and we would get to see them. I remember Charlie Boswell was down there. I thought he was the greatest thing that ever lived. He had beautiful form as a halfback. Boy!

The Omen

Fannie Buchanan, Jefferson County

Back in the twenties, what I remember first was Mississippi when I was about three or four. I was born in Mount Hebron, Alabama, but the family migrated to the Mississippi Delta, what they called it back then. While we were living in Mississippi, what we heard about was that the big river was always flooding and my mama was always afraid about that. It would overflood was what we would hear, but it didn't flood while I was over there.

One time, seems like we wanted to move from where we were to somewhere else and this white man came by—they called him a "riding boss"—and he was riding on a beautiful horse. I was too little to understand what was said, but when the riding boss turned his horse around to ride away, my mother threw a can at him. The next thing I remember was that we were living somewhere else, on another plantation. At that time, my father got what they called the pellagra and he couldn't work. We were very poor, but we didn't know that. Seems like we had something to eat and a roof over us and something to wear. We ate whatever there was to eat, like milk and butter and peas and greens, and a lot of that cane syrup. Just whatever was available. My daddy got better, and they used to go work on the levee when the river was threatening. They called it sandbagging. I remember I could see this train coming in and it was just people everywhere in the train, coming down to help with the sandbagging.

I saw my first movie about this time. It was Tom Mix and it was silent, no noise at all. I remember Tom Mix looked like he was sleeping and then he woke up. When he got up, he started coming at us, right at us, and we thought he was going to jump off that screen and walk on us.

My mother kept on worrying about the river rising and flooding us out. Along about 1926, they were working on an airport close to where we were and they put up some lights to shine at night so the airplanes could see how to come in. We were visiting a friend one night and my mother saw this light, a beacon light up on a tall stand, and this light was going round and round and it looked to us like it was just up there in the sky all by itself, going round and round. Mama never did like Mississippi, always afraid of the floods, and she got the idea that this light up in the sky was an omen, an omen telling us that a flood was about to happen. That's when she told my daddy that she wasn't going to stay there any more. She said she was going back to the hills, and that's what she called Alabama. My daddy told her that at the end of the year that she and the children could leave, so we left and moved back to my uncle's house in Gainesville.

We moved back to Gainesville from Mississippi in the late twenties. Well, it was out from Gainesville and I called it "plumnelly"—plum out of the county and nelly out of the world. It was interesting because I got the whooping cough, pretty sick, and my uncle gave me milk from a horse to help get me well. That's another reason I call myself a survivor. I was just a little girl, but I knew there was something out there beyond where I was. We had a fig tree and I used to climb up in that fig tree. Somehow, I could lay back and I would just space right out. My mother would pass by under that tree calling out for me and I could not answer her. My body heard her, but my spirit was gone. I couldn't think of places up in that tree because I didn't know where they were, but I just drifted—just drifted—taking myself out of that place.

That river flooded the year after we left and my daddy said that flood was awesome and he moved back to Gainesville, too. He came back with a horse named Charlie and a mule named Hattie and started farming again around Gainesville. We called all white people back then "Mr. Charlie," because usually we didn't know their names. We didn't have any contact with them, so they were all "Mr. Charlie." All of us lived with Uncle Perse for a few years and then moved to a place of our own. That house wasn't very good and we sometimes had to put the tub on one side while we slept on the other, and that tub was to catch the water when the roof leaked. It was a big house with a tin top but there were only three rooms and everybody lived together. We had never seen an electric light except in the stores and I didn't see an electric light in a house until I visited in Ensley in 1932. Living out there in the country, we didn't know about any depression because we had what we had always had, no more and no less. Everybody had about the same. I remember there was a white couple, lived on the riverbank, and they had a goat. We called them the "goat people." My aunt used to help them, give them things, and that white man used to come and play checkers with my uncle.

In 1936, I got married and I moved into Gainesville. Before I got married, I went to a school called Fremont and it had six grades. Our teacher was a man named Prime Lemon and I still don't know how he handled all those six grades. We lived out about three miles from the town. We would go to town on Saturday after working in the fields all week and I would meet my future husband, Wallace, up there. Sometimes, we would have a dime and we could buy a Nehi and some candy. When we went to town, there was nothing to do but walk around and visit with each other. I was seeing my future husband around town and sometimes he would come out to my house to see me. Wallace and my daddy worked together as field hands for the Rogerses, our "Mr. Charlie" at the time. Wallace came to see me one day and said something in my daddy's presence that offended him. Daddy told Wallace, "Don't you ever come to my house again." My daddy used to get drunk, so he got drunk and raised all kind of sand and Wallace left. But before he left, Wallace told me to meet him in town the next Saturday. Come Saturday, I had no intention of going to town because I wasn't worried about getting married. I was about eighteen and had been thinking about going to California to visit some relatives. My sister talked me into going into town, anyway. While I was in town, I bumped into Wallace, and they had something called the public square. It was nothing but a well and a little houselike thing where you could sit and watch the people come and go. Wallace and I walked up to the square, and on the way back, we met Wallace's daddy and he said to me, "Fannie"—that was his wife—"Fannie said come up there to the house." I asked what did she want and he said he didn't know. My sister and I went up there to the house. Wallace said, "Let's get married," and I said, "Huh?" and he said it again. I didn't say anything, and the next thing I knew they had sent out for the preacher and we got married

right there in the house. My mother-in-law had gotten the marriage
certificate about two weeks before that, but I didn't know it. See, we
had talked about getting married some, but I had been thinking
about going to California, and besides that, I had had enough of the
country. I didn't know about the outside world, but I knew there was
something out there past those cotton fields.

So, we got married that day. It was June 6, 1936. After the wedding, both of us were scared to death, so I just got back in the wagon
with the people I had come to town with and went on back home.
This was my wedding night. Wallace came to get me the next day
and we moved in with his grandmother. My daddy was so mad he
didn't speak to me for almost a year.

Sharecropping on Sand Mountain

E. L. Lovelady, Marshall County

We were sharecroppers down in Clay County where I was born. The
old house was like all the other tenant houses, two or three feet off
the ground with no underpinning. The house I was born in was just
four rooms with a hand-split wood-shingle roof. It sat up about three
feet off the ground on rock pillars, no block or bricks, just rocks.
My brother and I used to play under that house, play with bottles
and whatever to make roads in the dirt. We had a front porch there
which was the highest part of the house and a little back porch, a
kind of stoop where we would go in and out, you know, when we
wanted to. One time when I was about three years old and we had a
kitten and I would chase him around the house, and I mean I would go
after him and Mama would holler at me to stop chasing that kitten.
We had a closet beside the fireplace, and instead of going into the
closet, the kitten jumped in the fire. The kitten caught fire in there
and you talking about a cat screaming and squalling. The cat caught
fire and it was killed, pretty cruel, but I didn't realize what I was
doing. I got in bad trouble because of that and Mama tore me up.

We didn't have anything hardly to play with in the way of bought toys. We had to make our own fun. My brother and I played with toad frogs, dig a hole back in the dirt and put that frog in there and block him in, make a little gate and you know, all that kind of thing. My brother, Landress, was born two years before me, and since we all had to work, he was put to plowing early, like about six years old. I remember Landress trying to plow a mule on a rocky hillside. Can you imagine a six-year-old kid trying to hold a plow? He would cry and he would squall and fall down trying to hold that plow, but he was trying to learn and get by.

We moved to Sand Mountain when I was about nine years old. It was in the summer of 1937, early summer, and we moved on a ton-and-a-half truck. We had to hire somebody to move us up there, and we got all of our furniture on that truck, and it wasn't very loaded. We put old Betty, our cow, on that truck, too. When my daddy got through paying the man for moving us, all he had left in the world was two dollars. So, we got to Sand Mountain with two dollars, enough furniture to sort of keep house, and old Betty to milk. We were so poor when we got to Sand Mountain that we weren't about to make a crop on the halves, so we had to get out and hire out to work.

That fall when the cotton would begin to open, people would hire you to pick that cotton and we got about thirty-five cents a hundred. We stayed in the house with Grandpa for about three or four weeks 'til we found another place that had a little more room. I was almost ten and my brother was twelve and we started hiring out to pick cotton. My mama and daddy and we boys walked and picked cotton the whole fall as long as we could find some to pick. I remember we picked twenty-one bales of cotton that fall, two kids and Mama and Papa. We would walk two or three miles before daylight wherever we could find cotton to pick because we were trying to get in shape to get a little more furniture, some plow tools, and a mule and start making a crop.

I remember everywhere we went, we walked and we'd be there at daylight waiting to pick cotton. We always carried our lunch in a bucket and most of the time swung it up in a tree where a dog or a hog wouldn't get it. I remember one time we carried a lunch bucket a pretty good distance from where we lived. I don't remember who hung that bucket in the tree, but they didn't get it high enough off the ground. We got ready to eat, and boy, we were hungry and it was about noontime. We went for the bucket, but a hog had got into the bucket and just tore the food up, messed it up. We didn't have anything for lunch and we were about three miles from the house. Finally, a rolling store—which is a peddling truck—came along about 1:30. Daddy just happened to have some money, a very little, not too much because he never did have very much, and we bought enough from that rolling store to get us by. From then on, we made sure that the bucket was tied up high.

We would get to a place and sometimes waited for the dew to get off the cotton, but most times we started picking when it was pretty wet. If it happened to be cloudy and windy and there was no dew it was all right, but buddy, if it's clear and still, that cotton's going to be heavy. The cotton would stick to your hands, and I remember the burrs were pretty bad, pretty sharp. You had to go into that burr to pull the cotton out. I was always a good cotton picker, pretty swift, pretty fast. My brother was a little slow and I was better than he was. But now, my daddy was the hardest man to beat that I ever tried to beat picking cotton. You might beat him three or four pounds when you weighed up, but the next time . . . look out! He would have you beat ten or twelve pounds, along in there.

I remember eating as many as ten biscuits for breakfast, and I'm talking about good-sized biscuits, because as hard as we worked, it was a long time until twelve o'clock. My mother had to cook big pans of biscuits to last us.

We'd get started picking and Daddy would say, "Let's go, boys. Let's go. You're doing good." And man, we'd just work, I'm going to tell you. After a while, Daddy would get to singing old fa-so-la Sacred Heart songs. I didn't understand it but it was music to me. Entertaining. Sometimes you could hear a neighbor over a quarter-mile away trying to yodel as he was plowing a mule. Sometimes we'd get tickled at somebody trying to sing without a very good voice, but they were singing and they sounded happy, like they had something to sing about.

During the fall, when all the cotton was being picked and we were hunting for people that needed cotton picked, we would also pull corn for anybody that needed corn pulled. I can remember snow being on the ground, and a young boy like I was, being out in the field to help my daddy pull corn. But we were proud to do it because we were trying to help our parents survive and get in shape to rent a crop some place. And just imagine being able to farm on the halves. Now, when you farmed on the halves, you furnished the mule and the plow tools and the labor. The landlord furnished the house, such as it was, and the land and the fertilizer and the seed. You did all the work; you planted, you plowed, you harvested the crop, and you gave the landlord half and you kept half.

I believe it was in 1938 after we went through that cotton picking deal that we rented a place on halves. That spring, Daddy borrowed one hundred dollars to make a crop on. That fall, when we got through gathering and got everything sold, we had forty dollars left out of that one hundred dollars. Daddy only spent sixty dollars in that period of about six months from the time in the spring when he borrowed the money. So, you know, we didn't have much when we lived for six months on sixty dollars and five in the family. That's when we began farming on halves.

Everything was done with mules, you know, and our mules had names and our horses, too. We had two horses, black horses, and one of them was named Dan and the other one was Smoky. Our cow was named Betty, and of course, our dogs had names. We had a little feist dog, a black dog named Nig. One of the smartest little dogs I ever saw. You could go off out in the field with Nig, and she knew that you wanted a rabbit. She just seemed to know it and would jump a rabbit real quick. If you went into the woods, she'd tree you a squirrel. At night, we would go out into the woods and that dog would tree you a possum. Give her an hour or so and she'd find five or six possums. My brother liked to hunt better that I did and he wanted to stay in the woods, but Daddy kept us mostly in the fields. We did spend a lot of time in the woods, but that was times we were pulling a crosscut saw.

Now, we didn't name our hogs. That's one thing we didn't name because we knew that, sooner or later, we would kill them, and we just didn't want to get that close. You'd reach down and pet one, but you never named him because you knew that you were going to eat him for meat. We talked to our animals in different ways. You didn't call a mule. You whistled a certain whistle and he knew how to answer. When a mule brayed, he had to stop whatever else he was doing, like if you were plowing about eleven o'clock, the mule would stop and bray like he was saying he was hungry or thirsty. Horses would ninny. When you called a cow, you'd say, "Sook, heifer! Sook, heifer!" To run a hog away, you'd say, "Sooey, sooey!" When a hog got out, he didn't want to go the way you wanted him to at all.

Even when I was a young boy about eleven or twelve years old, I began to think about our lives sharecropping, about how hard everything was and wondering about my life. I wondered, is this the way my life is going to be? Am I going to sharecrop all my life? I could see some people who owned their own farms, but I couldn't see where we could get in any kind of shape to ever own a farm. Some few people even owned automobiles. My Grandfather Smith had an old '27 Chevrolet that he bought new, but it stayed in his shed most of the time because he didn't want to run it.

When we were picking cotton, I would have to go to the gin at night. We went to the gin at Albertville from the White Oak community. The pavement started right out of town and I looked at those houses that were so much better than the house where we lived. Those houses were painted and I lived in a sharecropper house that had never seen paint. Those town houses had to be warmer and the folks that lived in them dressed better than we did. They had electric lights while we had coal-oil lamps. All that time, I had been happy having nothing until I saw all of those people who had everything. Then I noticed that town people had better shoes than I did and most of them wore dress shoes and I wore old work shoes with dirt spilled all over them.

We wore overalls and my mother made guano-sack shirts. She made our underwear out of sacks, too. She put the sacks in wash pots and boiled them to get all the fertilizer out, but they'd have 6-8-4 or 7-10-3 or 6-8-8 printed on them, whatever the formula was. She would put some dye in the pot and boil the sacks and then wash them and they were always either brown or green. She didn't get all the numbers out of the cloth and people could see the numbers and say, well, he's using 6-8-4 or 7-10-3 or 6-8-8. We wore guano-sack underwear, and boy, it was rough as sandpaper. That stuff was tough, and she even made sheets out of fertilizer sacks and it was like lying on sandpaper. Later on, we got to where we could afford flour-sack sheets, and man, that felt like silk compared to fertilizer-sack sheets.

We seemed to move every year and try to do better, but never could find anything much better. Looking back, we had just the bare necessities to live. We had a bed, and most of the time, a bed in the living room. There was a bed in the room where the fireplace was, and sometimes two beds if the room was big enough. In the room where the fireplace was, we had the bed and two or three old straight-back cane-bottom chairs with some of the rounds broken and a nail keg or two. In the wintertime, that old open fireplace didn't do a whole lot of good when we had that north wind, I'm going to tell you, when it came up through those cracks in the floor. You'd have to get up every few minutes to get closer to the fire. What you were doing is getting warm on one side and freezing on the other. I remember, back then, girls' and women's legs would be a different color up to their knees from standing so close to the fire. We would have to get up every five or ten minutes to turn around.

We had a homemade table in the kitchen with an old Home Comfort wood stove. We got good food out of that old wood stove though, but I finally figured out why the food was so good. Everybody always bragged about how good the biscuits were off the Home Comfort wood stove, but they were so good because we worked so darn hard, buddy, when you sat down to eat, anything was good. I don't care what it was. We had an apple crate nailed on the wall for holding dishes and a cat hole cut in the kitchen door where the cat went in and out. The fireplace looked good when it got going, but I don't ever remember being warm in the wintertime as a young man. We had an old wash pan that was kept out on the back porch on a shelf with a water bucket and a dipper and a piece of homemade soap. We had to wash in the wash pan. Now, you kind of gave your feet a lick and a promise on a cold night, and that old cold water on the face, you didn't rub that on too hard, either. In the summertime, we just filled up a washtub out of the wells and the sun would warm it. We would take a bath about once a week, maybe.

Most of our wells were dug wells, but sometimes we would have a spring nearby. We wore our overalls about all week without changing because it was a lot of trouble to wash back then. You had to draw all of your water out of a well, then heat it. We had a big old paddle for washing. You washed the overalls, then laid them out on a stump or a block of wood and beat them with that paddle. Then you rinsed them in a tub of clean water. Those overalls got so dirty, they would just about stand up by themselves in a week's time after all that plowing and other work.

When I was a teenager, I was old enough to go to the cotton gin at night after picking cotton all day. I had to hook up the mules to the wagon and it would be loaded with cotton. The way we went, it was four miles to Albertville where White's Gin was. It would take an hour or more to get to the gin over those old bumpy, rocky roads. I'd get there and the wagons would be lined up at the gin and you would have to wait a long time to get your cotton ginned. Finally, about ten or eleven o'clock at night, you'd get ginned off and head for home. The road was so rough and bumpy you had to stand kind of on your toes in the wagon because it'd just jar your insides out almost. You had to stand up there because there wasn't any place to sit down. We had these high sideboards on for hauling the cotton and you just stood there and kind of held on.

I would be riding home and it would be a clear night, October or November, and you had frost and it would be cold. Maybe the moon would be shining and the clouds would move over the moon and it would get dark, then a little lighter as the clouds would pass over and you could see the white cotton in the fields again. I would pass by houses and couldn't see any light because most people had been in bed for a couple of hours, and you realized that it would be another hour or more before you would get home. Way off out yonder, you could hear the whippoorwills and do some serious thinking about why am I here and what am I going to do to make a living. Coming up to the house, I would see a light left on for me to see how to get in, a coal-oil lamp in the window. And when you got home, you'd have to take the mules out, feed them, take the gear off, and go on up to the house. Then, I would get in bed about midnight or after and think—it ain't long 'til getting up time about 4 A.M. and the whole thing starts over again.

Country Life, Lower Alabama

*Potato farmer and his family, Baldwin
County, circa 1940
(S. Blake McNelly Collection, University of
South Alabama Archives, Mobile)*

Salt Water and Seafood

Joy Buskens, Baldwin County

All the people on my daddy's side have always been fishermen. When they first came down here to the Gulf Shores area, everything had to be brought in by boat. From the beach area, there were no roads coming in or out. The area was virtually uninhabited except by fishing people. Back in the old days before ice or refrigeration, a fisherman would go out, net his fish, and bring them back to shore in live wells. These wells were big boxes with holes in them which were towed off the bow of the boat. Then they would take these fish by horse and wagon down to the landing and another boat would transport them over to the mainland. If the wind was good, they got them over to Mobile all right, but if the wind was bad and they were delayed, they would have to shove the fish overboard. My great-grandfather, John Steiner, had a boat and he would anchor his boat out from the shore, and the other boats—like oystermen and shrimpers—would come up and unload in his boat. He would take these catches to Mobile or Bayou La Batre to sell. When engines began to come in back in the twenties, they motorized those sailboats.

My father told that as a little boy, he was fishing with his dad and they got stranded down over on the bay side. On the gulf side, there was a huge boat that had foundered and washed up on the shore and they spent the night on this boat, sleeping on the sails. He said that for a long time, a man stayed on the boat hoping they could refloat it, but they never could, and finally all the rigging and fittings were stripped. Lots of times, we had these bad storms and many boats washed up on shore.

Back in the twenties, if somebody got sick, you got on a boat and sailed over to Mobile. It took a day to go over there, and another day to go to the doctor, and you were sicker when you got home than when you left. There were no doctors over at what is now Gulf Shores. When my little sister was born in 1943, my dad went over to the old drawbridge near Mr. John Lewis's place to use the telephone to call a doctor. By the time the doctor got to our house, my little sister was being born. During the war years, our doctor in Foley went to the war and I was delivered by his wife. My mother told about a time my grandmother was expecting a baby and the lady—a midwife—was sitting there with her and they were tired of waiting for that baby to come and my grandmother let out a deep breath—phewww—and blew that old kerosene lantern out.

When I was growing up, we had to be pretty much self-sufficient because we were cut off from the rest of the world. We had our own gardens and we had plenty of seafood: shrimp, crab, oysters, and fish, and we thought we were disadvantaged because we heard that people who lived in other places had steaks, pork chops, and ham, and we just didn't. We had a special treat on Saturday nights, because that was the night my grandmother brought hamburgers and Mama fixed hamburgers for all of us. When my grandfather was living, he had a record twelve-inch oyster shell and there were plenty of oysters then, but that is an era that is gone now. They used to have oyster planting grounds and it was just like your garden. Nobody fooled with your oyster planting ground, but that is a thing of the past.

My husband's family moved down to the Gulf Shores area in 1947. There was an old hotel down there built by George Meyer and it was called the Gulf Shores Hotel. There was a long pier down there, and then there was Bibb Graves who was governor of Alabama who had a cottage, and Dr. Holmes had a cottage, and there were maybe five or six others and that was it. People who always lived here wouldn't build on the beach because they were afraid of hurricanes. Sure enough, soon after that hotel was built, a hurricane came along and damaged it badly. In the forties, another hurricane came and filled the first floor with sand. They left the sand and moved to the second floor.

Mr. Meyer, who owned the hotel, made a deal with the state. The deal was if the state would build a road to Gulf Shores, he would donate some beachfront property to the state and that is the public beach and state park at the south end of Highway 59. Before the road was built, though, my great-grandfather and other kinfolks would charge a quarter to take you across down here at Callaway's Landing. They would let you stay for a day, and when you got ready to come home, they would come get you. That was back in the twenties. My grandfather told about one time Mr. George Brown brought a bunch of people over to go across to the gulf, and that was when women wore bathing suits down to their ankles. One lady stepped in the boat and her ankles were showing, and my grandfather called Mr. Brown over to one side and told him, "Don't you ever bring anybody back over here to go in my boat with that little bit of clothes on." When we grew up, people were very modest. After Labor Day, it was just dead on the beach. Everything just shut down as far as beach activities.

When we were growing up, my dad being a family man, sometimes on Sunday afternoons we would get on his twenty-seven-foot shrimp boat and go across to the gulf and play on the sand dunes. The sand dunes were very high back in the forties and it would take everything you had just to get to the top. Now, there are very few high sand dunes on the beaches. We thought we lived at the end of the world because we didn't have any sidewalks so there were no skates, and there were no picture shows. We had to drive twelve miles on a school bus to Foley to see anything, because everything went on in Foley. We thought we were underprivileged down here because there was nothing to do but go swimming. First full moon in June, most everybody would go over to the beach and hunt for turtle eggs. That was one of the things we did as kids—look for turtle eggs. We didn't find them too often, but that was one of the things we did. I was the middle child and the middle child was usually the one who stays in trouble, and I was the one who got to go shrimping with my dad in the summertime. It was really good for me, because I learned how to run a boat and he told me a lot of good stories out there on the gulf, taught me how to pick and head the shrimp, and how to clean crabs. Daddy didn't have any boys so I went along with him.

My daddy was real strict with us on morals, on dating, and we always heard, "What will the neighbors think?" and "Don't ever do anything to shame the family." I married my husband when I was seventeen. He was our neighbor and my daddy was concerned some because he said that my husband-to-be wouldn't stick to a job. But later on, my daddy thought the world of him. I still had one year left to go in high school when I got married. Up until then, the farthest I had been away from home was the county fair, Mobile, Bayou La Batre, Biloxi, and Panama City.

My dad liked to tell stories about hurricanes. His grandparents had a home on the lagooon. And in 1906, there was no way of knowing when a hurricane was coming, and the thing was, when the water got real high in the lagoon, old-timers would open up the mouth of the lagoon to let the water level go down. The reason for this was that they wanted to use the artesian wells up and down the lagoon. They used these wells for drinking water, and when the tide was up, they were covered. When this hurricane came up one night, my grandmother Callaway was like most women, worried about the weather, and was sitting there reading her Bible and listening to the storm making up. She heard this little thump out front and the dog started barking. When she went out to look, the water was already up to the gallery. All she had time to do was wake the family up and put the barrel of flour and my grandfather's violin on top of the kitchen table and they waded out in the night through waist-deep water, waded about half a mile until they got to the ridge where her brother, Bill Wallace, lived. They had to go over and under the blown-down trees to the ridge where they sat out the night. The next morning, they went back home and the house was gone and the fish nets were fourteen feet up in the trees. They found the family clock down the beach and it had stopped at two o'clock in the morning. My grandfather said that he looked across the lagoon to the beach and the trees that had been on the beach looked like umbrellas where the wind had turned them wrong-side out.

When I was a girl, my dad's big concern was what would happen to his boat during a hurricane. When he thought a storm was coming, he would move his boat as far as he could up to the east end of the lagoon where it would be sheltered. The mouth of the lagoon was closed and thousands of pounds of fish were in there, but now it is hard to catch a mess of mullet because the pass is open all the time. You could catch flounder. My grandfather told about the first time he went floundering and they had what they called a jack pan which was a pan they put in front of the boat. They would put wood in the pan and light it so they could see the flounder on the bottom. When they spotted a flounder, they could gig him. When I was a girl, that's how all the young men made their money. My husband would go out, and catching a hundred pounds of flounder was nothing. In the forties, there were three fish houses on the lagoon.

When I was growing up, everybody made a living in the seafood business. We would go up to the seafood shed and head shrimp. They would pay us so much a pound for deheading them, and this is what I did some when I was in high school. Then, my mother ran Callaway's Store over on the beach which was the first store going to the beach. There was a little store on the curb there called Callaway's that Uncle Calvin had. You could buy ice and gas and basic necessities like that. My mama ran that store over on the beach and we worked in that store with her, and my husband ran the fish house. But basically, people made their living from the water. Years ago, there was some farming down here, like oranges, and that's where Orange Beach got its name, and they shipped the oranges out by the schooner load, but that was before the land became so poor.

In the old days, my grandmother had a garden and my mother had a garden, but the land is so poor down here that you had to really build it up. We had to go to Foley to buy our main supplies when I was a girl. And isolated? We were so isolated that when the country had the Spanish influenza epidemic in 1918, we didn't have any deaths down here. Really, Gulf Shores was not an island until the thirties when they dug a canal from Mobile Bay to Perdido Bay. Back then, my dad decided that he was going to quit fishing and he went up there and got a job when they were digging the Gulf Intercoastal Waterway. He worked one day, made fifty cents, and quit. There were several boys who worked on the towboat who married local girls, but mostly, there was a lot of intermarrying of cousins because we were so isolated. They were worried at one time because cousins were marrying cousins and there was some fear that children would be born with birth defects. Everybody down here was some kind of kin, intermarrying and all. If you weren't kin when you came down here, you were before you left.

My daddy was not what you call materially well off being a fisherman, but when he died, there were over 450 people at his funeral. He was successful in that way, but I can't say he was a successful fisherman after the seine crew disbanded because it always seemed that he was too late. He hoped he would catch them, but they were hardly ever there. It never seemed to get him down because he thought, well, tomorrow I'll get them. My mother made all our clothes except hand-me-downs from cousins. She worked twelve hours a day at that store over on the beach and made seventy dollars a week. While she was working, my sisters and I took care of the house. One time when my mother was working, we were having a hard time with money. We had pancakes for breakfast every morning and that didn't seem bad to me. We never knew we were bad off because we had a nice house and a car and not all our friends had a car.

Road Building

Buster Hall, Clarke County

In the spring of 1922 after school was out for the summer, A. L. Payne, who was about twelve years old, went down to the Tompkins School area to visit his "country cousin" Forest Lee Mathews. At that time, a road crew was reworking the Grove Hill–Jackson dirt road. They were getting gravel from a pit on the property of D. C. Mathews and had been storing their picks, shovels, hoes, and dynamite in his barn. Two or three times a day the crew would set off a stick of dynamite to loosen the gravel so that it could be shoveled onto the wagons.

One Saturday morning when the crew was not working, A. L. and Forest Lee decided they would help out on the job by removing a big stump on the edge of the bank where the crew had been working the day before. The boys went over to the barn and slipped out several sticks of dynamite and the punch to make a hole with and headed for the gravel pit. They spent most of the morning getting four deep holes dug, two on each side of the stump, and attached the fuses. They had forgotten that they had to have caps to set off the dynamite.

They couldn't make the thing go off so they left the four sticks of dynamite under the stump and went over to their uncle Monroe

Halford's home while the Halfords were in town and whitewashed Uncle Tom's old black plow mule. They were mad at Uncle Tom because he had cussed them out at Christmastime for hunting on his land and this was a good way to get back at him. Uncle Tom did a lot of cussing the next day about what some so-and-so had done to his mule. A. L. and Forest Lee spent Sunday fishing and went to sleep Sunday night worn out and resting good.

They were blasted from their sound sleep early Monday morning by the greatest explosion that had ever happened in the quiet and peaceful Tompkins School community. Stuff was still coming down out of the sky when the two boys got to the front porch. Parts of the lot fence were knocked down, the top of the chimney was knocked off, and Mr. Dave's two fine horses, Woodrow and Pat, were racing madly around in the lot.

Neighbors started gathering and the man in charge of the work crew was telling everybody that he couldn't explain why there was such a tremendous explosion. He was telling that the first thing his crew did when they came to work was to place two sticks of dynamite under the big stump that had to be moved before the crew could begin moving gravel, and when they set it off, the whole world seemed to blow up. About this time, Mr. Dave Mathews came flying up in his Model T Ford and, seeing his family was unhurt, began showing Uncle Monroe what professional-type cussing sounded like.

Later in the day, A. L. and Forest Lee had a little conference and decided that it was time for A. L. to go home and it wouldn't be a bad idea if A. L. invited Forest Lee to go with him. It was okay with Forest Lee's mother. Forty years later, the boys were still afraid to talk about helping out with road building.

Home Conveniences

Tera Averett, Coffee County

We had an open well with a windlass and rope to let the bucket down into the well. The windlass had a crank which unwound the rope as the bucket went down. We carried the water to the house in buckets.

On the front porch, there was a shelf on which we kept the water bucket with a dipper in it. Everyone who wanted a drink used the same dipper. That shelf had a hole in it for the washbowl to sit so it would be steady when we washed. Nobody would ever think of going in to eat without washing our face and hands. There was a flour-sack towel hanging near the basin for drying.

For the kitchen, we had a metal wash pan for the same kind of washing, but at least once a week, usually on Saturday, we got our all-over bath in a wash tub. Every night, no one dared to go to bed without washing our feet.

As for an indoor toilet, the only one we had ever seen was once when we visited Grandpa and Grandma Byrd in Ozark. They had one. We flushed that toilet until I know Grandpa's water bill went sky high. They rented that house from the Holmans, and in later years, one of the Holman sons told me a funny story about when they put the toilet in. When the plumbers came to the house to install the commode, Grandma Byrd called Grandpa in town and said, "Curtis, come home. They are fixing to put the toilet in our house." It was a big event. Out at our house, we had what we called a "backy." I never knew why, but it must have been because it was so far back of the house we lived in. Inside the backy, we kept the Sears catalog and not for making an order or looking at the pictures. Sometimes Mama put a bag filled with small soft pieces of rags and a box of cobs from the corncrib after Papa had shelled some corn to take to the mill. Cobs that had been left in the trough when the mules had eaten the corn were hard, but the shelled corncobs were soft.

Animals and Peach Switches

Ben Meriwether, Bullock County

At Christmastime, I always got one nice present plus fruits and nuts which didn't grow in Alabama like English walnuts, raisins, and Brazil nuts. We always had plenty of fireworks and my mother liked to shoot off Roman candles. One year, Christmas came on Sunday and my mother told me not to shoot a firecracker on a Sunday. I couldn't help it and I shot one and got another trip to the peach tree. I remember three toys on three different years. The first was a windup train. We had company for dinner that day, and I thought those people would never leave so that I could spread my track down on the floor and play with my train. The next toy was a cast-iron fire truck with two cast-iron horses to pull it. In the summer, I dropped the fire truck out in the grove and it broke half in two. I cried over that and tried to tie it back together, but it wouldn't work. The third toy I loved was a little red wagon and I hauled things in it until it just wore out.

I raised a bull yearling one time, and when it got big enough to ride, I rode it all around. On rainy school days, I would ride the yearling down to the store, put it in a shed, walk across the railroad tracks to school, and ride it back home in the afternoon. One Sunday, my cousin Jim, Neal Hufman, and Roscoe Mathews walked down from Fitzpatrick to spend the day with me. We had a good time riding my yearling, all but Roscoe. He was a little on the heavy side and the yearling didn't like him. Roscoe would get on and the yearling would tear out for the house, go under it, and pull old Roscoe off. Late one afternoon, nearly dark, I was riding my yearling and he got too close to the fence and rubbed my foot. Man, that foot hurt and I cussed that bull. I didn't see my mother sitting on the steps and she heard me cussing. "What was that you said?" she asked me, and I knew I was headed for the peach tree again. Well, we had a black man working for us, and I said, "I heard Dusty say that," and I got out of a visit to the peach tree. After that, though, I looked before I spoke.

We milked eight cows at one time and my mother had regular butter customers in Montgomery. She sent that butter by parcel post, and why that butter didn't melt, I'll never know. She had a half-pound mold and a pound mold made out of wood. She would mold that butter, put it in a carton, and mail it to Montgomery.

One time, we bought a full-blooded Jersey cow from a man in Fort Deposit that was supposed to be a fine milker. The man told my mother that if there were children around, not to let the children get close because the cow didn't like children. Well, I was raised around cows and I wasn't afraid, so I went in the lot anyway. There was a big chinaberry tree right in the middle of the lot, and when I went in and the cow saw me, here she came, and I headed for that tree. I missed the low limb on that tree and the cow started chasing me around the trunk and me yelling "help! help!" all the time. Mother heard me yelling and got me out, but I was really scared that time. Another trip to the peach tree.

We raised hogs and had some pretty good ones. One day, I thought one of them was big enough to ride, so I jumped on his back. He turned and looked at me, pitched me off on a tree trunk and knocked the breath out of me. I didn't ever try that again.

Daddy was farming as well as running the store and we had several horses, never any mules. We raised one horse that was so clumsy he would walk along, stumble, and go down on his knees. One day, I was a little careless, got too close to the other end, and that horse kicked me it seemed about ten feet. One cloudy, drizzly day, I went out to the pasture to get the horses. I thought to myself, why walk? and climbed up on the back of one. He didn't like that and walked under a tree limb. That knocked me off the horse and I hit the ground. I decided I would walk the horses back to the lot from then on.

A Few Miles from Florida

Roger Marler, Lee County

My mama said that my granddad got to drinking pretty bad way back yonder. He was walking home one night after he had been nipping pretty good and it was a dark night and he was just trying to get to the house. The Ku Klux Klan was pretty strong back in those days and they operated a little different because they ranged a little further than just being against the blacks, you might say. They would come down on anybody who was sorry, or was a rascal, or wouldn't take care of his family. So, my granddad was coming home this night by the back way, pretty drunk, and had come through a pasturelike where the Klan was burning a cross. They didn't do anything to him, but he was so drunk that he imagined that they were after him for going home drunk to his family and just about scared him to death, but not enough to get him to quit drinking.

Later on, though, he heard that an airplane was going to be in town and they were offering airplane rides for two dollars apiece. He decided to take an airplane ride, and to celebrate this occasion, he decided to have a few before he went up so he could enjoy it more. He crawled up in that plane, pretty drunk, and the pilot got up in the air and started doing the loop-the-loop and twisting and turning and pretty well wrung that plane out. By the time they got down on the ground, my granddad was so sick and scared that my mama said that was just about the last time he took a drink.

Like everybody else down there around Opp, he farmed and planted a lot of cantaloupe and watermelons. Down there, they had what they called pie-melons which kind of came up wild you might say, and they were just about like concrete when you broke them open. Boys used to come up there from school and steal watermelons from my granddad and they would come into school and brag about stealing his watermelons. My granddad would plant watermelons in one place one time and another place next year to rotate the crop. One time, those watermelons got mixed up with those pie-melons which had just volunteered, and what came out was a melon which looked good on the outside, was just a little pink on the inside, but there was no way you could eat them because they were so hard. The boys lived close to me and I knew they were stealing. They came into school after they had raided that pie-melon patch and told me that we wouldn't have to worry about them anymore. They said those were the worst watermelons they had ever tried to eat.

I remember we had a couple of guys when I was in grammar school, twins, Earl and Jerald, and fight? They would fight with knives. Nobody messed with them because they were so big and mean. If they couldn't do any better, they'd fight each other. They got into a fight down there one time at that little old country school, and of course, we had outdoor toilets, and one of 'em stuck the other one down the hole in that outhouse. They had to send him home. I don't know how the other one got him through that hole. He was big for his age, but he was still in grammar school.

A friend of mine was telling me about his daddy and when they first went to using Ex-Lax when it first started coming out. Walter said that they came around and gave out samples to the kids in school and told them not to eat the sample but take it home and give it to their parents. It was a promotion, not a real smart promotion, because the kids all had to try it. It looked just like chocolate candy to them. There was just one outhouse at that school and it got to be real critical because kids were lined up outside that outhouse, and of course, some of them couldn't wait. A lot of kids went home early that day. It did prove one thing, though. Ex-Lax would get the job done.

Another buddy of mine told me this story. He used to live up in the valley, and I don't know why it is called the valley, unless there is a little valley between Lanett and West Point, but that is what they call that area. Anyhow, his daddy was in the merchant marines, and his daddy was a boxer when he was growing up. They wanted him to turn pro when he was about eighteen. Joe Louis was from down around Camp Hill and Joe would come down and they would work out together, and ride bicycles down to Lanett and all. This boy's daddy joined the merchant marines though and the kids didn't see him much. But when he would come home, he would tell a lot of neat stories and all like that. The family was pretty poor. They lived in kind of like the projects and it was called White Line, just a line of little small houses. They had outhouses at the White Line and there was one old guy that lived there had an old outhouse that was kind of rotten, kind of leaning a little bit. This fellow had a friend who was called Slim who was about six foot six and weighed about three hundred pounds. The boys kept telling their daddy that the outhouse needed fixing or should be replaced, and he kept saying, well, we'll get to it sooner or later, kept putting it off, you know. One day it was coming up a storm and the wind was blowing pretty good, and the two boys decided to go out and push over the outhouse, hoping their daddy would think the wind did it. They went to do it, wind blowing pretty good, and the outhouse toppled over. When it did, the door flew open, and big Slim rolled out. Old Slim never knew who pushed the outhouse over, but the john got rebuilt.

Five More Minutes

Willie Jiles, Bullock County

When I was growing up, we were farming and moving from place to place and all the houses were all about the same, shacks seemed like, but we were working other people's farms and we lived in what they had. I remember one house had a room without any floor in it at all. When my mama married my stepfather, there were two of us, my sister and me, and we worked on the farm ourselves. I just went through the eighth grade and mostly in one schoolhouse because we moved around but we were still close to that schoolhouse, and we walked to school when we went. All eight grades in that one school-house. Sometimes it was closer to walk to school than other times.

My stepfather worked in the woods, pulpwooding, and when I got about fifteen years old, I went in the woods, too, pulpwooding along-side of my stepfather. Back then, there weren't any white men pulpwooding with us, and the black men drove the pulpwood trucks, hauling that wood out of there. We would carry our dinner with us out there in the woods, and most of the time we would go back home at night, and sometimes it would be a pretty good distance away.

About the time I went into the woods—I was about fifteen, I guess, along about 1941 to 1942—Mama sent me to the store one evening for a few things. Now, that store was a good piece away and I had to walk it. They sold some little groceries and maybe some gas as I remember it. I started out, went down to the store and bought my stuff and hung around there awhile talking and seeing what was going on. Finally, along about 9:30, I started walking back home. I was walking along and I noticed that the wind was picking up a little and I could see these big old dark clouds starting to build up, just getting bigger and bigger and breaking up and coming back together again.

The wind started getting a little stronger and I saw the funniest looking sight up there in the sky. The sky started getting pink behind those black clouds and the wind started blowing a little harder and I picked it up a little bit, trying to get home, because I knew if nothing else happened, we were bound to get a good rain. I hurried up a little bit more and the wind was coming on good now and those clouds were getting blacker and moving faster and that pink color was behind those clouds. When I got to the house, it started sprinkling a little and the wind was really blowing now. I went in and got in bed first thing, and I hadn't been there but a minute or two when that tornado went right by the house, not on top of it now, but pretty close, and I heard this big noise somewhere in the house. That tornado must have been traveling, because it was there one minute, then it went on by and the noise was going away from us.

Everybody got up when it quieted down, and what had happened was that tornado just picked up our chimney and took it right out there in the yard. Didn't hurt the rest of the house, now, just the chimney, and we looked out there and hot coals were scattered all over that yard along with the chimney. It was nothing to do then, so we all went back to bed. Next morning, we looked out and that chimney was still out there in the yard, but that wind had dropped a lot of timber because trees were down everywhere that tornado had touched down. I thought about it then. That tornado went right down the road where I had been walking, and if I had hung around that store five more minutes, I would have had a free ride to Montgomery.

German Spoken Here

John Haupt, Baldwin County

In 1904, there was no such thing as downtown Elberta, but ten years later, there was a new town. The L & N Railroad, in order to encourage settlers to come down to the Elberta area when they built the railroad from Bay Minette to Foley, worked with the Baldwin County Colonization Company who had bought 55,000 acres of land from the Southern States Lumber Company. The lumber company clean-cut off all of the virgin timber from this huge tract of land and practically gave the land away because it was no longer profitable to hold on to it. The colonization company, which was based in Chicago, ran a lot of ads in German-language newspapers in the North, talking about the land of milk and honey in southern Alabama. They would sell the tracts at fifteen dollars an acre and the colonists could buy the land on time. These ads would run in New York, Philadelphia, Boston, Chicago, and St. Louis and other northern cities, and only in German-language papers. Ads were run in German newspapers and some of the settlers emigrated directly from Germany to Elberta. These ads ran from about 1904 through 1930.

After the lumber company had stripped the land, the entire 55,000 acres was totally bare of people. The cutover timberland was hard to clear for settling, much debris having been leftover from the logging operation. When people came down to look over the place, the corporation had temporary living quarters for them to stay in, and there were all manner of professions represented—farmers, businessmen, artists, and musicians. Around the turn of the century there were no towns in this area at all. Magnolia Springs had a settlement of sorts on the river, but otherwise there was nothing. Many people came and left after four or five years, disappointed that they didn't really find the promised land of milk and honey. They had to learn how to farm in Elberta. They had been told that the land was rich, but in reality it was sandy and porous and had to be fertilized every year.

The corporation organized excursions to come down to the property all during the year from all of the northern cities. They would bring these families down in Pullman cars, and on the sides of the railroad cars were these big signs proclaiming, "Excursion to Elberta, Alabama, the land of milk and honey, and we're going to make our money." They would park in stations awhile on the way down, and everybody would see the signs. They would take the prospects out to the farms and show them what could be done. At one time, there were a lot of Satsuma orange farms which were shown to great advantage. Most of the people would come down from the North with German as their only language and very few could speak English.

During some of this migration, I was about ten years old and could speak German as well as English, and the agent would get me to talk to the prospects and show them around our farm. This was in the early twenties, and the agent would bring all the prospects out to our farm in caravans of Model T Fords. I would take them out to the watermelon patch the first thing. I always carried a knife and would cut a melon and give them a rasher of melon and sometimes a slice of cantaloupe. I would get a nickel, a dime, or maybe a quarter from the people being shown around, but the agent in charge of the group would slip me a dollar, and that was a lot of money in the early 1900s.

You would go to town on Saturday night with a dime, and my father would want to see a nickel the next morning. My father was a miller by trade, but there was no wheat down here, so he had to farm. The main crops in Elberta during the big migration in the twenties were sweet potatoes, Irish potatoes, cucumbers, corn, and cowpeas. There was an indirect market for these crops, like feeding this produce to hogs and cattle, and there was a market for this meat in Pensacola and Mobile.

When my father came down and bought the forty acres we were supposed to settle on, he was told that it was three miles south of Elberta. There were no roads in the area, just dirt trails. After my father had come down and bought his forty acres, he brought my mother down to see the place. They arrived one evening, and early the next morning the agent picked up my father and mother in a surrey. They started following a trail, and after about a half-hour my mother said that we should be getting to the farm pretty soon since it was supposed to be only three miles from Elberta. The agent said, "It won't be long now, and isn't it romantic riding around in this surrey and seeing all these trees and the pretty land?" They traveled some more, and after about an hour my mother said again that we ought to be there surely by now. She turned to the driver and asked him how far it was from Elberta, and the driver said seven miles, and this didn't make my mother too happy.

By and by, they reached the forty acres and the agent explained that the company would clear five acres of the forty as part of the deal. They discovered a wandering stream coming through and the agent said that when it rained, they would have a good trout stream.

My mother rebelled and they all went back to town and my mother started looking around for a trade. They found an established farm about three miles from town and traded the land they had bought for the farm closer in. We moved in, my father, mother, and six children. I think my father must have gone through some torment for the mistake he had made, but my mother was a good trader.

After many people had moved in, there was very little to do in the way of entertainment. Between 1910 and 1920, there was an enterprising man named Captain Bob Foley who owned a landing at Hammock Creek and he offered overnight excursions down to Wolf Bay and the Gulf of Mexico. He would get up a party of about twenty people and sail on a Saturday morning, spend the night on the beach, and return on Sunday afternoon. He was so organized that he even took care of his customers' mules and wagons at the landing while they were gone. The trip down to the gulf took about three hours and the captain's customers would set up tents on the beach where they went crabbing, swam, and fished. They used dip nets for the crabs, and crabs were so plentiful they caught them as fast as they could pull them in. They caught mullet in the bay and fried them on big campfires on the beach. Sometimes they would find turtle eggs on moonlit nights and eat them regardless of the rubbery texture. There was always plenty of food, and liquid refreshment depended on the customer. Some were dry as powderhorns while others liked a little stronger stuff.

Most of these excursions were uneventful, but on one occasion, something happened that caused much apprehension back at Elberta. Captain Foley had found a piece of heart pine that was about thirty feet long, a rare treasure, and attempted to pull it back to his landing. He hitched the big log to the back of his boat, started back, and sheared a pin which disabled the boat. It took an extra day to get the boat fixed, an extra day on the beach for his customers.

When I was a boy back in the twenties, one of the ways I made extra money was catching terrapins and gophers and selling them to the peddlers who had regular routes through Elberta. The peddlers would usually come through the community on a Thursday and buy surplus produce and the gophers and terrapins and take them down to Pensacola on the weekend and sell house to house. What they couldn't sell this way, they would trade with the mom and pop stores. Almost every little store in Pensacola had gopher cages and the demand was good since many people considered gopher meat a delicacy. To get my gophers, I could dig them out of their burrows— a tough job—or trap them. They were fairly plentiful, so I usually had eight to ten to sell to the peddler when he made his weekly rounds. The peddler had a scale and paid me five cents a pound, and since the gophers weighed from three to eight pounds each, I could get from fifteen to forty cents for each gopher. When I had accumulated five or ten dollars in my piggy bank, my father and I would go down and make a deposit in my savings account which paid 3 percent interest. I ran a regular route catching my gophers and carried those gophers in that gunny sack back home, saving up for the peddler.

A Severe Case

C. J. Coley, Tallapoosa County

Back in the old days, many families were served by doctors who lived in their communities. The doctors got about with a horse and buggy. One of the best was Dr. R. A. Foshee who lived and practiced in the New Site community just outside of Alexander City. When he had finished his medical education, he set up practice in New Site and one of his first calls was to the home of a young mother with an ill infant down in Goldville. He hitched up his horse and buggy, and five miles later he reached the house where the sick baby was. He carefully examined the baby and reached his medical conclusion.

"This baby," he said to the mother, "has a severe case of locked bowels." The mother looked at Dr. Foshee with some surprise and said, "Why doctor, from the time I sent for you until you got here, this baby's bowels have moved five times." Trying to maintain his dignity, Foshee replied, "Lady, that is what I am trying to tell you. This baby's bowels are locked . . . wide open."

City Life, Upper Alabama

Promotion for Lyric Theater, 18th Street at Third Avenue, Birmingham, 1920s (Birmingham Public Library)

Magic City sign at Union Station, Birmingham, in the 1930s (Birmingham Public Library)

Everybody's Business

Robert Couch, Marion County

When I was growing up in Winfield in the thirties and forties, my horizons were limited. As a kid, I would sit on the curb there in town and I would look up and see the road curve up and over and around that hill and I would wonder what was on the other side of that hill.

A favorite meeting place in town was Mac's Cafe. Mrs. Willie B. McDonald and later her son, Willie B. Junior, had this really nice first-class cafe, and it was the only air-conditioned building in town. The bus station was in the cafe, too. The bus would be running mostly from Memphis to Birmingham, and sometimes from Tuscaloosa to Muscle Shoals and that was big entertainment. You would go and watch people get off the bus and go in the cafe to get something to eat. A lot of buses would come in and pull around in that big lot by the taxi stands. We had several taxi stands. They were all independently owned, but they had pooled their resources and had gotten a telephone. They found a big old metal mailbox somewhere and the telephone was in the mailbox right there across from the bus station. When the taxi drivers were hanging out and waiting for something to happen, they would stand around and tell dirty jokes, and then if the telephone rang, they would sprint for the phone.

Then, there were several big, or what we thought were big at the time, general type merchandise stores. Like R. W. Harris, Senior, and he sold everything under the sun, like baseball caps and fertilizer and hose. My grandfather had a store like that, and there was Sizemore and Ward's. In that store, you would walk in and right there by the door was a stalk of bananas, and bananas were real big treats. Sometimes, I would go in there and my Uncle Perv would give me one of those bananas. During the war, those bananas would come in with red skins for some reason.

My dad died when I was very young and my mother ran a beauty shop there in Winfield, so we were much poorer economically and lower socially than I realized at the time. The families in town, the ones who had the big cars and the big houses, were the ones like the man who ran the big grocery store who was R. W. Harris, and Dr. M. C. Hollis who lived in the big house up on the hill, and Mr.

Marvin Pierce whose family owned a lot of land and the ice house. When I was a kid, my mother would send me down to the ice house and they had these little bitty tiny ropes to carry the ice. You could watch them cut the ice and everything was dripping all the time. For about a dime, you would get a block of ice that you couldn't lift. They had a home delivery service for that ice, an old yellow truck that was a kind of cut-off convertible and it would go around town dripping, always dripping, and they would go and deliver to your house. You would have an icebox, and they would just go in your house, march right in, and put the ice in your icebox.

Winfield was so small, somewhere under three thousand people, that folks knew who you were, sort of an extended family kind of thing. One time, I had this thing to play hooky from school one day when I was about a senior in high school. My mother went on to work and I was home supposed to be sick, and oh-h-h, boy, I let on how I was so sick, and pretty soon, somebody came to pick me up and we lit out for Fayette, which was about eighteen miles away. We played around all day and got back home in time for me to jump in bed again before my mother got home. My mother came in and I was lying there moaning and groaning and she came over to the bed and felt my forehead and then she said, "How was Fayette?" Everybody in town knew I had played hooky and had gone to Fayette. You couldn't get by with much of anything.

Another time, I was feeling my oats and was going to drink a little beer or something like that and it was in my senior year in high school. Now, the whole state of Mississippi was *supposed* to be dry, but if we wanted to go get a beer, we went over to Mississippi because our county and all the surrounding counties *were* dry. You would go through Vernon and over the state line there and they had three beer joints—the Bloody Bucket, the Pines, and Midway—and most of the time, I would get caught by some of the adults from Winfield who had sneaked across for a cool one or two. All that got back to Winfield, too.

When we got ready to graduate from high school, we had gotten up all these elaborate plans and one of my friends was the local Dodge dealer. He had a demonstrator car and it was one of these long things with the fins and all, and it was pink and black and had chrome all over it and we thought it was the most wonderful thing in the world. We had found a local bootlegger and had bought a bottle of gin for this great occasion and we were going to the Silver Spur over in Columbus for a graduation party. We went out into the woods to a place called Mossy's Bottom about two months before graduation and we hid that bottle of gin, and somehow, we went back out the night before graduation and found that bottle of gin. Well, we graduated and took off for Columbus with some girls, and I didn't know you couldn't get in that place with your own bottle. When we found that out, I just slipped that bottle up under one of those girl's skirts—they had those big wide skirts—and I grabbed the bottle from the outside and we walked into the Silver Spur that way. We knew nobody would realize what we were doing, being such slick high school seniors.

I played football in high school. I didn't have all that much talent, but I was big enough and determined enough that I was honorable mention all-state along with this other boy. We tried out at Mississippi Southern and they offered this other boy a scholarship, but they wanted me to go to one of those junior colleges over there. I said, naw, I didn't want to do that, so I went on to North Alabama. Our football coach, Estes Hudson, was a really fine gentleman and made the high school hall of fame. To me, that was the greatest thing in the world, playing high school football, going down to dress out for a Friday night game, and putting on those clean white socks you had been saving up all week, and dressing out and going out there on the field, and all the cheerleaders turning flips and the crowd yelling. And then, getting up on Saturday morning and going downtown and getting all those pats on the back, if you won, that is. If you lost, you stayed busy around the house doing things.

The worst part of playing football was the practice. We would have to get up to practice about six o'clock in the morning when we started in the fall and we would be running laps and we crossed these I.C. railroad tracks, and across the tracks were some houses, and we would be running along and I could smell bacon cooking in those houses. Ah, that bacon smelled good and you knew you were in for a miserable day. Later, you would go home about worn out and it was hot, and then you would go back around three o'clock in the afternoon in that Winfield sun and you would do another one. And, in late August and early September, we would just about die in that heat. Then, a lot of us would get on that railroad track, a spur track that ran up to Brilliant where they had coal mines and Old Maude was the train that made that, and Old Maude would run up and back every day. We would get on those tracks right next to the practice field, and about a mile or two up those tracks and across this place called Rock Bottom, there were some underground springs that fed a pool. I mean it could be the hottest August day and we would dive in there, and I mean, you would come up with blue lips because it was so cold. It was the most wonderful thing in the world. That cold pool kept me going during those hot days during the preseason football practices.

As far as getting into trouble in Winfield, there was not much to get in trouble with. If you wanted to drink beer, you had a long way to go to get it. Something like drugs, you never heard of. Well, there was one person in town who was known as a "dope fiend," a nurse who was married to a cousin of mine. One time, three of us were sitting around town one night and one of the boys had the idea of stealing some hubcaps. I told them I didn't need any hubcaps, got out of the car, climbed a little hill, and went on home. The next day, I was lifeguarding down at the pool and the other two boys were in swimming, and in a little while the police came in and pulled those boys out of the pool. I was sitting up there, and scared? It scared the bejesus out of me because I knew that I was next. About a week or two later, the mayor called me and asked me to come by his office and I knew that the jig was up. I screwed up my courage and walked in and the mayor told me that someone had observed us that night and saw me get out of the car and go home and he just wanted to commend me for not getting involved. I wasn't any angel, but I surely was glad that I had left, and I don't know to this day who reported to the mayor. You certainly couldn't get away with anything in Winfield.

The Movement

Charles Wiggins, Jefferson County

I became active in the church and the church was the centerpiece for fighting discrimination. The church really spearheaded the total movement and all this was being done locally. You see, the black church has historically been the front-runner for any kind of injustice. About the only way the black people could be contacted for anything was through the church. See, the church attracted hundreds of people and most of the marches back then were organized in the church.

The caliber of Birmingham policemen at that time was so bad that a marcher would give his name and the policeman couldn't spell it. I took a group of kids down one time and they had been marching and I was standing there talking to them. Right there close to the city jail, a policeman drove up and said, "You-all are under arrest," and he looked at me and said, "Who are you? I want your name." I told him my name was Wiggins and he couldn't even spell it. He wrote something down on that pad, but my name never came up downtown because he couldn't get it right. This happened to a lot of people, getting their names wrong, and when a trial came up nothing happened because those names didn't exist. I knew some teachers who marched and they would make up names when they were arrested. Sometimes, the marchers would just give street names and the policeman couldn't even spell those. It seemed that in their own little world, the policemen were primarily concerned about putting you in jail and weren't too particular about getting your name right. Looking back, it looked like the caliber of policemen they had back then showed it might have been a period of "good old boys" on the police force, not that you pass an examination, not that you had the knowhow or had the physical requirements for the job. Say your daddy was a policeman and your son came along and he was going to be a policeman, too. All the boy had to do is grow up, be recommended, and okay, you were a policeman starting next week. Good old boys.

We called it the Movement, but the real name was the Alabama Christian Movement for Human Rights. I think the civil rights movement was festering for many years, not all at one time when it started getting the publicity. At some meeting, somebody said they had a problem down in Montgomery and a preacher down there had done a pretty good job of organizing. Somebody else said we need somebody like that and they sent for him. When Martin Luther King, Jr., came to Birmingham, I know some ministers—preachers—who said, "Hey, you leave things alone. We'll work out our own salvation. You go on back to Montgomery or wherever you came from. We really don't need you." But another segment of the blacks in Birmingham would say, "We need you, and you take those people and you organize us so we can make something happen." Once the Movement got started, these people out there who had said "go away" had to fall in. They couldn't very well sit out there after the Movement got rolling. King was the whole topic of conversation in the community because when people heard he was going to talk, they came. I mean they flocked in there. But King wasn't the whole show. He didn't do everything by himself. It was the Movement, a group of Birmingham ministers who came together and organized the effort.

Now, I'm thinking of a man—he's dead now, bless him wherever he is—had an undertaker place down on Southside. I was in the barbershop one day, and he comes up to me with a petition, and he made a little speech to all the men in there. He walked up to me and said, "Now, here's a young man and we're going to let him sign this petition and this petition is going to Martin Luther King, Jr. We want to let him know we're behind him." Well, I was a young schoolteacher and I said to the man, "You're a mortician. How come you're a mortician and carrying around this petition?" That man got mad and cussed me out because I asked him how come him, a mortician, is passing around something for people to sign. Bless him, wherever he is.

Right and Proper

Minnie Brown Sledge and *Mary Sledge Payne*, Hale County

Sledge: I was born in 1909 and grew up in Marion, right across the hill over here. My mother was left a widow when I was two years old, but we were moderately well off. I missed having a father. We had a nice house which was built in 1900. I had two brothers and one sister who was five years older than I was and I had to go where she went, and she didn't like that. When we played Old Maid, they always put the Old Maid off on me. My brother, Seymour, was two and a half years older than I was and he always looked after me.

I went to elementary school in Marion, about a mile out of Marion, and I had a friend who had a car and we all hung on that car going to school. I went to Judson for one year after high school. The matron of Judson was very strict on me and didn't want me to have anything to do with the Marion institute boys. She didn't want me to go to any of the dances over there and was so strict that I decided to transfer to The University of Alabama. At Judson, they were so strict that if you were caught with a deck of cards in your room, or if you danced in your room, you were shipped. Of course, you were not allowed to go out with the Marion institute boys. The boys could come over and sit in the parlor, but that was all.

My second year of college, I went up to the university. We had the train which came through Marion, and we would catch the train to go to Tuscaloosa. At that time, they had a hotel at Akron at the junction, and all the people from Selma and Greensboro and Marion would meet there and have dinner at the Ford Hotel. The train ran through twice a day.

Payne: I went to the dances at Marion. My mother was not the kind of Baptist that frowned on dancing, and besides, she knew that I would behave myself. We walked to the dances because it was only about two blocks. That was the most fun I ever had. I was a good dancer. They had live bands at the dances and they were held in the auditorium at Marion institute, and when they had big dances, they had bands from out of town. The girls at the dances came from Marion and around about there.

In the late twenties and early thirties, we would go to church on a Sunday and then the boys would come around and we would sit on the porch on Sunday afternoons. We enjoyed those porches so much because we didn't have air conditioning then, and we could sit out there and visit and see what was going on up and down the street. We had the old opera house on the second floor of a building here in the middle of Greensboro. We had public dances and everybody went, and they came from all around, and the dances were well chaperoned. We had real live bands to play for the dances at the opera house.

Daddy had an ice plant and they had wagons and mules that would carry the ice around town, big blocks of ice. I remember one old lady in town who wouldn't pay for anything she got on Sunday. She didn't mind getting the ice on Sunday, but she would wait and pay for it on Monday. People didn't have refrigerators at all, but got by with iceboxes. We had two Negro men who would go around with that wagon and mules delivering ice, and later on, Daddy got a truck, and they would hang off the sides as they went around. Then, Daddy put in a little ice cream factory by the ice house and we sold ice cream.

We always had plenty of food when I was growing up because we lived on the edge of town. Our house was built in 1829 and we had sixty acres of land out behind. We had quarters where the Negroes lived. We had the same cook for fifty years and she had a helper who took care of the rest of the house. Then, the lot man was the man who worked around the house. Every room in that old house had a fireplace, and one of his jobs was to build a fire in all those rooms every morning. We called him the lot man because he tended to all the livestock in the lot out by the barn. We had a big orchard and he planted the garden and took care of the orchard. Nobody had electricity and we had gaslights all around. I was talking to my nephew the other day, and he was wondering why all the houses here in Greensboro had those deep lots, and I told him that everybody in town used to have a garden out back. Sometimes they had a mule, and later on, there were just a few with mules who would come around and plow your garden for you.

I learned to drive by sitting in Daddy's lap. We always had some kind of vehicle. One time, we had an old green Chevrolet and we would get everybody to put up a dime and we would buy a gallon of gas and drive down twelve miles to the river. We loved to play in the Black Warrior River and ride in a little boat we had. We would fill up the car, and if we spent the night, we had to have a chaperon. Sometimes we used a tent and sometimes not.

Christmas was wonderful. We went out and got a tree and made our own decorations. We took sweetgum balls and dipped them in silver and hung them up on the Christmas tree by those little stems. We made our gifts because we didn't buy them. Christmastime was a great time for visiting, too. Family would gather from miles around at somebody's house and we would have plenty to eat and enjoy being with each other.

My mother worked with the Reconstruction Finance Corporation during the depression and with the welfare and she was with the Red Cross working the disaster areas of the South—Kentucky and Mississippi and different places. I was grown then and when she was gone, I would stay home with Daddy and keep house. Grandmother lived with us the last sixteen years of her life but she never spent but one summer in Alabama, and that was the year she died. She usually summered in the state of Washington or North Carolina. When she would go off to North Carolina, the train people would bring her ticket to our house for her.

While my mother was working with the RFC during the depression, she went to the first Chicago World's Fair with some other women. They would walk to the fair from the hotel. On the way to the fair, there was a shoeshine stand, and one morning, mother stopped to have her shoes shined. While her shoes were being shined, she heard one Negro man talking down the way and he was telling the other Negroes, "Yes, sir. You come down to Alabama and they will give you ten acres and they will give you a mule and you don't have to pay it back." He was painting a beautiful picture of this Garden of Eden down in Alabama and Mother couldn't help but say,

"That's not so." The Negro man who was doing all the talking looked around and saw Mother and he said, "Lawdy mercy, it's Miz Sludge." They never did say "Sledge," but "Sludge." She asked him where he was from and he told her Clements Bend. Mother told him she could name his deacons, and she started naming his deacons. Mother thought we already had more than we could take care of already and didn't see any need for more freeloaders down here.

A Letter from God

Jeanette Williams, Jefferson County

I was born in Birmingham's Southside in 1917. I got polio when I was four years and nine months old and that was the same year President Roosevelt had polio. People didn't know anything about polio back then and didn't know what to do for it. I lost the use of both legs and part of one arm. I went to a little private school on Southside, and at that time I didn't have braces or crutches. My sister and brother rolled me to school in a wagon.

My grandmother worked for the Stokely family, Judge Stokely, and the family had that big canned goods company. Before I had polio, I went all over the United States with my grandmother, because the Stokelys had a setup with the train where they had their own private car and they took my grandmother along to do the cooking. One of the things she told me about was the first turkey she cooked for the family. Mr. Stokely served the turkey, and when he got down to the frame, he had the turkey taken off the table because Grandma hadn't cleaned it. She didn't know how to clean a turkey and they had to teach her how. Back then, black people didn't have refrigerators and the food was just the basic, so after special occasions like Christmas, Grandma would bring home food left over from the Stokelys. She brought home turkey and black olives and things we didn't know anything about. We would take some of that food to school with us and we were very popular because we had everything most people didn't know about.

My grandmother lived there on the Stokely place. They had a place over the garage for the cook and the maid and I used to visit her up there. When the Stokely children outgrew their clothes, we would get them and we were the best-dressed kids in the neighborhood. When my grandmother came to see us on the weekend, she brought a basket of food and we looked forward to that. Times were hard in the late twenties and early thirties and food was a problem. See, my daddy worked at the school and he would bring home some of the surplus food, but the problem was, there were no labels on the cans, and we didn't know what was in there until we opened the cans. I believe one time, we ate some dog food.

Because my grandmother worked for the Stokelys, I got the best of whatever medical help was available in Birmingham, but there was not much available in 1921. After I graduated from lying flat in the bed, I was able to go to school in that wagon. When I got polio, my family tried everything they could to help me. People would come to our house with suggestions to try to heal me. I remember one man who came, and he talked like the Koreans, like you couldn't understand what they say, and this man was going to heal me. They would always want money for this healing and Mama would say, "If you heal her, your fortune is made," because she didn't have any money. So this man didn't stay long. It was a racket, see? Somebody told Mama that dirt had healing properties. So, every day when I was about seven or eight years old, Mama would dig a hole in the ground and sit me in that hole up to my chest and cover me up with dirt. She would put all my toys around that hole so I could reach them. We got all these good things from the Stokelys and my brothers and sisters would want to play with these toys out there. My brother wanted to play with something and wouldn't let me have it. I was all covered up with that dirt and couldn't get out of the hole, so he picked it up and ran off. I became sweet until he got up close and then I took that stove lid and tried to knock his head off. When I did that, Mama picked me up, brushed the dirt off, gave me a good whipping, and stuck me back down in that dirt. Sometimes, the neighbors would see Mama whipping me and they told her she ought not to be whipping me like that, but I needed it, and should have gotten more. Many times at night, I could hear Mama crying and I think she was seeing a bad future for me.

One day, this lady came by the house and told Mama that the Lord had revealed me to her in a dream and that she knew she could heal me. She told Mama to get some virgin olive oil and some virgin wool and she would heal me. So, my daddy went to the drugstore and got some brown wrapping paper. They would put the paper on the bed, put me on the paper, and this lady would massage my legs with this olive oil. One day a letter came in the mail. The essence of the letter was "my servant"—meaning Mama—"has disobeyed me. She was not supposed to leave the house and she is going to be punished. To atone for this, on a specified night, on a specified dark moon, you are going to a designated tree. You are going to dig a hole and bury so many silver dollars, bury so many quarters, so many dimes, and so many nickels." It was signed, "from God." My mama got a large envelope, put the letter in there, and addressed it to this lady's house. That was the last time we ever saw that lady. Mama said she saw this lady later on in a store and spoke to her. The lady said, "I beg your pardon. You got the wrong person," and that was the end of that lady. See, Mama had a little sense.

They would have these revivals in a tent and Daddy would take me. He would take me in his arms, and I would hold this leg up for some reason. When we went to this tent, you would write your name on a piece of paper and burn it up, and when you got in there, the man would call you by your name. I guess he wanted to show that he had some magic and you could believe he could heal you.

One of my mother's friends told her that she didn't see why I was going to school because I couldn't do anything but work with my hands, like embroidery. It didn't make Mama any difference, and I finished grade school and started high school. Mama made arrangements for a Mr. White to drive me to high school and pick me up in the afternoon. Back then, all the children had to walk from South-side to Parker High School, and they would line up on the street and get a ride with Mr. White when he came by to pick me up.

I've always had this sour expression on my face . . . look! My mama used to make me stand in front of the mirror and smile. She told me I wasn't ever going to be able to go around and do what other people did, so I was going to have to get into this world, and nobody liked to be around somebody who was always solemn. I have a harsh way of speaking and had to grin a lot to make up for it.

I don't know how my family handled all the medical bills because I had seventeen operations before I finished high school and this was in the thirties in the worst of the depression. One day, an insurance man came by and told Mama about the 365 Club. This was a club the people in Birmingham had formed to help people who had problems. What they would do is put in a penny a day for a whole year, 365 pennies, and they helped me with a lot of the operations. I spent about six months out of every year getting corrective surgery and the other six months in school. After one of these operations, I got my braces and crutches and could start moving around and taking care of myself. When I was about eighteen, the doctor wanted to do another operation. I wanted to know, "Can I throw away my braces? Can I throw away my crutches?" and the doctor said he couldn't promise me anything. I didn't have that operation and haven't had one since.

When I was at Parker High School, I got to be real good at public speaking. I spoke at Parker High School one time when Eleanor Roosevelt was there. I didn't have the kind of sense to be scared just because the president's wife was out there in the audience. Mama had schooled me so that nothing made me nervous. Besides that, I was a little mean and devious, and if you messed with me, I would get you told pretty fast because I had that little chip, right there on my shoulder. I graduated from Parker High School in 1938 and I was valedictorian of my class. When I made my speech as valedictorian, I told the story of my life and I could see people crying. Here I was about twenty-one and was a little older than most kids because for the past six years I was out six months each of those years getting operations. But all that time, I was keeping up with my classes. From then on, I began speaking at churches and clubs on a great variety of subjects.

Parties and Peach Seeds

Richard C. Boggs, Jefferson County

We were living in the Carolinas around 1925 and my dad heard about all the road building going on down in Alabama. He came down as a representative of heavy road-building machinery and we rented a house out in Avondale. About a year later, my dad bought a house just off Highland Avenue on Birmingham's Southside and the family settled in.

After about a year, I started high school at Phillips and we rode to school on the streetcars, those little small streetcars where one goes this way and another goes that way, down Highland Avenue past the country club and Forrest Park and on downtown. Even the wealthy kids rode the streetcars, but some drove to school in their own cars. We would get off downtown where the old YMCA was and walk the few blocks up to the high school.

I had some real nice friends there in South Highlands and Forrest Park, and the country club was there. We weren't members of the country club because we couldn't afford that. There was another nice group of friends over in Norwood at that time. We used to go over there and "pop call" some of the better-looking girls. Pop calling is when a bunch of boys would get together and just drop in on a girl without letting her know first.

We had a ball when I was in high school in Birmingham in the mid 1920s. We had high school fraternities and social clubs and they would give dances. The wealthier girls would have tea dances and debutante parties all during the winter season, and other buffet dances at the country club. I don't know how, but I got in that group. I got invited to all those parties, but there was no way I could reciprocate. I belonged to a little social club which met in the basement of a house around the corner from where I lived, fellow named Palmer Doggett. They had servants' quarters on the first floor and that's where we had a club room. For me, that was a big social step when I was invited to join the Jesters Club. We would give a ball once a year. In fact, all the high school fraternities and social clubs like the Manhattan Club and the Jesters Club would all give balls once a year. The balls would be formal, and it was an honor for a girl to be invited because we gave favors, like compacts or some little thing with our club emblem on them. Girls liked to go to a dance with a member because she was assured the first few dances with her date, and then the dance would open up for breaks. You know how people used to break on dances, like cutting in. We didn't have any refreshments as such but had live bands, well-known bands.

On dates, we didn't go to movies or anything like that. You went over and sat on the girl's porch. The sitting routine went on all through high school. A lot of us had regular dates, like I had a regular Sunday night date with one girl for a long time. We would be sitting there sometimes when the pop callers would come in and that would aggravate the hell out of me. One way to gauge how popular a girl was, was how many pop callers she had. Pop callers would drop in, play records, or just visit in general. I did a little pop calling myself, but of course, I didn't have a car and had to hook rides.

One fellow who was very important to me was a boy who lived on Highland Avenue. He had a very bad eye handicap and couldn't focus his eyes. One would go this way, and the other would go the other way, and he was always shaking his head to get them lined up. His father was a very wealthy man and his brother was a Rhodes Scholar and the family was very prominent. His family didn't want him to drive at night, so I would walk down from my house to his house and we would go out in the car, me driving. Well, as soon as we got out of sight, he would slip under the wheel and take over. I guess that's why we became such good friends. He was pretty dependent on me to get out of the house with the car.

His family did just about everything to get his eyes right. One doctor told the family that he thought it would help if the boy would get out and paint houses. So, the boy got out and got a job on a house-painting crew. At that time, he had a red Buick Roadmaster convertible with a whistle on the exhaust and a fire engine siren, and he had a raccoon coat he liked to wear. He would go to these construction jobs, drive up in a red convertible with that raccoon coat on, get out of the car, take off the raccoon coat, and start painting. Painting didn't do his eyes any good. He didn't go to high school.

His parents got him a private tutor in his home because he just couldn't hack it in high school. Well, he and I went out a lot together, driving off in his car and going to see the girls. His unusual eye problem didn't seem to bother the girls at all, and they thought it was a big joke that he was house painting.

Around the late 1920s and the early 1930s, we couldn't afford to buy liquor and Alabama was dry anyway, so we bought corn whiskey. We would go to these dances at the country club and some of the boys would go outside and slip a few drinks, then come back into the dance. The girls didn't like that. Those were the days when we would take a pull out of the pint bottle of whiskey, take a big drink of water, smoke a cigarette, then chew some gum. Then, you were feeling good. Of course, if the girl's family ever found out about it, you were out. We were young, then, and didn't worry.

At our house, we had a wooden garage out back with a wooden floor that the car drove up on. That floor was kind of rotten, the floorboards were a little loose, and I hid the whiskey under the floorboards. To make that old moonshine set up, we would go to the drugstore and buy charred peach seeds and pour them in the bottle, shake it around, and make it fizz a little bit, and you could age that moonshine in five minutes. I think the drugstore kept those charred peach seeds for that purpose. You see, what those peach seeds did was take out some of the fusel oil out of the whiskey, and then we would shake some of the whiskey out on the cork, strike a match, and light it. If it burned red, we wouldn't drink it because it would poison you. If it burned blue, it was all right; it was fine; it was good stuff.

Later on after I went to work at the bank, my little brother, Mark, called me up one day and said, "Dick, you better come on home. The garage fell down and we know what's under that floor." He was afraid my family would find all those bottles under there.

Another time, I went to an American Institute of Banking convention in Chicago. At that time, Alabama had a cap on alcohol, something like 2 percent alcohol in a brew they called "near beer." In Chicago, beer was legalized and we drank that regular beer, enjoying it because it was such an improvement on Birmingham's "near beer." I bought quite a few bottles to carry back to Birmingham to use for special occasions. I was still living with my family then and I put those special bottles of beer up out of sight in the butler's pantry. Then one day, my little brother Mark called me up at the bank. He said, "Dick, I thought I had better call and tell you that mom poured your beer out." My parents didn't drink at all. My stepmother had discovered that beer and just poured it out. She never said a word to me about it. Of course, by that time, I was twenty-two years old.

On My Own

Mae Mack, Jefferson County

I was born in Pittsburgh, Pennsylvania. My daddy was working in the mines and my mother stayed home having babies. She had babies like a cat had kittens, thirteen children, but then she moved to New York and I went with her, along with some more children. Well, we had an aunt in Birmingham who took sick and I had an older sister who came down to stay with her, and I came next. I was nine years old. When my sister came, she met this old, rich black guy and she married him and she took me with her. They gave me everything I wanted. This old rich black man was some kind of doctor and people came to his house to see him. Nobody paid much attention to me so I did what I wanted to.

My sister told me, "Mae, you keep your dress down, now," but I was moving pretty fast and I kept pulling my dress up and that's when I got pregnant. I was eleven years old. But I didn't know I was pregnant because nobody had ever told me anything, but my sister figured out what was going on when I kept on getting sick all the time. When that baby came—I was twelve then—my sister told me I had to quit school and take care of my own baby, but after about a month, I started back again. When I got back to school, I started messing around again and got pregnant for the second time. I was thirteen when that second baby came, and it happened with the same guy.

This guy was real nice looking, light skinned and handsome, and he had good hair. See, I was real dark, and I said to myself,

"Whoo-ee, Lord, I just love this man," because at that time, the light-skinned man went with the light-skinned girls, and he had just been using me, but I didn't know no better. After the second baby came, my sister said I had to get out and get a job. I got a job out at the Ingernut, like you going out to Tarrant City. I worked at the Ingernut when my sister went back to New York, and when she came back, she told me to get out of the house with my babies. I told her not to put me out because I didn't have any place to go but back to my mother, and she was still having babies herself. She gave in and let me stay there and I got a job down at a little cafe on Second Avenue, washing dishes. Washing pots and pans.

About this time, I met a guy from Atlanta, another older guy, and I met him on the streetcar, like they didn't have buses back then, but a streetcar that run on those tracks, you know. He told me I was a cute little fat black thing and he liked me. I told him about my children, but he didn't seem to care, and the first thing you know, he's coming to the house to see me, and the next thing you know, I'm in bed with him and I'm pregnant again.

My sister made him marry me then, but I didn't like him. I didn't want him for no husband so I took a fork to bed with me so he wouldn't mess with me any more. He got mad about that fork and said I was crazy and he never should have married me. We stayed together until my baby was about three years old and then he started running around on me. Then he left out, my sister sold the house, and there I was, no job and no house and three babies.

I got a job at the Domestic Laundry and rented a little shotgun house off First Avenue. I went down to the furniture store and got a coal stove, a living room suite, a bedroom suite, a rollaway bed, a kitchen cabinet, a table and chairs, three linoleum rugs, and I got all that for $150. I didn't have anybody to keep the three little girls while I was working, so I left those little kids in the house all by themselves for two months while I worked. The doors weren't locked so the kids played by themselves. I liked to went crazy. Then I found a woman to keep my kids for nothing.

I walked to work, all the way from Avondale to Fifth Avenue South. My shoes didn't have any soles in them—just the tops—and I would stick cardboard in the bottoms for soles. I would get the boxes from the grocery store. They would save me the strongest boxes because they knew what I wanted them for. Sometimes, I would get a big needle and try to sew that cardboard in the shoes. I would work all day, walk back to pick up the kids, and go home and try to find them some supper. Most of the time I wasn't eating myself and got down to about ninety pounds. I used to take one of their little dresses, lay an old dress on some brown paper, cut it out, and hand-sew their little dresses, two apiece at a time. There was a man who came through and gave me coal, said it was because I was struggling so, and he would come in and put the coal on a brown paper sack behind the stove.

We lived like this for five or six years and I didn't have any time for men then except for one thing. I went without food a lot of times so my kids would have something to eat, and I would do just about anything—except kill—to take care of them. I would have went with guys to feed my kids and have a place for them to stay. If I met a man, I would tell him, "Look, I got kids and they got to be fed and they got to have milk. If you can't give me money to help me do that, why honey, you can just go on 'bout your business." He would say, "You get just as much enjoyment out of it as I do," and I would say, "No, I don't. I'm just getting the money. That's all I want." Well, I was telling the truth. I had a hard time. I went with guys I didn't even want to go with, but by that time, I had learned a lesson. I made 'em use protection. I had it all figured out by that time and didn't want to make any babies.

I heard they were going to build some new apartments and I could get one cheap. I went down and they let me have one of those apartments for $8 a month and it was some change, I tell you. I had three bedrooms, a living room, and a kitchen, and I bought me some new furniture. I got a new living room suite, an end table, a coffee table, two lamps, some more rugs, a table and chairs, and a bedroom suite. I got all of that furniture for $350 and paid the man $10 a week.

Now, I was living better. I got a woman in the apartment to keep the kids while I worked and met another man who lived in the same place. He was OK I guess, but the first thing I know, I'm pregnant again. Now, I started getting sick down at the laundry and the man told me that if I had any more babies I was going to lose my job. So, I told him I was going to have to lose my job, because I was fixing to have a baby. There was another girl at the laundry who was always having babies, too. She told me, "Why, a man can just touch me and I get pregnant," and I told her I did more than that. I laid down with a man. Anyhow, I had to quit the laundry.

After that baby came, I got a job at Pizitz at Roebuck washing dishes in the store restaurant, then they taught me how to cook and bake. I met Jesse there that same year and started going with him. He told me he liked me because I had big legs and big hips, and I did. I wore a size twenty then. We got married and he moved in with me. I really didn't love him when we got married. I married him because his mother said he didn't need to marry a woman who was older than he was and had a bunch of kids. She even sent him off up to Chicago, but one day, he called and said he wanted to come home, so I sent him the money to get back. He sat around the apartment for a whole year, didn't work, and I told him, "Jesse, you are going to have to get a job or you're going to have to leave." He got a job and we had two more babies and we've been doing all right ever since.

Fifteen Acres in West Alabama

Jeff Coleman, Sumter County

My grandfather went down to Florida to help build a railroad. He moved to Muscle Shoals and finally settled down at Livingston. He built some houses and he built some stores. He was a contractor and a good carpenter himself. He built a house for a man and the man give him fifteen acres right on the Sucarnochee Creek. That's an Indian name which is supposed to mean "hog wallow," and he built a house out of some odds and ends on that land and that's where we lived through my childhood. My sister later built a house on that same site. That creek—we called it a river—starts over there in bloody Kemper County in Mississippi.

Before I came along, I guess the most excitement around Livingston was the hanging of the sheriff who turned bad and was a highway robber. His name was Renfroe and he's been written about. The crowd took Renfroe out of the jail and hanged him. He had been escaping and they hanged him not far from where my family lived, on some property next to our pasture out there on that fifteen acres.

I remember a time in Livingston when they had a big barbecue on the court square. They dug a big trench, at least it seemed like a big trench to me because I was a little boy, and they put the green poles across that three-foot-deep trench, and they put the whole hogs and calves on the green poles, and cooked the barbecue right there on the square. Then they put up sawhorses and put planks across the sawhorses for tables and that sort of thing. A big feed.

Another thing that was exciting to me when I was a boy, and I guess everybody else, was a big-time baseball game in Livingston. There was this fellow, Champ Pickens, who grew up in Livingston and was a little older than I was. Well, somehow or other, Champ got the Rochester baseball team in the American League and the Philadelphia Athletics to play a baseball game in Livingston and that was a real big thing in that part of the country. Champ was working for the Chesterfield Cigarette Company at that time, advertising Chesterfield, and Champ swung that game in Livingston somehow. I remember that there was a pretty good crowd, too, about 1,000 people.

We had a summer league for baseball. We would hire the whole University of Alabama baseball team to be the Livingston team in the summer. One year, the Alabama team didn't have a good first baseman, or the first baseman went somewhere else, and we had to get an Auburn player to play first base. The coach started out with a local boy as a replacement, the son of the banker, but that didn't work out. We played against those boys from over there at Macon and Electric Mills in Mississippi.

That fifteen acres of land my grandfather was paid for building a house, it was all right. We had five or six cows for milk. You know we didn't have milk delivery back in those days and my father had to do something with that fifteen acres. You couldn't grow a crop on it because it was sitting down by that creek, and the creek would rise and flood most of the property in the spring and often again in the fall. He thought that maybe he could grow some pecan trees because somebody told him that pecan trees could stand a certain amount of high water, so he made a deal with a man to plant some pecan trees. The man must have had another job somewhere because he came to plant the trees late one afternoon. I had never seen anything like this. So, he came in and put his dynamite down in some holes in the ground where he was going to plant the trees. I didn't know his system because he didn't have them all wired together, but periodically, one of those sticks of dynamite would go off. It was just like a little war going off all over those fifteen acres. He would blow a hole and plant the tree, and it was just before dark, remember. He planted the trees, but the high water gradually killed them. That fifteen acres was never any good for anything but pasture.

Getting the Word

Bob Hodges, Jackson County

Before television, we got the news in Scottsboro pretty much from neighborhood talk, from the radio, from the *Sentinel* and the *Progressive Age*, and from Bert Woodall and Veda Maude Sumner, the telephone operators down at the phone company switchboard. The phone method was my favorite way to get the news. You could call and find out from Bert or Veda Maude where the fire was after seeing the truck go around the square collecting volunteers, some of whom were pulling off grocers' aprons as they jumped on the truck, and you could find out if your daddy was still at the store, or if he had gone fishing, and you could find out if your neighbor was still in the hospital. The news in the paper was full of good things like what was playing at the Ritz and the Bocanita, what Bob Jones had said in Washington, and the Estill Fork column and the Woodville column and who had been down to visit with whom for the weekend. A revival was always good for a front-page story, and the high school game was fully reported.

One week, there was a picture in the paper of a brand new police car with two regular patrol policemen standing proudly on either side. "City buys new police car," the headline read, right on the front page. About a week later, the word got around that the new police car was chasing a car on the Guntersville highway, and one policeman told the driver that he was going to try to shoot the tires out of the escaping car. He leaned out the window and promptly put three rounds·through the radiator of the police car which ground to a screeching halt. The next week's paper carried a story on the last page which said, in total, "A high-speed chase of a drunken driver last week resulted in gunshots and damage to the city's new police car. The drunken driver escaped."

In Scottsboro in the early fifties, the word *sex*, as in the relationship between a man and a woman, was never used in a classroom or at church. Neither do I remember my parents ever sitting down and explaining it to me. My earliest recollection of any sex education was one December night just before Christmas when I was about thirteen. We were out caroling with the Methodist Youth Fellowship. We'd go up to a house, sing a few songs, and get some apples or oranges as a reward. When we got to this one house were a young and attractive widow woman in our church lived, she didn't answer the knock on the door. Somebody noticed a light shining at the back of the house. We went around back and sang a carol to that window with the light hiding behind a shade. There was a flurry of activity inside and the shade flew up, and standing there before the Lord and everybody else was the startled and quite naked widow woman. She had thrown up the shade to see who was in her backyard. Ever since that night, whenever I hear "God Rest Ye Merry Gentlemen," I feel a strange warmth, and I have fond memories of that carol.

Bo Davis, Pat Trammell, and I used to help Dusty Carter in the summer baseball program when we were in high school. Back in those days, the older kids were in what we called the Tiny Mites. Dr. Paul Dawson, a dentist, had two sons, Charles and Robert, and both played in this very intensely competitive league. I was an assistant coach and had to name a starting team each day for the Tiny Mites. Dr. Dawson was my dentist, and I remember my mother taking me there for a filling that summer. Just before Dr. Dawson began the drilling, standing there in front of the chair holding up a syringe of novocaine, he held the needle up to the light and gave a few test squirts. He told me to close my eyes and open wide, and then he said, "Why isn't Robert starting?" Robert never missed an inning the rest of the summer.

Back of the Bus

Icese Thomas, Jefferson County

It was a scary situation when the civil rights movement was getting going and I was right in the middle of it. Hundreds of black people would come marching by your door, trying to get you off the job and they would say, "Come on and march with us." I got off of work one evening, and it was in the summertime. Well, I went out of the building and locked the door and was walking down the street when a carload of white guys came cruising by. I heard one of 'em holler, "There goes a nigger and he be by himself. Let's get him." Back then, I could pick 'em up and put 'em down so I took off running. I was running down alleys and jumping fences trying to get away from those white boys and they were driving around trying to spot me. Finally, I lay down behind this hedge to keep them from seeing me and they drove up pretty close and one of 'em said, "Where did he go?" and then another one said, "I don't know where he went, but he sure is fast!" They didn't catch me that time, but that's the way it was then.

Along about that same time, I went downtown in Birmingham and I had my wife and children with me. We went into a store called Kresses. All these people were marching outside and they kept telling me not to go in that store, but I did because I needed some things for my baby. My baby had to use the rest room and I asked the lady there could I take my little girl to the rest room, and she said, "Niggers not allowed in there," and I said, "What did you say? This is my baby." Then I said, "Well, is there a janitor's closet? Can she go in there?" And the lady said, "Boy, you didn't understand me, did you? I said, no niggers use the rest room around here, period!" So, I took my little girl out of there, and when I got to the front door, I pulled her little panties down and she used the bathroom right there, right in the front door of Kresses, and I made sure that lady saw me. Out in the front of the store, there were two lines—a line of blacks and another line of whites—and they were throwing rocks. I told my wife we had little children and we got to get out of there. I remember right about then, Bull Connor was down there talking on a bullhorn and he was saying, "I'm not going to tell you niggers anymore. Break it up and get out of here." Me and my wife got out of there, walking, because we wasn't riding no buses or nothing. That was out. It was dangerous walking from town out to where we lived, but we made it.

Like, I got on the bus one evening and there was a portable sign about halfway down the bus and it said "colored." Picture this, I got on the bus, walked back to the back behind that sign. Then, the bus started getting full of white people so the bus driver got up and moved that colored sign further back so the white people would have a place to sit. Now I'm sitting in the white section and that meant I had to move. The bus driver looked at me and said, "What are you doing still sitting there, boy? This is the white section now." I told him that I had been working all day and that I was tired. He said something like "That's tough, but you got to move." I got up and moved, but that kind of put me over the edge, and I felt, right then, that I had about all I could take.

Gravel Hills and Flatlands

Jerry Oldshue, Lamar County

Sulligent is not an old town. About 1880, the Frisco railroad came out of Memphis headed for Birmingham and when it came back through that end of the county, several of the small communities around moved up on the railroad. So, it was one block, and then right down here on the north end was the depot, and any activity in the town was centered on the railroad street. The cotton gins and all were on the other side of the railroad. During World War II, a lot of guys went over to Prairie, Mississippi, to work in the ammunition factory, some more went to Mobile and Pascagoula, and some went to Birmingham to work in the steel mills.

The big industry in town was the cotton-oil mill. You brought the cotton in and you ginned it and they took the cottonseed and pressed it and you had cottonseed cake. They pressed the cakes and you got cotton oil. It smelled great. And the cheap sardines were packed in cottonseed oil and the good sardines were packed in olive oil. Supposedly, that was the largest cotton gin in the world. It was run with the old belts off the drive shaft and the belts would run the machinery, and sometimes, people would get their arms caught in the belts. This was a bad farming country, gravel hills back in there. The farms were down in the flatlands by the streams and the rest of the farmers were trying to scratch out a living up in those gravelly hills. Well, it turned out that about 1960 they discovered oil and gas and they got the wells sitting there chugging along and the people make a pretty good living.

My dad was the postmaster in Sulligent and he died when I was about five. We had four acres in downtown Sulligent on Vernon Street, and when my dad died, my mother went back to teaching in the elementary school. We had the house and it was paid for. We were poor, but nobody knew it, because the whole town was poor. I was thirteen years old before I figured out that we didn't have much money. I was a kid in the thirties and I didn't know times were bad. Dad died, but we got by. I guess it didn't cost all that much to live.

About once a month, the fellow who ran the grocery store killed a cow and you had fresh meat and you just bought what he had. If you wanted hamburger, you bought fresh meat and ground it yourself. I remember that grocery store, going in, and he's chopping the meat, and sawing, and the side of beef would be up there and he would cut a piece off for you. We bought milk from the lady across the street and I was in college before we had milk delivery in Sulligent. We had chickens and we sold eggs. During the war, we sold eggs for sixty cents a dozen and that was a pretty good take. Later on, we sold three of our four acres and I went to college on the profits of that sale.

Sulligent had a pretty good football team in the forties. When we graduated, about half of the football team, or more, got scholarships. The really good guys went to the big schools, but I was one step down, so we got offers from junior colleges in Mississippi. One of them was a junior college in Scooba, and anybody who hasn't been to Scooba is socially deprived. I can't remember that coach's name over there but he was one tough hombre. You had to go down there to try out and he didn't issue any hip pads. He didn't believe in hip pads for his football team. They put us in a room that didn't have a door on it. Well, it had a door frame, it just didn't have a door. And they didn't give us any sheets to sleep on. We had to sleep under newspapers. They offered us scholarships, but we didn't take them. Scooba? You kind of had to be going there on purpose to get there from here.

Moving South

Lula Fluellen, Jefferson County

In 1927, I was twelve years old when we moved back to Birmingham from New Rochelle, New York. My mother had to come back because my grandmother had taken ill and had to have somebody with her. Back then, there were no nursing homes. Families took care of family. My grandmother never did get any better, so the whole family had to come down here. My daddy had a good job as an upholsterer in New Rochelle and didn't want to come, but he finally moved here, too. He couldn't find a good job in Birmingham and finally got a job down in Miami as a mattress maker. That rascal went down there and made all kind of money and he forgot about us up here. The only time he came back was to my brother's funeral.

There was a big difference in New Rochelle, New York, and Birmingham for a twelve-year-old. Up there, when I wanted to go somewhere, anywhere, I just went. When I got down here, I was told I couldn't do this any more. So where you were supposed to go in the back door, I just went on in the front door. Sometimes, somebody would say something, and sometimes, they wouldn't. Like you had the elevators. You were supposed to just ride on just one, but whichever one came first, I just got on it. I saw no reason why it should be any different from where I came from. My mother instilled in us that all people are the same, but there are good and bad people wherever you go. In New Rochelle, we had integrated schools. In Birmingham, I went to a segregated school with all black teachers. I remember at New Rochelle, I had all white teachers.

One time, before I moved down here, my mother had to come to Birmingham to see about her mother and left us in school up there. The first morning Mama was gone, I went to school and my hair wasn't looking like it should have. My teacher called me in the cloakroom and asked me, "Where is your mother?" and I said she's gone to Alabama. She asked me who combed my hair, and I said my daddy did. She said, "Well, in the morning, you tell your daddy to let you come ten minutes early to school." She combed my hair every morning until my mother got back. I never got any different treatment up there from the other children because I was black.

The main difference I saw when I moved to Birmingham in 1927 was having to go to the back all the time, like in the back of the bus. There were certain places you knew not to go in to buy a sandwich or a hot dog because that wasn't for you. I couldn't ever see the reason in it. What difference did it make? When I was sixteen, there were just four of us in the house: my mother, my grandmother, my eighteen-year-old brother, and myself. Within three weeks, there were just two of us. My brother died in a swimming accident, and my grandmother fell dead out on the front porch. I don't think my mother ever got over losing my brother, and I know I didn't. He always protected me and was my best friend, and when he died, it never was the same again.

My mother got a job up on the hill at a hardware store. The man opened a grocery store in the other side of the building and she learned how to cut meat and all of that. We got by with the money she made and the money I got for playing piano at dances.

City Life, Lower Alabama

Street scene, Selma, 1935
(Walker Evans/Farm Security Administration
photo, Library of Congress, Washington, D.C.)

On the Florida Short Route

Denson Franklin, Coosa County

All the farmers came into Goodwater on Saturday and they would hang around the stores and talk. When evening came on, the black people enjoyed entertaining each other and the community with their music, playing the banjo and guitar and singing. Back in those days, there were no paved roads. There was a good chert road going north and south through the town and it was called the Florida Short Route. That's the road Yankees traveled on their way to Florida. Country people would come into town on Saturdays in wagons or in trucks which the plantation owner would use to bring his people into town.

In my father's store, I was assigned to about ten plantation owners to service and one in particular who was really big in the region. I was told what to let his people have and what not to have because all the purchases were charged to the big landowner. The tenants could have tobacco and they could have flour, and things like that, but my list told me exactly what each family could have. I had a box for each of these families. A lot of these big farmers raised a lot of provisions on their place and some even had their own gristmills down by some creek. I knew all these families, what their needs were, and who was about to get in trouble with the man in the big house. The farmers would bring their cotton in when it was harvested and my father would help them get the best price. We delivered groceries to townspeople. Many of the people in town kept cows and we delivered sweet feed and hay to the homes. Just about all of my father's store business was on credit and the big ledger in the front of the store was very important.

Back in the twenties, my father did a very unusual thing. He took a stand about the voting rights for black people. He was executive secretary for the Democratic party and when Al Smith was running for president, my dad registered every black person he could, most of them making a mark for his name. That was something in that day. Usually, the pastor would come with ten or twelve people and the superintendent of schools would bring some. My father was anti-Klan, too, and I would go to bed many nights afraid that the Klan would come for him. They didn't mean for me to hear it, but I could hear my father telling my mother, "If they come, I will be ready for them." He kept a revolver and could knock a bird off a limb with it. He would spin the cylinder on that pistol, lay it by the bed, and say, "If they come tonight, I think they will be sorry. They might get me, but I will get four or five of them." That was scary.

When I was four years old, I preached my first sermon in front of my father's store. I must have had an inclination for the ministry even back then. I would get up on a box there and four or five people would stand around and listen to me, some of my black friends, too. There was one man, a big fat man, who would stand there every time I preached, smoking a big pipe, just standing there listening. I would talk for about five minutes each time, and after I had finished, the big man would pat me on the back and say, "Son, you just keep on preaching. That's good." My father would laugh and say that the only regular parishioner my son has in his congregation was the chief bootlegger in the area. Uncle Pete stayed right there and heard me and gave me encouragement. I didn't understand what a bootlegger was, but I appreciated the encouragement.

I had taken lessons for the city band when I was about fifteen and learned how to play the trombone pretty good. A bunch of grown men organized the East Alabama Vagabonds, a dance band, and they played at Shocco Springs and a place called Clairmont Springs outside of Ashland. People had homes there, spent the summers there, and the Vagabonds played at each place one night a week. When Lake Martin was built, they started playing one night a week while the lake was coming in. They lost their trombone player one time and they called my father and asked him if I could play for them up at Shocco Springs for a dance. Good group of people up there for that dance, they said. I stayed with the band all that summer and most of the next summer. That was the days of "Shine on Harvest Moon" and "My Blue Heaven," and "St. Louis Blues" always came in there. I did the second round on that one with the mute, you know, the wah-wah sound with the trombone. I remember most of the songs of that day—"Three Little Words" and "Just a Cottage Small by a Waterfall" and "I Dream of Lilac Time."

I got in a dilemma because it worried my pastor that I was playing in a dance band. He knew that I was leaning toward being a preacher. We were having a revival there in Goodwater and I was ushering at the revival about the same time that I was supposed to be playing for a dance up at Clairmont Springs. The orchestra didn't start playing until nine o'clock, so I went ahead and ushered for the revival and left a little early to rush up to Clairmont Springs. Right after I left, they called for the ushers to come forward and give out some literature. Somebody whispered that I had gone to Clairmont Springs. That shook me up, and it wasn't long after that that I made a decision to go into the ministry.

Lemon Sodas and Cotton Mills

C. J. Coley, Tallapoosa County

I was born in my parents' home in 1902 in Alexander City down on what is now Church Street, about halfway between the big Russell Mill plant and the Avondale Mills factory. Back in those days, we called Russell Mill the knitting mill and we called the Avondale mill the cotton mill. I grew up like any other small-town boy on an unpaved road and I can remember that in the winter, the street would get so bad that even wagons would get stuck. The town began to grow in direct relation to the growth of the two big mills. Alexander City was named for the president of the Savannah and Memphis Railroad, a Confederate general named E. P. Alexander.

When I was a teenager—this was between 1910 and 1920—it was the custom for all ages to go down to the Central of Georgia Railroad and watch the passenger trains come and go. Every morning about nine o'clock, a passenger train would arrive from Columbus, Georgia, on its way to Birmingham. The train would stay long enough for the passengers to get off and others to get on. Postal service was also provided by the passenger train. There was a slot on the side of the baggage car for letters to be dropped in, and the baggage mail clerk would work up the letters while the train was moving between stations. One of our favorite pastimes was to watch the engineer when he came down from the engine to oil his "wheelers" at each stop. We really admired the engineer who could blow his whistle with the greatest virtuosity and the large, strong firemen who shoveled in the coal.

After high school, I worked a year in a bank, then went on to The University of Alabama. When I came back to Alexander City, I developed an alcohol problem, left the bank, and founded the first chapter of Alcoholics Anonymous in Alexander City. Even after this experience with alcohol, I decided to run for probate judge. A lot of people thought I was overly optimistic about my chances due to my past record of excessive drinking, but I ran and won, and held that job for the next fourteen years. I left the judgeship to run a bank and stayed in the banking business for the balance of my working life.

My father was a merchant, he and my uncle, and they had a business called Coley and Sandlin, a rather big affair for a small town. The store had two entrances to it, about the size of two store buildings now. They had men's and women's wear on one side and farming tools and groceries and things of that kind on the other side. Now usptairs, they had a millinery department. This is rather interesting. Back in those days, ladies had one or two hats that they had trimmed every year. Our millinery department had what they called "hat trimmers" on the second floor and ladies would come and get their hats trimmed every year so they would have new headdresses. In church where they would have the singing, one of the things that attracted the people to the new hats was the way the hats shook when singing was going on, watching those flowers dancing about. All women wore hats to church back then.

My father's business closed in about 1914 when the boll weevils ate up all the cotton. My father suffered severe monetary losses but never took bankruptcy. He paid all his debts. During the summers, I would be a runner for a store, delivering groceries. Back in those days, people would order groceries from the store, and the groceries would be delivered to the house and would be charged. I can remember back in the 1920s, I would take a date in a car and drive up in front of Carlisle's Drugstore, sound the horn, and a soda jerk would bring the Cokes out to the car, complete with cherries. Cokes were a nickel apiece and the soda jerk would charge them. Think of that! Back in those days, the big soda fountain drink for country people was lemon soda, served in a big glass with a lot of foam on it. What they would do, those country people would come into Carlisle's Drugstore, and it would be three or four or more. Every one of them would order a lemon soda. Then one of the men would say, "Have one on me," and they would drink another one, and wind up drinking several lemon sodas at one sitting.

On Saturday, country people would load up the town. We had so many blacks here, and of course they were good blacks, but they would just bunch up here and there. Occasionally, a policeman would have to go up to a group of blacks who were talking and laughing and gathered up on the sidewalk and ask them to move so that folks could walk by. People would come to towns in wagons, mostly, and some of them had buggies, but whole families would come, and they would put these cane-bottom chairs in the wagon beds for the ladies to sit on. You would say, now what did these people do all day on Saturday while they were in town? Well, they would go in these stores and the ladies would sit back there and wait and they wouldn't even think about shopping for anything.

Back in those days, the young men out in the country would gradually come into town to live. Their idea of greatness was to get a job in a grocery store or something like that. The housewives in town from good families would take these country men in as boarders. The housewives would give the men three meals a day and a place to sleep and it would cost the boarders about half of what they made, maybe twenty dollars a month. When these ladies would go down to the grocery store to do their shopping, they would always ask the grocer what he suggested for dinner that day. Now, dinner was at midday. The night meal was called supper. One day, one of these ladies asked the grocer what he suggested for dinner that day, and he said he had some really good-looking cow's tongue that she might like to serve. The lady said indignantly, "I don't want to serve anything that has been in any animal's mouth." As quick as a flash, the grocer asked, "How would you like a dozen fresh eggs?"

I went through the depression working in the First National Bank of Alexander City. We had two banks in town back in the thirties, and neither one ever came close to failing. Sometimes, our mills did cut down to running two days a week, but they never closed. We had sawmills as well as the textile mills and everybody kept going, somehow. One of my jobs in the early days in the bank was dealing with currency. We were a national bank and national bank currency at that time came in large sheets, some sheets being five-dollar bills, some ten-dollar bills, and some twenty-dollar bills. My job was to stamp the names of the bank president and the cashier on each bill, take the scissors, and cut each bill out.

When I first started working in a bank, the tellers stood behind iron grilles. A man would come up to the window with a bank passbook to make a deposit and we would take the book and make the entry. Once a month, he would come in and ask for his book to be balanced. Before Franklin Roosevelt took us off the gold standard, I handled a lot of gold coins. In the midtwenties, and through the thirties, we would come into the bank at 7:30 in the morning, sweep it out, and open for business at 8 A.M. We stayed until five in the afternoon, except on Saturdays when we stayed open until 9 P.M. We loaned principally on crops yet to be harvested and on cows and other stock, and on some real estate. All our loans were short term, like a farmer got a one-year loan. When I started in the banking business, my salary was forty dollars a month, and when I got married in 1932, I was making sixty dollars a month. I felt fortunate to be earning that sixty dollars because it was during the depression.

Latchkey Child without a Key

Mary Frances Tipton, Dallas County

My mother grew up in a large family in Lowndes County. She grew up out in the country since my grandfather was a farmer. There were no schools in that part of the county then so they had a governess who lived there in the house to teach the children. My mother stopped going to those little classes they had up there in the top of that house, and now this is according to one of her sisters, my mother was always too modest to tell it, but one day, she just stood up and left the room because, as she told her mother, she knew more Latin than the teacher did and she figured it was time she left. A couple of years after that, now this was about 1910, she got permission from her parents to go to Selma to go to business school there. My parents found a place for her to stay with some of their friends. She was the first to leave home and start a career. After she finished the school, she got a job with a Mr. Callen who was a cotton buyer down on Water Avenue. She met my father through friends of hers in the Methodist Church and they got married in the midtwenties.

My parents did not set up a separate home for themselves after they got married. My father's mother was a widow, and there were some younger children at home, so my father took my mother into his mother's home. And there they all lived—my father and mother, his mother, and my father's two younger sisters who never married. Well, I was an only child, but I thought that was normal, growing up in a household with all those adults. People always assumed that you had all these adults to spoil you, but you also grew up with all these expectations. What was amazing to me about that household that I didn't realize until I was grown was that those women got along together. They worked things out between them so that my mother ran the household even though they all worked. My mother did the hiring and firing of the servants, paid the bills, did the meal planning, did the grocery shopping, and generally ran the house.

The house we lived in in Selma was built in the 1890s, a one-story white frame house. My two aunts still live in it. It was a house with a wide hall down the middle with rooms off to either side, very tall ceilings and tall windows and a little sleeping porch on the back.

We had a woman who came once a week and took wash home with her, but we sent the linens to the steam laundry. When I was in school, I was close enough that I could walk home after school. I had no trouble getting in the house because we didn't even have keys for the front door. I don't ever remember the house being locked. I was a latchkey child without any key.

Seven Miles Behind the Jail

Leon Davis, Coffee County

Well, Elba was built on a square with a courthouse in the middle with a flowing well right there on the square. In fact, they call Elba the city of flowing wells. There was a flowing well in one corner of the court square that had a pool around it and it had a water fountain where people could go and get a drink. Artesian wells. The swimming pool was fed by one of the artesian wells and the water was always just freezing cold all the time. They put plants around the pool in town and they put fish in the pools like goldfish, but they were bigger than goldfish, colored red and orange and so on.

I was born in 1931, and all my life, when people talk about 1929, most people around the country would say that was the year of the big stock market crash and the big problems around the country. Well, around Elba, Alabama, the big thing down there was the flood, and that was the first time that the Pea River and the Whitewater Creek which converge right there within three hundred yards of the high school building showed serious high water. This was the first flood Elba ever had and, of course, it just washed away the town. In Elba, everything is dated from 1929 with the flood. After the flood, there were some weird stories. They say that one of my uncles spent the night in a tree with a rooster.

Following the flood, my daddy laid by his crops that summer, and found out that the WPA was building a levee. The WPA came in and just encircled the town, up above the town and around it and come down by the Whitewater Creek where it met the Pea River, and on down by the river past the town, and then on around the south side of the town. Roughly three sides of the town were enclosed. This was to keep the floodwaters from coming back through. It worked, I guess. The farmers, in late July and August, took the mules and scrapes and hired out to help build the levee. My daddy did that to make some money.

As I grew up, that levee was there and we didn't think much about it. It held the water off pretty good. Some water got into the town in

1985, but not a whole lot. Now, in 1990, we were down visiting in Geneva which is further down the Pea River near the Florida line and my stepdaughter called me early in the morning and said, "You might want to call your folks in Elba. They're evacuating up there." So, I thought about where my brothers and sisters lived and they lived out from town a little and I didn't think they would be affected. But later on that day, I saw the courthouse in Elba on TV. You know that the town is built on a square. The whole town was flooded, the water coming up to the second floor of the courthouse. Now, that's a sight to see—your whole hometown under water.

Of course, Geneva has a levee around it, too, and the people down there were sandbagging and so on and my wife and other folks were making sandwiches to help out. There was quite a stir there. It turns out that what happened in Elba was that the water came in on one side of the town, the water just rushed in, and it just flooded into the town. If they had not built that levee all around the south side back in the WPA days, the water would have continued on downstream. They had created a collecting tank there that just held the water. A lot of people feel that if they hadn't built those levees in Elba that Geneva would have caught the brunt of it. But the dam held the water in Elba and it just stayed there. I tell people I grew up in Elba behind the jail . . . about seven miles behind the jail, so I never worried about flooding when I was a boy.

I played baseball and basketball in high school, but no football. I went to high school in 1946, and in those days Coffee County, Alabama, had a bunch of junior high schools and four high schools. As long as I can remember, those junior highs had basketball teams. We played basketball all the time. It was like that old Jerry Clower story where Marcel Ledbetter was asked why he wasn't in school that day and he said wasn't no use in going because the basketball was flat, didn't have no air in it. I had played basketball three years before I went to high school and I don't believe Elba had won a basketball game through the war years. We had three people who came in from the junior highs who made the first team in the tenth grade. I played basketball three years in high school and we just had two people who lived in the city limits who played basketball. See, we played good because we hadn't been contaminated by football.

I went out for football in 1946 and I was probably about five-ten and weighed about 130 pounds—wiry as they say—and I went out there and I guess I was about fourth-team right end. What I really was was cannon fodder for the first teams. I remember two people very distinctly on that team. One of 'em's name was Pete Martin and the other'ns was Earl Twilly who played tackle. The thing I remember was the impression those two guys made on me. Both of them weighed about 190 pounds apiece and they had just gotten back out of the army. We had several people who had been in the army. Pete's brother played in the backfield and he had been in the military. They discouraged me considerably and I just went out for football one year.

One day we were having tackling drill and I was paired off with a kid about my size. You tried to get somebody your size so you wouldn't get killed. We were bumping each other around and I turned my ankle. Now, the football coach was also the basketball coach and he knew I was a pretty good basketball player, so he just told me to forget football for the rest of the year.

One night during the middle of the football season, both football coaches went up to Troy to scout a game. On the way back, a drunk hit them and they were hospitalized for a long time. There was an engineer there in town named Stanley Clark and he had played football at Mississippi State and they got him to take the football team for the rest of the year. Now, Stanley Clark got up one of the gosh awfulest ideas I ever heard of anybody having. He took the football team from Elba High School to Starkville to see Mississippi State play Hardin-Simmons. That's when Shorty McWilliams was playing at State. Somebody said they saw Shorty come around a corner in his car and it was so long that it had hinges in the middle to get around that corner. The crazy thing was that the football team went to Starkville in a trailer truck, if you can believe that, a flatbed trailer truck. The deal was that Dorsey Trailers, the biggest deal in town, donated the services of the truck for that trip. I remember we came through Montgomery and stopped at the *Montgomery Advertiser* building and they came out and took a picture of all the boys on the back of that big flatbed trailer. We must have had about forty boys on the back of that truck. We went over on Friday and stayed in the old gym on the State campus, supposed to sleep on the floor, but I don't think any of the boys slept any at all. We watched the game the next day, and since Stanley Clark was from Greenwood or Greenville or one of those town in the Delta, somehow we wound up going to Stanley's hometown to spend Saturday night. People in Elba gave us crates of apples and crates of oranges to take along on the trip. I'm sure there were a bunch of worried mamas when that truck left town, and I still don't know why my mama let me go. It was a crazy trip.

The Latest News and Barbecue

Hardenia Johnson, Marengo County

I was born in Cedarville a little after 1900. I was reared by my grandparents. I had an uncle in Birmingham, and when I got big enough, I went up there to stay with him. When my mother moved to Demopolis, I moved back to Demopolis, but when I was ready for high school, I went back to Birmingham to stay with my uncle again. I liked living with my uncle and his wife because they didn't have any children and I was the only young one living in the house. When I would leave there after school was out for the summer, I would come back to live in Demopolis with my mother and step-father. When I would come back to Demopolis in the summertime, I didn't miss anything because when I was in Birmingham, I didn't do anything but go to school, come back home, and go to church. So far as going out to parties and stuff like that, my uncle didn't allow me to do that. He was a strict old fellow. I didn't start going out with boys until I had finished high school and had moved back to Demop-olis, but even then, I didn't go out. Boys would just come to the house and visit.

I got married in 1924 here in Demopolis. We had a lot of black businesses here in those days, cafes and upholstery places and those kinds of things.

The *Demopolis Times* belonged to the Georges and very few black people took the *Demopolis Times* because there was very little black news in the paper. One day, Mrs. George stopped me on the street and asked me how I would like to write some news about black folks for the paper, and I thought I would enjoy that. When Mrs. George first asked me about writing for the *Times*, she said she would pay me. I told her, "You don't have to pay me. I'll be glad to do it for nothing." We didn't have any special pay. Sometimes, she would meet me on the street and would say she hadn't given me any money this month, and she would give me a check for fifteen or twenty dollars, and that was all right because I was just getting a kick out of writing the news.

I started writing news about black people in the 1940s. At that time, my husband and I were in the cafe business and I guess Mrs. George figured that I knew what was going on in the black community. Besides that, I had eight children and I was active in the Morning Star Baptist Church, supervisor over the Baptist Training Union.

I've been around Demopolis a long time and I've been friends to all of the people around here and we didn't have black and white, you know. All my children grew up here and they all worked. My boys carried papers. Since the early 1940s there have been several different editors at the *Times* and I still write for the paper, and that's been over forty years. I started getting the news after people found out that I was writing for the paper. They would bring me the news and I would ask about it, like when people have homecomings and family reunions, deaths, and parties, and all that stuff and I wrote about it. Some weeks I have a lot and some weeks I don't have much, but I have really enjoyed it down through the years.

About our cafe, it was in 1936 during the depression when my husband was working for the railroad, and he got bumped. Mr. Pickett, he's in Mississippi now, told us that if we could find a place to open a cafe, he would lend us one hundred dollars to get started. We found a place and opened. There was an old fellow who taught me how to barbecue and we cooked whole hogs. We got our hogs out of Montgomery because we didn't have a packing plant here. We fixed real food, dinners for everybody, and they came in and sat down to eat. The first day, people just knew we were going to open up, and that first day, we just served hot dogs and drinks. We had so many people we couldn't set them down. Hot dogs were a nickel and hamburgers were a nickel. We just did barbecuing on weekends, mostly. We started barbecuing for everybody, blacks and whites, catered parties, anybody who wanted Brunswick stew I would fix it for them. We did things for the paper mill, and everybody in town knew us. We catered for the country club, civic center events, and all the churches. That cafe helped us put eight children through college.

I am really proud of my eight children. All of my children finished college and they all have good jobs. Most of my children are in the teaching profession because that was the thing to do when they were coming along. I have one daughter who was the first black teacher in the Westside Elementary School when it was integrated in 1967. She was twenty-five years old. She didn't have any problems when she started teaching there when they integrated the school. That first year, I believe she had about five black children in her class.

House Calls

Ben Meriwether, Bullock County

Daddy ran that store for about two years and did pretty good with it until he came down with malaria fever which affected his heart. He couldn't run the store, so after I finished the school in Fitzpatrick in 1922, I took over the store and tried to run it myself. But I was just fifteen at the time and did not know as much as I thought I did.

Daddy stayed in Hill's Hospital three weeks back home, then he was in Dr. Horn's hospital in Birmingham for six more weeks. With all the money going to hospitals and doctors, our money began to dwindle away and we didn't have enough to keep the store stocked. The Meriwether Store in Fitzpatrick gave up the ghost.

Daddy came home from the hospital, still sick, and had to stay in bed most of the time. One day, he was real bad, and I knew he was having a heart attack. I went for Dr. Darnell and he came real quick and managed to pull Daddy through.

Doctors made house calls back then. The doctor would come in, give you an examination, then go sit down at the dining room table. He sat that black satchel down and would ask for a newspaper or a magazine. He'd tear off several strips of paper about two inches wide and three inches long and reach for a bunch of vials he carried in his bag. All the vials had dry medicine in them. He would pick out the ones he wanted, pour some in the caps for measurement, and pour it on another piece of paper. After he had measured out several of these, he would take his pocketknife out and mix it up all together good. Then, he would take the little strips, lay them all out flat, run his knife blade in the pile, get as much as he wanted each time, and pour each knife-blade-full on separate slips. Then, he would fold these strips up, twist the ends, and each one was a dose for you to take. If you took them like he told you, you would get well.

Day's Work

Railroad dining car and
waiters, Montgomery,
1923
(Alabama Department of
Archives and History,
Montgomery)

Sorting tomatoes, Blount
County, 1945
(Alabama Cooperative
Extension Service photo,
Auburn University Archives,
Auburn)

Costs a Little More to Go First Class

Ulysses Terry, Jefferson County

In 1941, I couldn't see any future with Loveman's Department Store, the war looked like it was coming on, and I was ready to move on to something else. I applied with the Pullman Car Company in Birmingham. They had an office on the fifteenth floor of the First National Bank. I had found out the superintendent's name, a Mr. Stiles, and when I told him that I had been a window trimmer at Loveman's, I think he gave me some extra consideration. I hired on to be a Pullman porter. They started me off at $120 a month. The first thing I did after I was hired was to go to school and they had the school in one of those Pullman cars right here in Birmingham. There were twelve of us who were hired at one time and they showed you how everything on a Pullman car operated. We stayed on that Pullman car for twelve days learning how to make a bed and learning all the rules and regulations plus everything about that car from one end to the other. They knew business was going to pick up if there was a war and they would need a lot more people on the railroad. See, they were taking a lot of cars off regular service to haul soldiers, but wherever my name came up on the list, that's the run I made.

I started making regular runs after that training, New York and Miami, and then all over the country. I hauled some of the best of people and hauled some of the worst. I never will forget the first regular run I made because I didn't know what was going to happen. This was a trip to Memphis and some other places, but I got along fine. There was a porter for each Pullman car, and I found out pretty quick that the Pullman porter was responsible for his car and every passenger in it.

A porter had to know how to operate all the mechanical parts in there like the air conditioner. There would usually be three Pullman cars running together, and if the air conditioner went out in your car, you had to know how to hook it up with the other two cars to get it going again. Each one of the porters in the cars would help each other out. We worked for the Pullman company and not the railroad and if you didn't cooperate with the other Pullman employees, you couldn't work very long.

The reason that you don't see Pullman cars like you used to is because the Pullman company, being separate from the railroad companies, had to depend on the railroad to sell the space in the Pullman cars. The railroad got so they looked like they weren't particular about selling this space, so the passengers in the Pullman cars started falling off. When they fell off and they got down to one car instead of three, then the Pullman conductor was out of a job, not to mention the porters. Sure, I had to join the union when I first took the job. We had a good man who was head of our union for a long time, a man named Randolph, and the railroad union tried to get him to combine his and theirs to make one big union, but he didn't. Later on, I was on the grievance committee for this district and we had a right to question the railroad about why they did this or that. Like when I first started working, I was the low man and didn't get much choice about runs I made, but it didn't make any difference to me because all I wanted to do was work. I would go anywhere, anytime.

I was traveling all over the country and the Pullman company didn't pay any expenses while we were on the road. Say, I would get to the end of the run in New York, they had a place for us to sleep, but that was all. Even when we were on a run, we had to pay for our own food on the dining car.

When I started with Pullman in 1941, civilians had to have a little money or they never would have been on a Pullman car. As far as tips were concerned, some were nice and some were generous because I tried the best I could to make everybody have a pleasant trip. When I started in 1941, the Pullman company didn't have too many compartments or roomettes. Those Pullman cars I started on were the kind that looked like a regular seating car in the daytime. But at night, we would pull down the beds from the overhead and make up the upper and lower into bunks with curtains over both. I could pull down one of those beds and make it up with my eyes shut. You would pull it up and shove it and it would drop in place and I could convert those seats into berths as easy as breathing.

You always ran across some low-down passengers, but I found out one way to handle them. You know he's low-down and you know what he has in his mind as soon as he gets on the car, but you make out like you don't recognize it. I got so that I could read a passenger as soon as he stepped in the car. I didn't mess with a passenger unless I thought he would jeopardize my job. I remember, I was going up 35-36, going to Washington, and we were on the regular old Pullman open cars. And a lady and her little boy were in my car, and this little boy would get to the end of the coach and just come flying down the aisle, running as fast as he could. So, I went to the lady and I said, now I know that this is your son, but you are not supposed to run up and down this car, because you never know when this train will make a sudden stop or go around a curve. I said the Pullman company would not be responsible for that child if he got hurt, and I wish you would stop him running. She told me that her boy knew what he could do, and not to tell her what the boy could do or couldn't do. Pretty soon, we went into one of these sharp curves and the boy fell down and bumped his head and that woman just about had a fit. I said, well ma'am, that's what I told you, he might get hurt. The woman didn't like the idea of me telling her anything. She was raising so much sand that I went and got the train conductor and the Pullman conductor. The two ladies in back of this woman said, the porter told her, Mr. Conductor. He told her what could happen to that child. The mother got mad about it. I got those conductors there in a hurry because the accident had happened on my car and I was responsible for everything that went on in there. That was three people from the railroad looking at this lady, and she finally quieted down. She didn't let her little boy run in the aisle anymore, though.

After a while, you get the hang of all the slick operators. Some people went to Florida in the winter who couldn't afford to go to Florida. And, what they will do is they will get on a train and go down to Florida and spend a lot of money, and then on the way back, something will happen they say is the railroad's fault and they try to sue the railroad. If you work for the Pullman company, you get to know all that stuff, and you have to be careful anywhere you go. And cheap? I ran across some people who would beat you out of a nickel. One time on a run from Chicago to Birmingham, a woman stopped me and said, "Porter, would you get me some cigarettes?"

At the next stop I bought these cigarettes for her, and you know, when I got back on that car, she wouldn't pay me. She was changing Pullman cars in Birmingham going to Jacksonville and she knew she wouldn't see me anymore. I told her, all right lady, thirty-five cents won't make me and it won't break me. I wouldn't make a fuss with a passenger for thirty-five cents.

I had a case heading north on the Birmingham special. After we left Chattanooga up there, one man said to me, "Porter, wonder if you could rustle me up a couple of club sandwiches." He said, "I don't feel like going to the dining car." I went down and brought him some club sandwiches, and I gave him a bill and he said, "All right, I will pay you before I get off." This man was in a room and I knew he was getting off pretty soon. We left Roanoke and I went there and rang the bell, but he wouldn't answer. I went and got the conductor and told him that man owed me some money and I had rang and rang and he wouldn't answer. The conductor banged on the door and told the man to open up. He wanted to talk to him. The man still wouldn't open so we took the door off the hinges. That man was sitting up on his bed with his suitcase packed, ready to get off the train. The conductor told him, "Pay this man what you owe him," so he paid me and I didn't say nothing to him and he didn't say nothing to me.

One thing they told me when I first started with the Pullman company was "Don't see too much." One time, the train conductor came up to me looking for one of his passengers. See, they had seat numbers, and that conductor hadn't seen this man since he got on the train and he was looking for him. I told him I hadn't seen this man, but a little later on I saw a man slipping into one of the berths where this lady was. I knocked on the panel and asked the man if I could see his ticket, please. He hollered back out through the curtains that he didn't have to show his ticket to me. I told him if he wouldn't show it to me he was going to have to show it to somebody, and that's when I went to get the conductor. We stayed out there in the aisle trying to get that man out of that berth, but he wouldn't budge. Finally, the conductor told him, "Mister, we are about to come to the Mississippi line, and Meridian isn't too far away. If you stay in there with that lady and cross over into Mississippi, they are going to get you for white slavery and haul you off to jail." After a minute, the man stuck his head out through the curtains and said, "What did you say?" And the conductor said, "White slavery, mister. You are taking that lady across the state line for immoral purposes and they are going to lock you up in the Meridian jail." The man ducked back in the berth and slid out in a minute looking kind of sheepish and shook up. The conductor told him to go back and get in his regular seat and he wouldn't say anything about it. That man didn't move out of that seat until we got to New Orleans.

On-the-Job Training

Robert Couch, Marion County

The first job I had was working in a drugstore there in Winfield, and what I was supposed to do was empty the trash cans. My mother had a beauty shop and it was right there over the drugstore, and a dentist was next door. You might say I was raised there in my mother's beauty shop. She had kind of an apprentice thing going in the shop because she would get some white girl from out in the country, a little country girl, and I say white girl because there weren't any blacks around there, and she would bring the girl into town and let her be our live-in housekeeper. If this girl was good, and if she kept house good, Mother would promote the girl to the beauty shop, letting her sweep up and do shampoos, and if she kept being good, she would promote her up to assistant apprentice beauty-shop operator. Mother was the first beauty-shop operator in town, and sometimes one of these girls would go off and open her own beauty shop. Naturally, when one of the girls would move out of the house into the beauty shop, Mother would go out and get another girl to move into the house and the cycle would start again. Pretty good arrangement.

We raised chickens at home and I was supposed to feed and water those chickens twice a day, and bless their hearts, I don't know how any of those chickens ever survived, because I missed quite a few of those feedings.

When I was about fifteen, there was this Herbert Webb and he was still in high school and he really had a nose for business. He had a pickup truck and delivered the *Birmingham News* and he had a seventy-five-mile paper route. He would pay two of us a quarter and we would stand on the side of that pickup truck folding and throwing papers for about three hours every day. One time, Wayne Penneger talked me into going halves on a plug of tobacco. I had never smoked or chewed or dipped anything, but I told Wayne I'd go in with him on that plug. We divided up the plug and we started out on that paper truck with full cheeks. That old truck was bumping and weaving and I got sick from that chew of tobacco. Bad sick.

Later on, I got a job in a grocery store. The man and wife who owned the grocery store were always fighting and they would have some knock-down and drag-out fights. The second day I worked for them, I went over to go to the store with them, and one of them told me that they couldn't go in that day. They gave me a paper sack with some change in it and told me to go on in and open up. Yes, sir, I was down at that grocery store all by myself and the reason was because the man and his wife were having this big, terrible fuss and couldn't stand to be together. So, I opened the store by myself. I was down there trying to figure out what to do and this traveling man came in. He was trying to sell some cigarette rolling machines, and since I was the only one in the store, he laid some powerful sales talk on me. I said, yeah, that looks like a pretty good deal, so that guy just sold me all kinds of those cigarette rolling machines. The owner didn't like it, but he should have been there.

Later, I worked in a store that was owned by my uncle, but my main job was the one that everybody wanted and that was a soda jerk at the old-fashioned soda fountain. The pharmacist was a Mr. Shirey, a little bald-headed man who smoked a cigar all the time, and he typed up all the labels on the prescriptions with two fingers on an old Olivetti typewriter. Mr. Shirey was a little short man and a deacon in the First Baptist Church and he was a character. That cigar was always sticking out of his mouth, and when anybody in town whipped out their pills, there was usually some cigar ashes in there, too. We had screen doors on that old store, and I used to think that dipping ice cream in the summertime would be the best job in town, getting next to all that ice cream and they said I could eat all I wanted free. But that got old in a hurry. I can remember on a Saturday afternoon reaching way down in that can and trying to scoop up that ice cream and getting all that sticky stuff on my elbows.

Greatest Job I Ever Had

Tom Ogletree, Talladega County

My family was in the restaurant business in Alex City and I worked there as a kid. I did it all. I did everything there was to do in the restaurant business. In between my senior year of high school and going to play football at Auburn, I was manager of the Kowaliga Beach restaurant, which was one of the four or five best restaurants in the state of Alabama at the time. I had all kinds of restaurant experience from my family's place and the boss had all kinds of faith in me and gave me the restaurant to run that summer. By the time I got to college, like so many other things, I had been around the restaurant business all my life, more or less compelled to work in it, and vowed that if I could ever get the hell away from it they would never get me involved in it again. Looking back, with the experience I had and the education I got, I should have gone in the fast-food hamburger business and made a quick million.

When I was in law school at The University of Alabama, I worked for Bert Bank at the radio station and also worked for Bert Bank secondhandedly because I was the Schlitz Beer representative on campus. In those days, all beer distributors had reps on campus to assure that if a fraternity or other group was going to have a party, and if they were going to buy beer, that they were going to use your brand. My job was to contact them and basically negotiate how many cases I was going to give them to entice them to buy some more. Greatest job I ever had.

Nothing but Work

Willie David Jenkins, Hale County

I worked on a water truck down in Hale County, and you know about that. On them dirt roads with that gravel on there, well, we had to work all night long, 'cause wasn't nobody out at night and I be on the back of the truck, didn't care how cold it got or how rainy it got, you got to stay warm, 'cause if you fell off the back of that truck, you had it. See, white man driving with lights on all night long, spraying that road and patching it, and the gravel truck come along dumping gravel on that county road because that's all we had in Hale County.

Before that, I drove a tractor all night long. They learned me how to do that. Mr. James showed me how to do that. He cranked that tractor up and put it in one gear and so I cut land down in that swamp all night long. They has been some what would fall off that tractor and that disc harrow would cut them up. Get sleepy, got to stay awake, 'cause you know how them discs is . . . they cut you up. See, you be driving that tractor and you fall off and then them discs come along and cut you up. Now when you breaking land you got to be real careful, but when you disc, you just breaking it up, going around in a circle, down in a circle, that's right.

I married Lilly when I was nineteen. I moved over there in a little old shotgun house Mr. James Clay had on his place out there in the field and they let us stay there. Well, we were still on the same place, but I had a little wife then. In 1940 I was twenty years old and we left the place. We went on up to Moundville and started working by the day and that's where I met Mr. Rives. They come from Birmingham to Moundville and we build a Standard Oil terminal. They had me and another boy doing the work and they had these great big mules and we had these big scoops moving that dirt with two mules because those scoops were as wide as that table. And you had a handlebar on it and you had to hold that down, you know, and if you ain't strong enough to hold it down, it will flip you over, you know that. You got to keep it aimed right and them mules is still pulling.

From then on, Mr. Val Rives, that's Mr. J. V.'s daddy, they liked me so well they wanted to pay me twenty-five cents an hour and that's something I ain't ever got. Them other fellows didn't like me getting all that money and they told Mr. Val he couldn't pay me that money 'cause it was messing up. Mr. Rives said he would pay what he wanted to but they wouldn't let him. Well, we got through with that job and then the Riveses got a job up in Tuscaloosa. Oh boy, I had a uncle staying up there. I walked up the railroad track from Moundville to Tuscaloosa and spent the night with my uncle and walked back to Moundville the next morning.

Me and Lilly walked up the railroad tracks to Tuscaloosa from Moundville, 'bout fifteen miles I reckon, and stayed with my uncle again. I was following Rives Construction Company, you see, hoping I could get on with them. This was about '41 or '42, long in there, and Rives was starting to build a Standard Oil terminal. I got to working with them up there and they started giving me fifty cents an hour. Some others found out I was getting that big pay and they had to stop that. It was too much. Then, you know what they went to doing? They went to paying us in an envelope. They told us to not let them others know what they was paying us, so we didn't. I worked there with them a good while and then my wife got a job.

When Mr. Val Rives finished that job, they come back to Birmingham. I left everything I had in Tuscaloosa and come to Birmingham looking for work. My wife got pregnant and then Sonny, he was born, and we come up here. Mr. Rives, he like me, see, and it wasn't like it is now. All the white folks wanted to know is do you work, and if you work, you can get a job. Nowadays, you got to have education. See, now I ain't did nothing but work and everybody knowed I worked. 'Cause I liked working, 'cause wasn't no way for me to get anything without working. You know I like pretty girls, and I like pretty clothes, and I like pretty shoes and stuff like that.

Now, when I come up to Birmingham, I knowed my brother's wife's brother and he was staying over on 39th Street, and me and Lilly and Sonny come up to Birmingham in nineteen and forty-nine and I started working for them Riveses again. Now, you got to remember, when I come to Birmingham, I couldn't read and I got lost every time I come out the door. I couldn't even tell people where

I live and I walk, I walk, I walk trying to find right over here on 1st and 39th Street. When I kind of learned how to get to work, I didn't have no trouble, but I still had to walk. Didn't have no money for the bus, 'cause we didn't have no money to get something to eat. We got ten cents and we buy a quart of milk for a dime and a piece of corn bread and Lilly and Sonny and myself ate on that quart of milk and that piece of bread. And sometimes, you had to borrow that dime, sometimes, that's right, and we did good, I thought. Now, don't get me wrong, but see, I didn't work every day 'cause lots of days it rain and rain and rain and stuff like that. But I didn't care 'cause later on, I have that truck greased and have that truck fixed. You know how I learned how to drive? I be a helper on that truck right down there with Mr. Rives. I learned how to be a welder 'cause first I be a helper. And then they let me drive some and my job was keeping them pumps going, and I keep them going night and day and cared about that job more than I did about home. And, I was making a little overtime, see. Then we got a weld truck, and Mr. Rives put me on the weld truck, and we had a big weld machine setting on the back, and we had oxygen and tall tanks and we had strops around to keep them tanks from turning over and hitting one another and stuff like that. I went and went all over the country, I mean to Memphis and Milwaukee with them white folks. One place I didn't go was Alaska.

Then, Mr. Bob got a big contract to lay pipe and I went with them, see? And I was a brush boy, and what that was, I brushed them welds, and I learned to operate a rigger. We run a line all the way from Nashville down to the river and a backhoe would dig this big ditch, see, and we laid pipe all the way from the terminal to the river.

When I come to Birmingham I didn't have no car and didn't have no furniture excepting a stove and a bed and that was it. We lived in one room with a fireplace what burned coal, but the old man we was staying with had rules and one of them was he wouldn't let us close the door. All the winter long we didn't close the door, that's right. Another old man, Willie Drake, got me a room down on 37th. Pretty soon, I learned to drive good, so see, here's what's happening.

They hired Mr. Powell out at Center Point and they told me to learn him how to fit pipe. I learned him how to fit pipe and then he turned around and be my boss, he sho' did. That's right. He took that job and put me on the truck. But don't get me wrong. Mr. Powell and 'em, and Mr. J. V. and 'em, and Mr. Val and 'em, what they did was this. Mr. Powell go ahead on, he go to Nashville or go somewhere else, and he give me directions on how to get there. But I had to be there time enough for them to go to work, don't care how far it was, and I drive all night long, and sometime I run the window down and get some fresh air, and I stop awhile and sleep awhile and stop to get a milkshake and I be ready to go again. I be on one job already and then hit the road, and what they did was give me directions, the number of the road. See, I could read numbers, seventy-five and stuff like that, but this was the thing. He give me the numbers all the way to Nashville, but when I git to Nashville, I was worried about it 'cause all I know is where I 'sposed to go, like Standard Oil terminal.

What I do is this. I stop and ask some of them white people where is the terminal and I got by that way. What he telling me didn't mean nothing 'cause I couldn't read street signs, see. When I leave, I ask some white folks, now how do I get to Detroit or to Chicago or wherever I be going and they tell me how far to go and they draw me a little map, and somebody else tell me where to go. I had a credit card for gas but I had a problem with that, too. It's pitiful, and it's a shame to say this, but I fill the truck up and drive the truck 'til it be empty, and they wouldn't sell me gas because I were black. What I done was carry gas in the back of the truck in the weld machine, see, and get a siphon hose and siphon that, and that's when I couldn't get no gas. I drove that truck 'bout twenty-five years, and all that time, I couldn't read. Now, Mr. Powell, he try to learn me to write, write my name and all that stuff. He try to show me how to make a J without picking my pencil up. You know what I did? I pulled a mark down like this, and put a mark over like that, and go back over the top of the mark and make a J. I never did learn how. I never did learn how to write until I be sixty-four years old and that's after I got hurt.

Special Delivery

Vern Scott, Talladega County

When I was sixteen years old, this was in 1928, I started carrying special delivery letters for the Talladega post office riding on a bicycle. Today, you don't hear of special delivery letters, but back then, there were lots of them. I would start out of a morning with around forty-five letters, and I would then go back to the post office and get anywhere from six to a dozen. I would go back about two o'clock and get as many as twenty-five. Then, at 3:30, I might have some and I might not since there was only one train. Go back at seven o'clock and I'd have six or eight or ten at night. Well, that took me on a bicycle back and forth across town about four times a day.

Back then, there were still a lot of old fellows here in good financial shape and if I saw one of them out in his yard—they all had big old houses over on the south side of town there—why, I would stop and ask them questions, and here was a teenage boy asking questions, and they would tell me all about it from the time their granddaddies came in here. So I had so many of these stories, I got interested in the history of Talladega. This post office job was full-time because I had to drop out of school and go to work. I did this work for nearly four years and got around town so much I knew every pig track in it, and the people, too. In 1924, they paved the principal streets but most of the streets in town weren't paved.

Back in the twenties, stockbrokers called Talladega "stockbrokers' town." This was because so many people owned stock. What happened was that there was a fellow here, John Hicks, and he made money in different kinds of ways, all perfectly good business deals, and one of them was speculating in cotton. When he speculated, cotton seemed to go up every time. He started Talladega National Bank and he convinced all of his friends that you could make money buying stocks. Many of these men got in on the ground floor, buying stuff like U.S. Steel and Coca-Cola and General Motors and companies like that. All of those things went wild and split and resplit through the years, and when I got to Talladega in 1927, I noticed that all of these old men I delivered those special delivery letters had big houses and big cars.

They all had those big cars, but you hardly ever saw them drive them. You could see them every day walking to town, set under the trees around the courthouse, and talk and whatnot and then they would walk back home. Well, when I was carrying special delivery letters, the man who carried the mail could handle it ordinarily, but when the first of the month came around, he had so many magazines he had three big mailbags. He put those big mailbags in his car and he got me to go along to help him. He would give me the mail and I would trot and put the mail in the box and come back to the car. I noticed that all on that side of the town there would come a handful of dividend checks. Looked like nearly every house on that side of town would be getting from two or three to half a dozen or more dividend checks every first of the month. I knew what was in those envelopes.

Wheat Fields and Termites

Jerry Oldshue, Lamar County

I remember I got a job with the Ogden store in Sulligent when I was growing up. Got two dollars a day. It was Ogden but everybody called it Oglins and I got this job there on Saturdays, kind of a salesman, you know. And I worked in a grocery store some, and one summer, I went out to Kansas to the wheat fields. We got the job of hauling the wheat to the elevator. I figured this was great. We would be there sitting in the truck and all these other guys were out there working. But it turns out, you pull up there and they load you up with the wheat, and you sit there with this tremendously long line to get to the elevators where they take the wheat off, and when they take the wheat off, you drive back and get another load. The joker was that you didn't get any time off to sleep. You were supposed to sleep in the truck, see. Take a catnap when you could in the truck and eat sitting in the truck. After about a week and a half, we decided, well, we aren't cut out for this work, so we meandered over to Moline, Illinois, and got a job in a tractor factory. What we were doing was moving big heavy blocks off the production line, and after three or four days, we decided we weren't cut out for factory work and came on back to Sulligent and dug ditches.

One of the best-paying jobs I had in high school was working for a construction company that my best friend's dad owned, you know, small, one house at a time kind of thing. We also dug a pit for gasoline tanks. It was supposed to go about sixteen feet down and we dug it with shovels, so at sixteen feet down, you couldn't throw the dirt all the way out of the top of the hole. So you had a platform, and the fellow in the bottom threw the dirt up on the platform and the one on the platform threw it out of the top of the hole. It took us darn near two weeks to dig that hole big enough to get those tanks in. Ten hours a day and thirty minutes off for lunch. I stayed with them a couple of months, but business began to slow down and it's August, you know, and he had us out there breaking up concrete. Breaking up sidewalks and those little culverts that went over the ditch. I was out there swinging at one of those culverts and broke the handle to the hammer. I went up to Mr. Graham and I said, "Mr. Graham, I broke your hammer here." and Mr. Graham said, "No, you didn't break my hammer." And I said, yes, I did, and he said, "No, you were moving so slow the termites must have eaten it."

Working the Jitney

Robert Mardis, Jefferson County

Back in the late thirties, we were living out in West Birmingham. One of our neighbors was a chef on the dining car for the Frisco railroad and Mr. Pickens was a Pullman porter and they inspired me to go with the railroad. My brother and one of the Pickens boys were one of the first ones to get jobs with the railroad. I was only seventeen years old but they began hiring younger fellows and that was a break for me. Before I started with the railroad, I used to meet my brother down at the terminal station after he would finish a run and he would give me all the change he had—no dollars, now—but the change. He finally got tired of that and told me he was going to get me a job.

There was a man in the dining car on the train called the steward. My brother talked to him and they gave me a job on the spot. The first job I had on the railroad was working the jitney, and what that is, you have a basketful of sandwiches and drinks and you go through the coaches selling these to the passengers. You work the jitney until you had enough seniority to move into the dining car. There were two of us working the jitney and we would start out with the food and drinks and enough money to make change. One of us would work the Jim Crow coach—that's the one the blacks rode in—and part of the other coaches, and one would work the Pullman coaches because a lot of people just didn't want to go in the dining car. We carried that food and the drinks in a big basket with a strap to go around your neck and wore an apron or a white jacket, kind of like busboys wear.

I made my first run from Birmingham to Jonesboro, Arkansas, and I knew the railroad was for me. I really felt grown-up and independent because they paid us $235 a month with the tips on top of that. Remember, I was just seventeen years old and schoolteachers back in Birmingham weren't making but $75 a month. When we got to Jonesboro, the railroad had an arrangement for us to spend the night at a boardinghouse, and the first thing I wanted to do was go looking for girls. Fortunately, we didn't have to look hard because the girls were looking for us. See, back during the depression, the best jobs a black could get was at the post office or on the railroad and I had one of the better jobs a black could have back then. I found out that every town we passed through, we would pull into the depot and a bunch of girls would be out there waiting, just like they wait for a sports star or an entertainer today. We were careful, though, because the older boys had warned us about all of that.

Once, when I was working the jitney, I came into a coach loaded down with two baskets and I left the coach door open. The train was going through Mississippi then—and you know that is rough—and a big old white fellow told me to close that door. I just kept on going like I didn't hear him. When I came back through the coach, he just got up and slapped the fool out of me. I went back to the kitchen and I was mad and crying and I got me a butcher knife because I knew the Lord was on my side. A friend of mine was back there and he looked at that butcher knife and asked me what was going on, and I told him. He told him, "Let me handle this. You're nothing but a kid." He went back there and whipped the fool out of that white man and they put that white man off at the next stop. We were lucky we didn't have a lynching right there. Nobody got up to help the white man because my friend looked almost white himself, real fair, pretty hair, and everything. That was the only tight spot I got into during the eight years I was on the railroad. The rest of it was fun.

Ginseng and Possum Hides

Cullman Powell, Walker County

We were living in Coal Valley when the depression came and that just about folded us in. The mines let the men work just enough to pay their due bills. For extra money, the men would go out and cut cross ties for the railroad and you didn't cut out the cross ties, you hewed them out with an ax. They got twenty cents a cross tie and you did good to get three a day. In the fall of the year, they would go in the woods and dig ginseng. Now, ginseng is a root that the Chinese and Japanese use for medicine. If you got a cigar box full of those roots dry, you would have enough money there to buy all the kids one suit of clothes apiece. You would take that ginseng over to the hardware store and they had a man who would come down from Jasper and buy ginseng and possum hides and fox hides and things like that.

Me and my brother would help out the family by working on this man's farm and we would take our pay in butter and milk, work all day from daylight to dark and get one little cake of butter for it. Then, we would go down to my other granddaddy's farm and work until we had a crop laid by, and then we would hire out some more.

When blackberry season came along, we would pick them and sell those blackberries for ten cents a gallon, and people still thought that was too much. We would do all kinds of stuff to make a little money, like cut wood for people and hire out to the store to clean out their warehouses.

One time, we hired out to clean up a man's warehouse and we worked all day. That night, he said he didn't have any money to pay us but he could give us some cowboy boots. We were just little old kids but we said, sure, that would be ideal, getting some new cowboy boots. Those cowboy boots turned out to be some of those old-fashioned ladies' shoes that buttoned up the side, and had a heel about that high, and you could kill a spider in a corner with the toes. We wore those shoes home that night and my feet were so sore the next morning I couldn't wear them anymore.

Another thing I did to make money was to pick cotton. They said they were going to pay a dollar a hundred, but the way they weighed the cotton, you never got a dollar. One day, a girl my age and I were picking cotton and I went down the line with her, row for row, and when weighing in was done, I weighed fifty pounds and she weighed up a hundred and I haven't figured that out 'til yet.

Fit to Print

E. M. Danenberg, Jefferson County

Looking back over many years of covering many stories as a newspaper reporter, I seem to remember some of the small things that happened vividly as I traveled around Birmingham. Remember Bull Connor? One time, I was standing close to Mr. Connor and he made a statement that he wasn't going to have those black folks and white folks "segregating together." I wrote it just like he said it in the paper and he denied saying it to his dying day, but I was standing right there when he said it. He wasn't about to let those folks segregate together.

Back before radio and TV, see, there was this man who worked for the *Birmingham News* named Henry Vance. The *News* building was on 4th Avenue and 22d Street, and Henry arranged to have one of the windows on 22d Street closed off, and he would get up there in that window and call the world series. He would sit up there on a ledge and call the game from the telegraph. The Associated Press would tap out the plays and what was happening and Henry would interpret the telegraph and call it just like a radio announcer, filling in the gaps with his own imagination. Henry would sit up on that ledge announcing the game and there would always be a big crowd down on the street listening to him. This went on for years and it got to kind of be a Birmingham tradition at world series time, going down to hear Henry Vance call out the world series. The weather wouldn't be too bad and people would stand around and listen to what was going on.

During the depression, I was the Ensley reporter for the *Birmingham News*. Like a lot of other banks, the Ensley bank didn't open one morning. I went down there to cover the bank closing that day, and close by was an elderly black man on the steps of the bank. He couldn't understand why the bank didn't open and turned around and asked another man, "What's happening with this bank? I can't get in there." The man told him that the bank was busted. Closed. Busted. The black man stared at him and said, "You mean this bank done busted right in my face?" That was a bad day, but to me, that old black man's comment was funny and I wrote about it.

Another little incident I'll always remember with a smile. Years ago, there was a man who had a restaurant and a night club down on Morris Avenue. He had brought in an elaborate floor show, but he had neglected to set up a cover charge to get in the place. So here comes this man into the restaurant. He sat down at one of the better seats near the stage and orders a cup of coffee. The waitress asked him if he wanted to buy a meal or something and he said, "No, there is no cover charge here and I just want to see the show." The waitress went back and told the owner about the man out front at a ringside table who had just ordered a cup of coffee. He just wanted to pay his fifty cents for a cup of coffee and get all the benefits. The owner realized he was being had, so he volunteered to take the cup of coffee out personally. He drew a hot cup of coffee, went out to the table, stood beside the man for a few seconds, and poured the hot coffee on his head! The man took the owner to court. I wouldn't tell the owner's name because he was really embarrassed by that incident.

Another unusual thing I remember happening forty or fifty years ago happened out close to the steel mills. There was a man named Virgil Pearson working for TCI and TCI had built a big bunch of houses out there for the mill workers and they had Virgil to take over these houses as supervisor. There was one fellow living in one of these mill houses who said he wasn't going to pay any rent. He said that he had been working for the company for forty-some-odd years and he had never paid any rent, and he wasn't going to now. Virgil went to see him, and the fellow told Virgil that he was just wasting his time, that he absolutely wasn't going to pay any rent. That afternoon, Virgil had the man's furniture put out on the front lawn, brought in a bulldozer, and bulldozed the house flat to the ground. Virgil told me what he had done, and I said, "I can't believe you did that, Virgil," and he said he would take me out there and prove it. "He couldn't do that to me," Virgil said. Pretty drastic, but there is more than one way to skin a cat.

I spent a lot of time back in the old days covering the police beat and had a lot of buddies in the department. During the depression, on 21st Street near 1st Avenue South, there was a place over a garage called Madame Murphy's Emporium. Madame Murphy had her women up there, a kind of house of ill-repute, and she had plenty of whiskey, too. This place was about as bad as it can get and everybody in town knew about it and wondered how in the world she could stay in business. She had the place elaborately decorated and even had the usual red light in the window. I had a real curiosity how this woman, in flagrant violation of the law, could go on day after day, month after month. I asked a detective about it and he said that Madame Murphy was the best friend the police had in Birmingham. I said, "Tell me how that happens, because I don't understand it." The detective said, "Well, look. We get these safecrackers. They go into a business, put a blanket over the safe, blow it open, and relieve the owner of its contents. The first place they always go is Madame Murphy's. They buy her whiskey and visit with her girls."

Nobody ever knew what that woman's real name was and everybody just called her Madame Murphy. What she was doing, she would call the police and say that she had these two men in the place and they had a big bankroll, spending like crazy. The detectives would rush over, let the men leave the place, and pick them up a little distance away. They would never come to the house because that would ruin the whole setup. Madame Murphy's wasn't the only house in town. There was one down on 8th Avenue, and another one up on 2d Avenue, but the police would raid those places. Madame Murphy was very useful to the police and she stayed there a long, long time.

I worked for the newspaper a long time and covered a thousand stories during a time when Birmingham was growing, writing about the doings of the little people as well as the big ones, writing about the tough times of the depression, the colorful political scene, the night scene in a column called "After Midnight," and the always fascinating activity down at the police department. What I remember most were the people involved in these stories, little vignettes in daily life. For instance, there was a morning many years ago when Joe Denaburg had a little business called Levy Loan Company, a pawnshop was what it was. I happened to be in the store that morning and here comes this man in with his wife. The man said, "I'm in a big bunch of trouble, Joe. The minute the court opens, I've got to be there to pay that fine, and if I don't, the judge told me he would put me in jail. He already gave me two extensions." Joe told him, all right, what are you going to put up for collateral? The man told Joe that his wife was going to sit here in the back of the store until he could get to the bank to get the money. He told Joe that his wife would be the collateral. Joe looked at me and then back at the man and he said, "We don't take *people* in here for collateral, fella." Joe said, "Besides, the minute you leave, suppose she wants to go somewhere and gets up and walks out? What am I supposed to do?" Now, Joe was the kind of guy that would let you have the shirt off his back, but he wasn't about to let money go for a fine with a man's wife as collateral. He had to have something he could hold in his hand.

Ole-Time Religion

Perdue Hill near the Alabama River, Monroe County, 1984. The Perdue Hill Presbyterian Church is in the foreground, the Barbara Locklin Baptist Church in the background. (Michael Thomason photo)

Three Kinds of Mothers

Burton Troup, Marshall County

What we would do up on Gunters Mountain is go to revivals, and they just had revivals in the summertime. We knew we would be going to that revival that night so we would sweep the wagon bed out and have it all ready for hay and a quilt spread over that hay for the kids to sit on. The wagon was made so you could stretch it out, and you would stretch it out on a coupling pole and we would jump up on that coupling pole to get in the wagon. Then there was a spring seat up front, and my mother and daddy couldn't get in the back and go up there and crawl under that spring seat, so my daddy would step there on that double tree. I can just see him getting in that wagon and then Mama would put her foot up on the hub of that wheel and Daddy would pull her on up on the wagon. We would go about two miles and we would get to the church early every time and the families would stand around and talk, talk, talk.

Then we would get in there when it came time for the preaching and I guess the seats were just for the adults because the kids would be standing in back. Then the preacher would start. You just don't know how different babies cry. There are about three different kinds of mothers at church. One, the first time the baby cried, up she'd get and go out with the baby. Another would just take her time. The baby would cry-cry-cry but she would finally get up and leave with the baby. The last one wouldn't do anything, just let the baby keep on crying.

And of all places for the water bucket, it would be up close to the rostrum and they would just make a trail up there getting water and pick up that dipper—everybody drank out of the same dipper—and they would just drop it right back in the bucket. And that poor preacher, just up there preaching away, and here a woman would get up right there in front of him and make a pallet down on the floor for her kids when they got sleepy. I know that just about the time he thought he had somebody converted, a baby would scream out. I guess there would be five or six pallets laid down in front to put the kids to sleep.

Summer Was for Baptizing

Houston Cole, DeKalb County

We went to the Methodist Church every Sunday, McNutt Methodist Church out there on Lookout Mountain in the Loveless community. Now, Coon Rock, where I was born, let me tell you how it got that name. There was a little creek, Johnny's Creek, and it came over a ledge and fell about fifteen feet and that's where we got our water supply. It got its name because coons would gather around midnight at this spot and flirt with other coons and folks started calling it Coon Rock.

We would go to church and what would happen is that the boys would sit together, and the girls together, then the women, and most of the men would sit over together in what we called the amen corner. There was always a bunch of "ameners" every Sunday morning. Church would start at nine o'clock in the morning and go to about 12:30 or one o'clock and the preacher would preach for at least an hour and we kids were always ready for him to get through.

At the end of the service, the preacher used to ask sinners to come up to the front and confess their sins. In other words, you weren't a Christian at that time and they would have a bench there where the sinners would come and bow down and pray. I went up one time, and while I was down there on what they called "the mourner's bench," I heard somebody just crying and patting me on the back, and crying and patting me on the back, and I wondered who in the dickens was that. I looked up and it was the mother of the boy next to me and she had got us mixed up. When she saw me, she just moved over to her boy and started the same thing again, crying and patting him on the back. This was called going up to the mourner's bench. When you were down at the mourner's bench, the preacher would stand over you and pray and pat you on the back and some mothers would come up and cry. Some mothers would come up and shout. We had shouting in church at that time. It was one of the entertainments because there were always three or four mothers who would always shout.

They were emotional, you see. There was not much Christianity in it.

When we got baptized in the Methodist Church, we got sprinkled, but the Baptists would dunk you. We had a big time when we would go to the creek when the Baptists would finish a revival and watch the baptizing. I watched one woman come up out of the water and she looked at the preacher and spit that water out of her mouth and said, "This is the second time you've baptized me, and you ain't gonna do it any more." The Baptists saved up all their baptizing for the summertime after they had their revivals, what they called Big Meetings, because the creek got a little cold in the winter up on that mountain.

All-day singings were kind of a social event in the community. People would go in and listen a little bit and get up and walk out. They would walk out during church services, too. They would just get up and walk out and talk awhile and come back in. Well, the services just lasted so long that nobody thought anything about it. Everybody would bring lunch and folks came in wagons and buggies and some rode horses and mules, mostly mules. And those singings really would last just about all day.

Moving Words

Bill Dean, Escambia County

I preached for the first time in my home church down at Brewton. I preached on the subject of following Jesus. I used the scripture where Jesus came by and called on James and John and Matthew and they immediately followed him. I think my sermon was about seven minutes in length. There was this little woman, roly-poly and short, who sat right in the corner and always went to sleep during every sermon. Even during the seven minutes I was preaching, she still went to sleep. I had been encouraged by the regular pastor to stand in the door and greet the people when they came out after the service. I was standing there and this little lady came out and she came up to me and said, "Billy, that surely was a good little talk, son. You'll have to do it again sometime."

That night, I had to preach again. Now, the regular preacher was away and most of the congregation knew that there was this young fellow just out of high school and he couldn't preach a lick, and besides, he had preached that morning and probably wouldn't have anything more to say. There were very few people in the church that night, and those that were there were sitting toward the back. In the center section of the church, two little beginner-class boys were sitting in the second row and on the same row toward the end of the bench were two little girls about ten or twelve years old. Right in the middle of my sermon, the two little girls got up and moved one row back. I thought it unusual, and in a minute, the little fellow next to the aisle got up and walked all the way up the aisle and stopped at the next to the last row to the back.

He leaned over and spoke in one of those little kid's whispers, which is not a whisper at all, and said, "Mama, Jimmy wet on me." You could hear it all over the church, and you know, not a one of those people in that church laughed. I knew they heard him because I could hear it all the way to the pulpit. What I wanted to do then was say, "Let's all stand for the benediction." What had happened was that little Jimmy had wet his pants and it started flowing down that pew and the two little girls saw it coming and they had moved out of harm's way. But the poor little fellow sitting next to Jimmy had no warning, so it flushed up under and flushed him good. Being an inexperienced kid and not accustomed to preaching anyway, I just thought if I could get through that sermon without breaking up, I could probably handle anything that ever came up in my future ministry.

Answering the Call

Icese Thomas, Jefferson County

Now, the Lord called me to preach when I was twelve years old, but I didn't want to preach. I got into some serious things, like I got hurt real bad when I was a teenager, and I was lying there hurt real bad and I heard a voice say, "If I let you live, will you preach my eternal word?" I couldn't talk because I had gotten this piece of steel in my neck but I heard this doctor say, "Take him on upstairs because I doubt very seriously if he will be living in the morning," and I heard that for sure. I was lying there and I had lost—what you say—air to the brain, but the next morning, I was alive and I told the Lord I would preach for him. But when I got well, I still didn't want to preach.

Later on, I guess I was in my late twenties, I was still wrestling with this thing, feeling the call, but putting it off. One day, I got off of work and was going home and this preaching thing was just about to get me down. I went by—guess you would call it a bootlegger's house—and I said I'm going to stop by here and get me a little something to keep these voices from talking to me. I went in that house and got a little shot of stuff and carried it on home. I was sitting there on the sofa and my wife was in the kitchen, when all of a sudden, I heard this voice again. It said, "Preach my word or die," and this time, I mean it was different from what it had been. I yelled out, "Mae Dean, stop playing with me. Don't play with me like that 'cause that's not funny." Mae Dean walked up to the door and said she didn't know what I was talking about. I sat there a minute, debating whether to drink this stuff I had brought home, because I had promised the Lord I wouldn't do that any more. I got up and went into the kitchen and poured some of that stuff into a glass. Mae Dean said, "You ought to be ashamed of yourself. You are a Christian and a deacon in the church." I told her I didn't care and I was tired and needed something to relax me.

So, I poured that stuff and started to drink it and I just started throwing up. I went back and sat on that sofa, looking out the window at that house across the street where I had got the stuff, thinking maybe that woman had put something in there to make me throw up. Right then, that voice said it again, said, "Preach my eternal word . . . or die." I jumped up and went upstairs and started praying and accepted the call. I called my pastor, thinking he might laugh at me, but the first thing he said was, "How you feeling there, Reverend?" Called me "Reverend." First time he ever called me that, and I told him I wanted to answer the call to preach. I been preaching ever since.

Not Your Usual Baptistery

Ben Meriwether, Bullock County

In the summer of 1923, there was a revival down at the Baptist Church and I joined the church on a Thursday morning. During that revival, we had an unusual amount of rain, a whole lot of rain, and the old creek was spread out over the public road out there in front of the church. So on that Sunday afternoon, instead of having to go in the creek to be baptized, I was baptized right out there in the middle of the public road where the water was up to my waist.

What a Beautiful Sound

E. L. Lovelady, Madison County

We boys went to church mainly just to see the girls. That was one big thing we went for. We enjoyed the all-day singings and dinner on the ground and we had an awful lot of them back then. The churches always kept the windows raised because there was no air conditioning and sometimes you would be sitting up in that church and hear people for a mile away. And what a beautiful sound it was, as all the voices sounded out with the old songs like "The Old Rugged Cross," "At Calvary," and "Blessed Be the Tie That Binds," and a lot of them.

Corncobs were used for a lot of things back in those days. Sometimes we would carry some of them to church in our hip pocket and stick them up in the exhaust pipe of some old man's car. Two or three of them right behind the other, and when he cranked that car, that thing would pop and cobs would fly out of the exhaust pipe like bullets. Sometimes we used Irish potatoes for the same job. Sure, I remember going to church.

I Never Reached Perfection

Tera Averett, Coffee County

On Sunday morning, everyone was scrubbed clean and we put on our Sunday dresses and went to church. Uncle Alph stood by the church organ and led the singing. I thought the organ looked so strange because it didn't look like the organ Papa bought for us in 1910. The church organ was short and it didn't have the mirror and the tall top like our organ at home. But the music was just as sweet as the whole little church full of people sang the gospel songs like "The Sweet Bye and Bye" and "Jesus, Lover of My Soul" and "There Is a Fountain Filled with Blood." I wasn't too sure about the one called "When the Roll Is Called Up Yonder, I'll Be There." They told us that we had to be good if we expected to go to heaven. I tried to be good, but I found out that I wasn't good. It was years later that I learned that the Bible tells us there is none good. No, not one.

In the summer, every church in the area had a "protracted meeting." Today these meetings are called revivals. As children, we went to Klegg to Methodist Sunday school, and once a month on Sunday afternoon we went to the Methodist Church that met in the Klegg schoolhouse. The circuit-rider preacher had so many churches that he could not come to Klegg on Sunday morning, but he brought the same message that told us to "give our hearts to Christ" and not to sin. I can remember so well where I sat on a long handmade bench one Sunday afternoon thinking, I am not going to sin next week. But you know, I never did reach that perfection. As teenagers, we attended protracted meetings for several weeks in the summer. It didn't matter whether it was at a Baptist or Methodist church, and occasionally a Holiness Church. At the Holiness Church, we sat in the car at night and watched the people sitting under the brush arbor.

The Baptists at my mother's church had services all day for about a week. They carried trunks full of delicious food and served it from a table built in the churchyard. For the life of me, I cannot know why we never got ptomaine poison from food that was carried there in open wagons and was left in the wagons until dinner time. But never once did I ever hear of any illness from spoiled food. We had never heard of a refrigerator. It was only in the thirties after I was married that I got an icebox, but even then we had to go to town to buy ice.

If there were church services at night, the children did not go to a nursery because there weren't any. The children slept on quilts at the rear of the church. For churches which had morning and night services during the protracted meetings, it was arranged for the visitors to go to a different home every day for lunch. Sometimes the same ones stayed for supper before church time.

For the Baptist churches, a baptismal service was held at the end of the week at a nearby stream or a tiny pool just large enough to get baptized.

Mama's church finally decided to start Sunday school in the one-room church building. To accommodate the different classes, little spaces were cut off by hanging sheets from wire strung to form rooms.

Getting There

*Eden, St. Clair County, 1936
(Dorothea Lange/Farm Security
Administration photo, Library of Congress,
Washington, D.C.)*

No Other Smell like It

Robert Couch, Marion County

The big deal in Winfield was the depot. In 1887, the Frisco railroad came through, and at one time there were eight passenger trains that came through. I can remember a time when some of my family moved out to Oklahoma on account of health reasons, and they loaded up the whole family on that train, including all their worldly possessions, and went west. They put the wagon, horses, and cows, and everything else and took off for Oklahoma.

When I got older, the farmers on a Saturday would all come into town in their wagons. Those wagons had these little tongues sticking out the back of the wagon and we would run while the wagons were going and jump on the back of that wagon on that tongue and ride down to the bottom of the hill, get off, and run back up the hill to get on the next wagon.

The depot was kind of like the center of Winfield, and right outside behind the depot, all the people in the town would congregate—country people, that is. That place was kind of reserved for those farmers to park their wagons, mules, and horses when they came into town.

I can recall when the first diesel engine came through Winfield. We were all up north of town about a mile or a mile and a half and we were playing baseball in Jim Green's pasture underneath the town water tank. And the pasture kind of came down, like this, like a V, and when you played, you played on a slant and jumping cow-pies was commonplace. But that day, when we heard that diesel coming down the track, we dropped everything and ran like mad down to the depot just to watch that diesel engine go by.

Before the diesel engines, the trains were pulled by steam locomotives and they had to have a lot of water. Right there by the depot, there was a big water tank right by the railroad tracks and this big tank was constantly dripping. The steam trains would come down the track and the locomotive would stop there under that tank and there would be this big long pipe, and the fireman would pull this pipe down and fill up the boilers. When I was a boy, Winfield had a full time flagman, Mr. Looney, and he had a big silver sign that said "STOP" on either side, and his job was to get up when a train was coming, hold the sign up to tell people that a train was coming. That was Mr. Looney's entire job with the railroad, hold up that stop sign when the train was near. Now, Winfield had quite a few trains coming through, but not all that many, and when he was not holding up that sign, Mr. Looney would sit down over there by that water tank on a little stool and light up his pipe. When all the kids in town would come down to watch the trains go through, they would sit down and talk to Mr. Looney. Not many grown-ups could give the kids that kind of time. What with watching trains and playing baseball and talking to Mr. Looney, our days were pretty well filled up.

The town itself had the depot as a hub and Letha Mae and Luther Wells ran all the activities down there. The depot had this little bay window out front that you could see the train tracks from both ends, and they would sit there with their telegraph going. That depot had a special smell and no other smell was like it in the world. That telegraph would be clicking all the time. We would go in and visit with the Wellses, and this is the place where the newspapers came in and you'd get your express packages here at the depot. They would put all the outgoing mail in a sack and hang it on a post right there by the railroad track, and when the train came flying by, a man on the train would stick out a hook and snag the mail bag as the train went by.

Back during World War II, troop trains would come through all the time, and the soldiers were packed on those trains, and when the train came through, soldiers were hanging out the windows and raising cain, and if they could see a female on the street, they would really let out a yell. Some of them would write their names and addresses on a piece of paper and throw it out, hoping some good-looking girl would pick it up and write to them.

Raised on the Toothache

Ben Meriwether, Bullock County

Pretty soon after I was born in 1907, my mother's brother, Dan Dugger, talked my daddy into moving the family from Fitzpatrick, Alabama, over to Iuka, Mississippi. The only way to get there was by train. My mother and I had to leave Fitzpatrick on a night train to Montgomery, spend the night, catch an L & N train the next morning at eight o'clock; go to Decatur, getting there at 6 P.M., and wait in the depot until midnight; catch a Southern train to Sheffield, get there at two in the morning, wait in the depot until five o'clock; get back on the same train to ride the last twenty-seven miles. Three hundred twenty-five miles and thirty-one hours from Fitzpatrick to Iuka.

Daddy had the railroad set off a boxcar and he loaded one end of the car with furniture and all our belongings. In the other end, he loaded the horse, cow, dog, cat, chickens, feed, two barrels of water, and he put in a cot and kerosene stove. Mother fixed him lots of food. It took him three days to get to Iuka from Fitzpatrick.

Early in 1913, Daddy had to go to Fitzpatrick and he carried me with him. That's when I saw my first automobile, if you can call it that. A man had taken his buggy, put a little gasoline engine in the back, attached some chains to the back wheels, and had a little stick to guide it. He cranked the engine, jumped in, and went down the road. It looked funny to me, a buggy going down the road with no horse pulling it. A year or two later, a salesman came out from Montgomery to take Daddy to town to buy the fall line of ladies' hats, shoes, bolts of cloth, and other little items for the dry goods department in the store. The man came in a Model T Ford pickup truck with a young man driving. They took me with them and it was my first ride in a car. We got about ten miles from the store and it came up a big rain. We stopped to put up the curtains, and by the time we got the curtains out, found out how to put them up, it had quit raining.

The next time I rode in a car was when Mr. Pugh bought a Model T. They sent it out by a young man who was to teach Mr. Pugh how to drive and he asked me and two of his girls to take a ride. We got five or six miles away and ran out of gas. Gas stations were not real close together back then. The boy driving had to walk about two miles to get some gas, and when I got back home, I was late for supper and Mama was heading for the peach tree. I got by because Daddy had said I could go.

Now, my daddy was a good-natured man, always jolly, never saw a stranger, and everybody liked him, but he could get mad. One cold Sunday, we drove up to Fitzpatrick to go to church. After church, we headed back home in the buggy on those muddy roads in a cold, drizzling rain. Those buggies came with curtains you could put on in front and each side to keep out the wind and rain. About halfway home, one of the few automobiles around came up behind us and the man blew his horn so he could get by. That man kept blowing his horn and Mother tried to get Daddy to pull over, but he wouldn't. Finally, he grabbed the reins, pulled over, and let the automobile by. My dad was so mad by then that he jumped out of the buggy in the mud and rain and started walking. We just sat there for awhile and let him walk, and he was walking fast. When he had walked nearly a half a mile, we started on and caught up with him, stopped right beside him. None of us said a word and he got back in the buggy and Mother drove on home. Not a word was said, and it was never mentioned again.

I was raised on the toothache. One time, my mother made an appointment with a Dr. Fordyce, a dentist in Montgomery, to fill some cavities. My parents put me on the seven o'clock night train to Montgomery all by myself, and I really thought I was a big shot, riding the train alone. A grown cousin met the train and took me to a picture show and I spent the night with him. The next day, he took me to the dentist. That afternoon, I caught the afternoon train back home. Oh, I was proud of that trip and did a lot of bragging.

One time, I had been down at the store on a Saturday, and it had been raining for several days and the roads were muddy, mud-holes all along. My daddy decided we would ride horseback that night, so we saddled the horses and started home. About a mile from home,

Daddy was riding that clumsy horse that had kicked me one time, and we rode along, just walking the horses. Daddy's horse stumbled, went down on his knees. Daddy slid out of the saddle and down the horse's neck and sat down in a big puddle of mud and water. He sat there like he was stunned and I couldn't help but laugh. That really made him mad. He got up, pulled his pistol out of his pocket, pointed it at the horse, and was going to kill that horse right there. That scared me, and I rode up close and begged him not to do it. He looked at me, put the gun back in his pocket, but he wouldn't get back up on the horse. He walked the rest of the way home. I wanted to laugh, but I didn't. He sold that horse right after that.

Years later I bought my first car there in Montgomery and carried my daddy to work one day. He was on the police force. On the way, I ran into a wagon. The back wheels on that wagon rolled over my front fender, across the hood, and down the other side. It didn't hurt the car much. The colored man who was driving the wagon got out and said, "Boss, you thought I was going to stop and I thought you was going to stop. Neither one of us stopped." I couldn't help but laugh. Daddy hadn't said a word, but then he handed me something and I asked him what it was. He said it was a ticket for reckless driving and having an accident. He walked on down to the police station three blocks away and never looked back at me. Boy, was I upset about that. Taking my daddy to work at the police station and him giving me a ticket. It sure made me a more careful driver, though, especially if Daddy was in the car.

Going in Style

Rob Maulsby, Marshall County

About the turn of the century in Decatur, my grandmother ran a tearoom. Men would come to eat there. My father's sister helped my grandmother in the tearoom and became interested in a Colin St. Clair who was foreman of the railroad roundhouse there in Decatur. This was for the L & N. Colin had saved his money and had obtained some stock in the railroad. Occasionally, he would go to the stock-holders' meetings in Nashville, I think, and he found out that due to the shortage of materials and whatnot that they couldn't get new engines for the line. He came back home and made a study about train engines. At the next board meeting of the railroad, he said that he would like to make a proposition. He said that they had enough steel and enough know-how in the roundhouse down at Decatur to build two engines. He said that they wouldn't be regular engines, but he submitted plans for his own engines. He told the board that they would relieve other engines for the main line. The board bought the idea and Colin went back to the roundhouse in Decatur and built the two engines.

These homemade engines were so good that they were occasionally used on the main line. My aunt married Colin St. Clair in 1911. St. Clair had such a reputation after building the two engines that the president of the railroad sent his own private car down to Decatur to be reworked. This coincided with the time that my aunt and Mr. St. Clair were to be married. When the president's car was ready, the president told St. Clair to write his own ticket and go anywhere in the country he wanted to on his honeymoon. They took a honeymoon on the president's car, down one coast of Florida and back up the other coast and back to Decatur. That was a very private honeymoon, just two people on the president's car for a month, just going in style.

My father was a short little fellow, about five foot three, but he loved horses and would sit up real straight on a horse. He moved south with Grandpapa in 1888. He happened to be in Chicago in 1895, and that was the date of the Great Race. Many of the famous car drivers of the day were there. That particular day, he was walking down toward the Loop, and he saw people running down the street. He noticed a lot of smoke and a bunch of people yelling and waving and he turned around and saw these motorized buggies going by. He went back to his hotel room, and later on he went to the livery stable to be placed on the register to rent a team of horses for that coming Sunday. He was going to a monthly meeting at the Baptist Church and needed the team to arrive in style. Of course, the more you paid, the better team you got and the better harness with more colored ribbons, and you reserved this far in advance to get a better rig.

At that time, he thought nothing would replace the horse, but these racing cars were on display at the livery stable and stirred a little interest in him. Later he was at the livery stable in Chicago, about 1903, and there was a 1903 Oldsmobile and he was enticed to drive it around the block. At that time, he was working for International Harvester in Birmingham, setting up and installing machinery, big wheels that ran gins and mills and so forth.

A little before 1910, the first automobile was delivered to Birmingham. This was an International Harvester high-wheel buggy. It came into the railhead with the wheels off of it. There were demurrage charges piling up waiting for this northerner to come down and set it up. The time came when the man should have been there to take over the sales and delivery of automobiles, but he never showed up. The demurrage charges were piling up, and the International Harvester people asked my dad to go down to the railroad, assemble the car, and bring it to the International Harvester store. He went down, assembled the car, and brought it back to headquarters, and it was displayed in the window.

When the first motorized buggy was sold, it was sold to a farmer way out in the country, and the company man still hadn't arrived from Chicago. Dad was asked to deliver the car to the customer. This was the first automobile in the state and you didn't have any filling stations, no service, no good roads, just buggy paths. He took what gas he thought he would need for the trip, packed his tool kit, and started out. He got out in the country about half a day and started using more oil than he thought he should.

Somewhere out there in the country, the car quit running and he settled in to fix it. He got the car pulled up to this farmhouse and started looking around for some stuff to repair the car. He started taking the engine apart and borrowed a pot from the lady of the house to collect the oil. He took some cheesecloth and drained the oil. He kept all of that and took his knife and whittled out a wedge and melted the babbitt out of the bearing into this pot the woman had given him. He reset the one-cylinder engine and took a rope he found on a fence, held the rope together with a pair of pliers, and pulled the babbitt around the crankshaft. He took the shaft apart, put new bluing on it, got the bearing set, poured the oil back into the engine, fired it up, and delivered the automobile. This was how one of the first automobiles in Alabama was delivered.

Down through Helena

Libby Fitts and *William W. Collins, Sr.*, Bibb County

Fitts: I remember the days when they brought the national guard into Coleanor, down close to the coal mines, and they brought them in on a train. I remember all those soldiers were standing in the doors of the train with their guns and the reason they brought them in was because of the strike. I didn't know anything that bad was going on.

Collins: See, the sheriff would have to ask the governor for the guard, and the governor would send them in. They come in over there and used the schoolhouse and took the children's schoolbooks and burned them and all, and when the strike had settled down, they pulled them out.

L & N run over the southern route from Woodstock over here to Blocton to the depot and we had a roundhouse, and at one time there was four engines that stayed there all night. They had a keeper and a helper there. What the roundhouse did was turn the engines around. Had a passenger train, now, come out of Birmingham of a morning, come down through Helena and down through Roebuck into Gurney Junction to Boothton and Coleanor and Piper, pulled in there and backed out when it got ready to leave. Then we had train service from Blocton to Tuscaloosa and the conductor was a man named Joe Lee and he was a bad, bad man. Don't think he wasn't.

Fitts: A lot of students would ride that train into West Blocton High School. My town was Piper. It's out toward Montevallo and there's not anything there much now, but it was a pretty good little town when I was growing up. Our town had a commissary and a post office and a payroll office and a depot. They say that the railroad tracks coming into Piper were the most expensive thirteen miles of railroad in the world at that time, that little stretch between Coleanor and Woodstock. They had to build so many trestles, you see, between all those hills and gullies.

A Railroad Town

Denson Franklin, Coosa County

When I was a boy, Goodwater was a railhead, a little town of about 2,000, and most people worked in Sylacauga or Alexander City. The trains used to stop there to get coal and water. The water was pumped from Hatchet Creek and there was a big coal chute beside the tracks. The railroad kept a lot of people employed. When I was a little boy, I enjoyed sitting on the bank and watching "the Floridian" pull in and stop and watch all those people eating in the dining car. I would watch as the waiters served the diners, moving around inside the car with a towel over their arms or over their shoulders.

Most of my daddy's business in the store was railroading and farmers. With the farmers, he would do what you called "furnishing," supplying the farmers with just about everything they needed, and they would pay him off in cotton. He furnished anything from a thimble to a Studebaker wagon and all kinds of groceries, overalls, shoes, and cloth. He would have a couple of warehouses full of cotton when the farmers would pay off in the fall, and he watched the cotton market carefully, because just a penny one way or the other would make a big difference.

Railroad camp cars were out in front of our house quite often. There was a siding out there and people were always working on the railroads, two or three crews all the time, and they would stay in those camp cars. They served good meals on the camp cars and my father, being a merchant, sold groceries to them. As a boy, I got to know the supervisor and the scratch boss, the second man. They would invite me to come in and eat with them, and I would pull up a chair and eat.

Railroading was a big factor when I was growing up. I got to know most of the engineers and firemen and people who worked on the train. Goodwater was halfway between Birmingham and Columbus, Georgia. Back in those days, they used what they called a local. Freight trains would pull into town in the late afternoon and the train from Birmingham would be exchanged for the one from Columbus. The engines were turned around on a big turntable right in front of my home, and the thing was so well balanced that two men could do it. Goodwater was a railroad town.

Drives Out Real Good

J. Torbett Crocker, Jefferson County

Back in the thirties, I started to buy some cars. I could buy an old Model T Ford for $2.50, $3.00, $4.00. I would fix it up, buy tires for twenty-five cents each, and sell the cars for $10.00. From the Model T's, I bought a 1926 green coupe, called it "Gardenia." I named all of my cars. But Gardenia's engine was real sloppy, and it would go rattle-rattle-rattle, so I took the pan off, put the oil back in, but the engine was so tight it wouldn't start. I got Henry Love down from Ab Johnson's filling station to work the crank. He was on the crank and I was on the starter, but we still couldn't budge it. Finally, we got somebody to push us to get us running. That was Gardenia.

Later on I had "Sweetpea," a 1927 Ford convertible with no windshield. I would take a cardboard backer that used to come in shirts and bend it backward and cut holes in that backer so I could look out. It was cold as hell in the wintertime, but the cardboard knocked most of the wind off and I could see to drive through the holes. No top and no windshield. I paid $18 for that car, and in 1935 I traded it in for new Ford and got $125 trade-in. My new Ford was the most beautiful car in the world. I was going to college then and working for Republic Steel at night. That car was the most expensive Ford made and it sold new for a little over $800.

One time, two couples got in my new car to go down to Montgomery to see Auburn play Birmingham-Southern. Lyle Baxter and I were sitting back in the rumble seat and Norma Jean and the other girl were in the front seat and Norma Jean was driving. We were going down the highway with the top down and Norma Jean asked the other girl to hold the wheel a minute while she adjusted her hat. The other girl had the wheel all right, but she was watching Norma Jean adjust her hat instead of the road and we rammed right into a telephone pole. It wrecked the car and we missed the football game.

Sometimes, a bunch of boys would go down for that game and we always stopped to eat at the same restaurant. None of us had any money, so when we would get through eating, we would leave one at a time and when we passed the cashier, we would point back at the table. Finally, there would be just one guy left. He would saunter up to the cashier, and when he got even with the cash register, he would just take off running. We did that to the same restaurant many times and it's a wonder they didn't have us spotted.

Country Roads

Buster Hall, Clarke County

When I was growing up in the early 1900s, the roads to the settlements near Thomasville were especially bad, the red clay of that area famous for its striking qualities and it wouldn't take but a little water to work up that clay into a terrible mess.

The county commissioners back in those days didn't have any money to improve roads and the only work crews were the citizens of the county. There was a road tax of five dollars, and people had the choice of paying the five dollars or working five days on the roads instead, and most people chose to work on the roads because a dollar a day was good pay.

The road from Thomasville to Grove Hill and on to Jackson was just two deep ruts with a mud-hole thrown in every one hundred yards or so, and the men would cut young saplings and cross-lay the mud-holes and hills forming a sort of bridge for vehicles to cross over. There were very few cars back in those days and most of the traveling was done by mule and wagon. Near my home was an especially fine mud-hole, impossible to get over during the rainy season, and we made big money letting travelers go up through our field. We charged fifty cents a car to get around this mud-hole, and some days we would make as much as $1.50. Three cars. That's what we called heavy traffic. That road was so bad that several students from nearby towns had to board in homes near the school during rainy months.

Rural mail carriers really earned their pay over those bad roads. They had a terrible time delivering the mail and many days they would go as far as possible on their routes in their little T-Model Fords, get stuck, and borrow a horse or a mule from a nearby farmer and continue until they got all the mail out. It was really an all-day affair and many times it was way in the night before they got through.

Then one day, Mr. McKee of Leroy moved his road construction crew into Thomasville and started to work on old Highway 5. My brothers and I would sit by the road and marvel at how fast those fellows were building that road. They used slip scrapes pulled by mules to move the dirt. A man would take hold of the two handles on the slip, and as the mule moved forward, the slip would fill with dirt, the man would guide the slip to where he wanted to dump, let 'er go, and start all over again. They used heavy plows to break up the hard dirt so the slips could move in. It was many years before they filled up all the mud-holes in the county.

A Rough Ride

E. L. Lovelady, Madison County

Before we moved from that first house, we had made a two-wheel homemade cart to get around in. The cart was an axle, two wagon wheels with some shafts put to it, and no springs. You talking about a rough ride, but buddy, there wasn't no spring to it at all. You hit a bump and it was rough. It had a box seat. Mama would go to town with a mule hitched to this homemade cart and would be carrying a couple of dozen eggs. That's all, no money, seven or eight miles to trade those eggs at the store. She would get eight cents a dozen. I've heard her say that was what she got for them. But she traded them for baking soda, matches, coal oil, or whatever we needed in the house.

We raised just about everything we ate, but there were some things, of course, you couldn't raise. But can you imagine driving eight or nine miles in a wagon or a buggy or a homemade cart with two or three dozen eggs and no money? A mule walks about four miles an hour, so you're talking about two and a half hours each way. Now, that's pretty hard times. Mama got a letter in 1933 from a cousin down in south Alabama, and the letter said, "We're liking it fine where we are and eggs are up to ten cents a dozen, and I sure hope they've gone up for you." Now, wasn't that something?

Around the Mills

Workers' houses owned by
Republic Steel,
Birmingham, 1936
(Walker Evans/Farm
Security Administration
photo, Library of Congress,
Washington, D.C.)

Carborundum molding
machine, Alabama Marble
Company, Gantt's
Quarry, Sylacauga, 1920s
(O. V. Hunt photo, Alabama
Department of Archives and
History, Montgomery)

Gobbler's Knob Revisited

C. E. Bracknell, Jefferson County

I grew up in a little community just north of Ensley and the Ensley steel mill. It was a mill village, you might call it, kind of like a mining camp, only it was for steelworkers. That was all that lived up there, steelworkers. Some called it Gobbler's Knob and some called it the Quarters, but that meant it was steel mill quarters. My father worked for the U.S. Steel for awhile, and me and two of my brothers worked there. The Tennessee Coal and Iron Company owned that camp, of course, and you had to work for the steel mill to rent a house up there.

The first house we lived in was a four-room house and we lived in two rooms and another family lived in the other two rooms. We finally got a house, a whole house, to ourselves and it was just a frame house and it wasn't underpinned or nothing. For a while, we didn't have any electricity and we used coal-oil lamps before they put the electricity in. For water, they had a hydrant out there on the hillside and everybody got water out of that hydrant. We had to haul that water to the house, but we didn't have no sinks or bathtubs or nothing like that. They charged . . . run about two dollars a room, and a four-room house would cost you eight dollars a month. We had a privy out there on the hillside and they had them cans they set out under there and a wagon that would come around and change out them cans, two mules pulling that wagon, and we called it the "ice cream wagon."

I went to a company school there, and I mean everything centered around that company. They had good schools, though, a whole lot better than the city schools, and they were steam heated and every-thing. They had buildings there where we could have our activities— singings and dancing and everything else. They had playgrounds with swings, merry-go-rounds, and what have you, and they fur-nished us all the baseball equipment we wanted. They had the finest teachers you could want and most of them were Yankee teachers. I don't know why they got Yankee teachers, but every once in a while, you might see one from Tuscaloosa, like that. The teachers had a big house they lived in close by and we called that the teachers' cottage. Oh, they had a fine home up on top of that hill.

They had a volunteer fire department that took care of the mills and all the camps. They had one of these old carts that had a hose wrapped around it with big high wheels, and when there was a fire, they pushed the cart. They had a whistle down at the mill they called "Big Jim" and it was blowed with steam. It stood up in the air maybe fifty feet. Big Jim would blow at 12:00 and 12:30 in the daytime and the same at night. If they had a fire anywhere in the Quarters or rail mill or foundry, they had so many blasts for the Quarters and so many for the foundry, like that. Then the firemen would know where to go because they didn't have telephones or radios or nothing. Lot of times, I would be laying in the bed at night and I would hear Big Jim, and I would lay there and know where that fire was.

There were four of us Bracknell boys and nobody messed with us much. But when we would go into downtown Ensley, people got a notion that we were hoodlums and we lived across the tracks. We would go into Ensley and a policeman would follow us around if there were four or five of us. People would say, "Aw, that's all them kids from up on the hill." Up on Gobbler's Knob, we didn't have any policemen other than the company guards, and they wore uniforms and all, and that was the only law we ever saw. We called them the TCI Braves for some reason. If you ever had to have any kind of lawman up at the camp, you called the TCI Braves.

When I was growing up, we had all kinds of foreigners living in the camp. We lived next door at one time to some Italians, and then we lived in the house with some Polish people. Up there, we had Slavs, Greeks, Italians, Polish, and Lord knows, there were some other kinds of people. There were some up there that couldn't speak our language because they came directly from the old country to work in the mills. I remember we lived next door to some Polish people. Their name was Jarvis and the woman raised geese. I was a boy and I would be out there looking at them geese and she would come out there and blah-blah-blah at me and I couldn't understand what she was saying. I figured she was cussin' me out, though. I had been told by old man Pete Harduval—he was a Greek and had a cafe—that when the Italians first come over here that they had a kind of stockade built, a wire pen, and some buildings inside where they would stay at night. People didn't hardly look on them as human beings, but old man Harduval said he would see the guards bring them down there and put them in those pens. This was a little after 1900. When I was growing up, I never thought nothing about them being foreigners because we played with them just like anybody else.

Most of these foreigners were Catholic, but my folks were Baptist. We didn't have a church out there on Gobbler's Knob but a woman came from North Birmingham every Sunday and taught the Sunday school. For a long time, they had the Sunday school at our house. Brother Bryan would come out there every once in a while to make a talk.

There wasn't much of what you call a social life out at that camp. About all the women did was go visit the neighbors and the neighbors would visit us, and sometimes they would stay all night. There wasn't much to do, to tell you the truth. They had a picture show down in Ensley that some would go to occasionally, but not much. We didn't have no kinpeople up there because most of them was down in Bibb County. Every once in a while, we would ride a train down to Tuscaloosa, and then go over to the M & O depot and ride another train down to Bibb County. We didn't do that too much because it took a whole day to get down there.

When I went to Ensley High School, it was about two miles and we walked there and back. My daddy bought a Model T Ford in 1923, a tin lizzie, and it was the first car he ever bought. People would come down there just to look at it. They was some that had cars. One family had a Buick, and we looked up to them, kind of.

I was sixteen when I started working in the steel mills. I had to get a minor's release to go to work. I took the streetcar and went down to Birmingham and went to the board of education and two or three other places. Back then, I never thought too much about nothing but having a good time. My father, he worked for the mills, and during that school vacation, my mother thought I ought to be working so my father got me a job in the machine shop as apprentice boy making seventeen cents an hour. I worked there 'til time to go back to school. My mama wanted me to quit and go back to school, but my daddy seemed like he didn't care one way or the other and I just kept on working. The machine shop was a great big place, about two hundred feet long, I suspect, and they had planers, shapers, drill presses, and mostly lathes. They done repair work, whatever they needed in the mill, blast furnaces and open hearths. You had to work four years as an apprentice before you could become a machinist and machinists made fifty-five cents an hour, a little bit better than being an apprentice. All this time, I was living at home and just had to walk about two blocks down to work. Back then, we worked six days a week and they paid off every two weeks. My daddy took ten dollars for board every two weeks. I was making so much money, I didn't know what to do with it.

I had what they called a sweetheart, and on Sunday I would borrow my daddy's car and they called it going riding, didn't go nowhere, just riding. We would go round what we'd call the loop. We would leave Ensley and go out to Mulga, Bayview, then go on and kind of make a circle around and go through Edgewater and Wylam to Ensley and come on back up the hill. It wouldn't take no more than two hours, but we would have that car packed full of people. My daddy had what they called a touring car, and most of the time there would be six or more people hanging on. That touring car wasn't too wide and we would be scrouged in there. Some Sundays, we would just go back in the woods, bunch of boys, hunting sweet shrubs and things like that. U.S. Steel owned all this land around here, what Belcher Lumber Company didn't own.

Here's another thing about Gobbler's Knob. Nineteenth Street come up the hill. That's where that viaduct is right now, and way up on that side was the black quarters and on this side was the white people. The black people had a fine school up there, their own, and we had one, too. We never had a bit of trouble with black people. We would play ball with them. The company had a ball diamond down there with a grandstand for people to sit and each plant had a team. The black people worked in the same place we did, but they didn't have the same jobs. Like the open hearth and the rail mills, and we had black people in the machine shop but all you ever see them doing was sweeping. Back then, a black didn't have a dog's chance to get a good job, but the union come in and they fought for them black people to get in the line of promotion.

Well, they had two lines of promotion: the white and the black, just like they had the water fountains and the rest rooms and all for the different ones. They had a water fountain that was a square box like that, and over here they had another one and a sign over each one that said "colored" and "white." Those signs stayed up there until the sixties. The union balked for having it all the same. We didn't have any trouble with the blacks because they didn't make any trouble. We had a bunch of the best black people I have ever seen down in the mill.

There was no sign of a union when I first started working in the mills in 1925. They didn't get organized until Roosevelt took office, about from '36 on. Like if you was a craneman, you stayed a craneman and that was it. You couldn't move nowhere else to another job. When the union come in and put in what they called a line of promotion. A craneman was in job class 8 and that paid so much, and the next class was a 9, then 10, and on like that. If a job come open in job class 9, a man in class 8 would step up. If you was in line for it and had the seniority, you got it. For a long time, they was a few that wouldn't join the union. I held out for a long time because I had a mind of my own and the company had been good to me. I would tell 'em, why should I join? I remember the dues was a dollar and a half a month and I said why should I pay that when I already got a job? They would come by to talk to me on the job, and that was against the rules, but the company wouldn't do nothing about it. I was just torn between one and the other because you hated to work with a bunch of men and be the only one not in the union.

When they were organizing, a bunch of men would just get together outside of the gates. They was my buddies and my friends, and they thought they could better theirselves. Finally, they just kept on after me, on and on, and I said I would just go ahead and sign the card. Finally, they got a meeting hall up there in Fairfield. The union just kept gaining a little at a time, plus the government would help them. Mr. Roosevelt, he actually forced some companies to recognize the unions.

Finally, somewhere along in the thirties, the NLRB, they made the company hold an election in the plant and each employee could vote if they wanted the union or not. I don't think you had to be a union member to get a job at the steel mill, but I didn't know anybody who wasn't a union member, but there were some. They just didn't fellowship with you if you weren't a member, and you know how that would be.

When they laid me off in 1929 after the depression hit, I was just off for about two weeks. I didn't worry much because I was living at home and I was young and had a little money. I hadn't went nowhere hunting a job when I got off and didn't care. Then, one of the guards and I had gone fishing about two weeks after I got laid off, and after that, he went into my daddy's place in Ensley and told him that there was a job open in the sheet mill in Fairfield. He told my daddy to tell me to come in. Monday, I went into the employment office and they sent me to Fairfield to operate a crane. I had never operated a big crane and I went down to talk to the chief electrician, and he asked me if I had ever operated a big crane. I told him I had operated little ones and he said I could handle it then. He told me to come out to work on that Sunday. He put me up on one of them big cranes and I done fine.

That first day I worked with the millwrights picking up those mills. Mills was what they used to mash steel into sheets. I was just supposed to work for two weeks to fill in for a fellow who was sick and then I would be off again. My two weeks was up and it was on payday. Back then, they paid off in cash and we lined up to get them envelopes, and I was standing up in that pay line and a dressed-up man come down the line and asked me, "Are you getting laid off?" And I said, "I'm done laid off." He said he needed a craneman and told me to come on back in the morning, and I been working right there ever since, up until 1972. It just seemed like everything fell in place for me.

I got married right in the middle of the depression, in November of 1932. We stayed at my daddy's house a few days and I got me some rooms and got out. We went out to Ensley on Avenue F, two rooms and a kitchen. I know people told me, said, "Bracknell, I don't get it. I understand you voted for Hoover." I did vote for Hoover because my father had always been a Republican. They said, "Here it is in the middle of the depression, and you are voting for Hoover?" My daddy was in the loan business by then, and he had an expression when somebody wanted to borrow some money. He would turn them down and say, "That's the way it is." "That's the way it is" fitted me voting for Hoover. Sometimes my daddy would say, "It's hell when it's thisaway, and it's thisaway now." There was a lot of good business out there in Ensley right on up through the sixties, mills running and everybody working. Things were hopping around the mills then.

During the war when so many women came in, we had to help train them there in the mill. The men resented the women coming in, because they had to show them what to do and they called it "carrying." Carrying them women. They brought some women in and they would put them up on the crane with me to learn them to operate a crane. Most of them women, they wanted them to be cranemen, and they would put them up there on the crane with me and some of them would stay three months. The funny thing of it was, we would train them and they would get to be fairly good, then they didn't know what to do with them because us regulars were still there. The superintendent talked to me about it and asked me would I change jobs and go over to another crane and let this woman have my crane. I wouldn't do it and that was the only time I ever refused to do something that I was told to do. It looked like what it was they wanted me to do was to leave my crane and give it to a woman. They left her up there and she worked it when I took a day off or went hunting or something like that.

Finally, they took a bunch of these women down on the floor and put them to wrapping and crating, where they wrapped the sheets, putting heavy paper and straps around them. The women finally took lightweight jobs, mostly. When the boys went off to the army, their time went right on, and when they came back after World War II, they got their old jobs back. The company wanted all the women to leave and thought that is what they would do. Some of them women raised a ruckus and filed somewhere and the company had to give them back pay.

I never had any trouble with my bosses in over forty years working in the mills except for one thing. One time the company had a big drive on for the Community Chest and they wanted 100 percent participation from every employee. The heads of United States Steel got with them people up there and said they could get all the employees to sign up. I always despised to be made to do something that I didn't think was right. They kept on hammering at the men out there and hammering at me and a handful of others who wouldn't sign for Community Chest. They actually called me into the office off my job and talked to me and wanted to know why I wouldn't sign. The superintendent of this plant told a bunch of us one time we didn't have to sign up for nothin', and that was when the union was trying to sign us up. I told them I didn't mind the few pennies they would take out of my pay, I just didn't want to be forced to do something against my will, and I wouldn't sign it. They threatened to fire one man who wouldn't sign it. I would give it to them, but I wanted to get my time. I wanted it in my hand first. They wanted to cut it through the payroll so they could say they were 100 percent. The head of the department was a man I thought a lot of and he would put his arm around me and say, "Come on, Brack, come on now and sign this if you don't do it for nobody but me." One time he told me that for every dollar they cut out of my pay, he would take it out of his own pocket. So, one day he was talking to me and I said, "Well, go ahead and give me the paper. But I don't want to." I signed it, and the company was 100 percent.

Saints Had to Live

Bud Dean, Elmore County

A standard tradition down around Tallassee was going to work in the cotton mill pretty early. I started when I was sixteen, for thirty cents an hour. You were moving up on the economic and social ladder then. I went to work full-time then and worked twelve hours a day, get so sweaty it was like you ducked me in a pond. Those old brogans would get filled with sweat and you could just hear it sloshing around. Worked like the dickens and enjoyed it.

My daddy went to work in the old cotton mill this side of the river in 1899. My aunt was two years older than him, so she got his pay and then she gave it to Grandma.

You had to be mighty thirsty to drink water out of the water buckets there in that mill because they were just sitting out there, and the lint was flying everywhere and it would settle on that water. Everybody dipped snuff and chewed tobacco in the mill then, and they would take that dipper and kind of scrape that lint and the snuff and tobacco off the water in the bucket to get a drink. A little retarded boy named Will Short toted water from under the bridge on the Elmore County side of the river up to the mill, all five floors, and it really kept him hustling. There was a big spring down there and that's where he got his water. Just a little bonus there, didn't cost nothing.

They got an hour off for dinner at that mill and my sister and my older brother used to carry dinner every day to the workers when we lived in town. They would turn out school for an hour and you would hit it atrottin' and you'd run to this house and that house and get the lunch pails and hustle down to the mill to the workers. In that lunch bucket would be fried meat and cooked vegetables and sweet potatoes and fried apple pies and whatever the wife could fix. There were slim rations at times.

They paid once a month at four o'clock on Saturday evening in a little envelope they called a ticket. Daddy made a little less than six and a half cents an hour which was six dollars a month and that was working from six in the morning to six in the evening and until four on Saturday afternoon. He was thirteen when he started working in the mill and Mama started when she was just nine years old. Her mother had died and that was just the way it was then, not that her daddy wasn't a good man. Grandpa Spradlin was a good old saint, but saints had to live. When my Grandpa Dean died, my daddy had seven little sisters, and they held the family together. No welfare, no commodities, no food stamps, but they had a damn sight more than they got now. They had hope and honor and you see what kind of nation they made. It was scratch or starve and that was the name of the game. Us three oldest boys dropped out of school to work and an aunt on each side of the family took one of the girls apiece and helped them in school. Now, the girls had to have books and decent-looking clothes but us old boys had to make it any old way.

A Terrible Thing

J. Torbett Crocker, Jefferson County

I was going to school at Birmingham-Southern in 1935 and 1936 and working for Republic Steel at night. I got attached to my job and making money, so I left school for a full-time job at Republic. I got a full-time job because the union went on strike about that time and the company needed people. They wanted me to go out on strike, too, but I said, "Hell with you. I need the job." I was what they called a scab, and union men didn't like scabs. They would get on a streetcar looking for scabs, and if they found one, they would throw him out of the window. The company would send trucks around to pick us up for work and bring us food in the plant.

There were about nine hundred people in this plant and we mainly made coke for the steel mills. They would run the coal into this long trough, and underneath the trough they had gas burning. Then the coal would burn for a certain time, a pusher would come along and push the coal out into a big car where it was scrubbed with water. Then, it was coke. I was a water tender. We made steam to generate electricity for the plant. Most of the coke we made went to the Republic Steel plant in Gadsden.

A terrible thing happened when I was working at that plant. I was making thirty cents an hour and had a bunch of blacks working for me, emptying these big gondolas into a pit. One day, one of them said something smart to me and I hit him and knocked him down in that pit. It was small coal in the bottom so it didn't hurt him. He crawled out and I saw him walking over to the superintendent's office. I thought, oh-oh, I'm going to get fired now. Pretty soon, I got called to the superintendent's office. He asked me, did you hit this boy? And I said, yes sir. Then he said, did you hit him with your fist? And I said, yes sir. He shouted, "You supposed to hit 'em with a board." That was embarrassing, I tell you.

They Filled Every Room

Vern Scott, Talladega County

Back in 1928, Bemis Bag Company, they were prospecting for the location for another plant, and naturally some of the local fellows wanted them to locate in Talladega. Man in a bank here named Henry Lane, he dabbled in real estate and another man, Henry Thornton, both were anxious to get the mill located here. But the place they would have liked to locate, place about a mile south of town here, good flat farmland, about half of that location was owned by a man named Benny Cogman. Cogman was a businessman and he was always dressed neat, always wore a derby hat, and stingy as could be. Better watch him, too, because if you were dealing with him, you might come out on the short end.

Well, Lane didn't want Cogman to know about the factory deal because if he did know, he'd jack the price up so high on the land that he would run the factory off. Cogman went to Lane's bank every day and Lane caught him one day and said, "Benny, my farm down there is not making any money and I'm either going to sell it or buy some more and get bigger and see if I can make some profit. Now, your land is right next to mine, so what will you take for yours?" Cogman made a reasonable price and Lane said, "Well, let's put that in writing. I'll just put $150 down to seal the option, and if I decide to buy it, I'll just put the money in your account. And, if I don't, well, you can just keep the $150." That sounded good to Benny so they signed up, and as soon as Benny left the bank, Lane put the purchase price in Benny's account and turned around right away and sold the land to Bemis Bag Company.

Day or two later, Benny found out about the sale to the bag

company and came in the bank just raising cain. He wasn't going to honor that deal, he told Lane. Lane told him the deal was done, and that's how the bag company came to Talladega. That bag company ran right through the whole durn depression and had about 1,100 employees. Big payroll in a town of about 6,000. They made both cloth and paper bags, but they made the cloth bags out of the same material that you made shirts out of. The reason for that was that they were selling the cloth bags to the flour companies and folks would make clothes out of the flour sacks, and that helped them sell the flour.

It came out in 1940 that they were going to build a big powder plant down at Childersburg. That's what all that surveying was for because they were going to have this plant down there about four miles wide and seven miles long. They spaced the buildings out so that if one of them blew up, the whole works wouldn't go. Folks fell in there and started building that powder plant, and soon after, we heard that they were going to build a bag plant out here on the edge of Talladega.

What they were doing is making that powder down there in Childersburg and hauling it up to Talladega for packaging. They came out here on the north side of town, built that factory, and overnight almost, the population of Talladega doubled. Clay County and Randolph County didn't have any industry, and Chambers County didn't have much, and those people all fell in here to get jobs. They rented every room they could get. If a fellow had enough basement under his house, he made some way you could sleep down there. They filled every vacant upstairs room downtown, and I mean every one, and for awhile, a bunch of them slept in their automobiles up north of town until they could get a place to live. Some of them slept in chicken houses and garages and anything that had a cover over it. With all that increase in population, people fell in here opening cafes and such.

Well, they would take powder from Childersburg and they had people out here putting it up in raw silk bags making artillery charges, and they were going at it night and day. At the Anniston Army Depot, Lord, they were making everything up there. They would take these bags full of powder and ship them on up to the

Anniston Army Depot. They would take these bags and put them in steel drums and send them to Anniston, and up there, they would send them right on up to the front.

Some Kind of Bad Place

Billy Miles, Marengo County

Back in the depression, about 1936, I worked for my father in the neon sign business. I was about nineteen or twenty years old and single. I had come down from Buffalo, New York, and Alabama was the first place I came to in the South. We stayed at the old Molton Hotel. I remember going around the corner and eating in a dime-store lunch counter and the lunches were nineteen cents. I was in a nice restaurant one night across from the hotel, eating at the counter, and some state of Alabama agents came in the place and seized several cases of beer stacked up there on the wall. Beer was illegal, but that didn't make any difference in Birmingham. To me, being in Birmingham was just like being in the wild West.

My dad told me one time when he found out I was going to take a job at a paper mill that all I was going to do was to get my hands dirty. He told me I ought to use my head. I listened to him and I thought of some of the things he had been in, and decided that I wanted something more permanent. I went in the paper-mill business in 1937 and started in Jacksonville, Florida, and then I went to Valdosta, Georgia. In 1956, they had a big change in management in the Valdosta plant and they paid me off because I was one of the newest people there. Another fellow there was in the same boat and he was coming to Demopolis to work for Gulf States Paper. I came to Demopolis, looked around, and decided to take a job in Alabama.

Some people came by my house in Valdosta and said they heard I was coming to Demopolis, and I said I was, and they said they certainly wouldn't go to that place. All the people in that plant were crazy, they said, and I wondered what I had got into. When I got to Demopolis, I was getting a thousand bucks a month from my old job on a six-month payoff, and a thousand bucks on my new job, and I was floating in money.

I had a boss at Gulf States and I called him General Halsell, a big general in World War II, and a graduate of West Point. The owner of Gulf States, Jack Warner, liked to hire retired military. The first day on the job, I asked General Halsell what he wanted me to do. He told me he wanted me to go out there in the mill and see them getting a job together. I walked out there and they were all working, and about the time I got close to the job, I seen a man walk up to a fellow and hit him in the head with a hammer. The fellow went down and the man who done the hitting ran out into the woods. I was thinking, hot damn, this is some kind of bad place. I went back and talked to General Halsell and told him what had happened. He said, "Well, that's just the way it is."

Then, one day, I was sitting in my office working on some plans for organization, and a girl came in my office, good-looking woman, man, she was a good-looking woman. Came in there and said she wanted to talk to me, and I asked her what she wanted to talk about, and she just backed up against the door. "I want to talk to you about getting a job," she said. "I'm not smart enough to work for General Halsell, but I think I'm smart enough to work for you." That's exactly what she told me, and she pulled out a book and said that she had to pay these coupons off on that Ford she bought. I kind of backed up a little bit and didn't know where to go. You get caught in a funny situation like this and you get run off, for sure. All of a sudden, I heard some laughing, and it was General Halsell and his secretary and the purchasing agent out there and they were playing a joke on me. They were just laughing like hell. We scared you, they said, and you can bet they did, because I hadn't been there but a month.

We started up this paper plant here in Demopolis making pulp. Jack Warner, who owned this Gulf States Paper Company, came along and told me one day that when we got up to making 2,000 tons a week that he would buy me a hundred-dollar hat, and that's when you wore those big fedoras, you know, and one week we made 2,100 tons. The next thing I know, here comes this man coming in my office and he's got this big box, and in that box is one of these derbies like Churchill wore. Jack Warner was as good as his word and I still have that derby.

Walking the High Line

S. L. Pinson, Jefferson County

In April of 1930, I got a chance to go to work for U.S. Steel in Fairfield and got a job in the billing division at ten hours a day, twenty-five cents an hour. There was no overtime back then, no unions, no nothing. This was a big mill, even then, and there were a lot of people working out there, at least 30,000. I worked in that billing division for seven weeks and got a little promotion over to the cost accounting office. This was very nice because I went to eight hours a day, five days a week, and this was paying me about sixty-six dollars a month. That wasn't so bad because I was single and there was a depression on and a dollar went a long way.

My parents moved back to Georgia so I got a place in a boardinghouse at Wilks Station and paid five dollars a week board. Wilks Station is on the Bessemer Car Line, between Bessemer and Fairfield. I walked back and forth to work, about two miles across there over the hill, across what they called the High Line, which was a railroad track. I walked that High Line to work, and if a train came along, they had places along the line where you could get off to one side.

In April of '32, they called us all in and said that they were going to keep all the married men and all the single men would have to get laid off. I left Birmingham and went back over to Georgia and stayed with my family on the little farm they had over there. I helped my daddy around the farm, and on Saturdays, I would go into town and work at the A & P for about eighteen hours and I got two dollars. About that time, the banks had closed during the depression, and the manager of that A & P had to take the cash he had taken in that day and go down to the post office and buy a money order to mail it in to Atlanta. There was no other place to put the cash since the banks were closed.

They had told me at the mill that they would probably be calling us back, so in July of '33, I went to Birmingham and checked with them to see what was going on. They said they would be calling me back in September, so I went back to Georgia knowing I was going to get my job back and got married. I came back to Birmingham in September with a new wife and my dad's old Model A Ford. Everything my wife and I had in the world came back to Birmingham in that Model A. We drove that old car until 1937. We rented a little four-room house in Wilks Station for five dollars a month.

There was a furniture store in Bessemer and we went down there and bought some used furniture, and the man told me, "If you will pay for it in ninety days, we'll give it to you like cash." So we bought what we could pay for in ninety days, and then we would go back and buy more when we had the money. We started on the basis of living within our income, and if we couldn't buy for cash, we just didn't buy it. Things were a little uncertain, you might say. That little house just had four rooms, with a little front porch and a little back porch, and an outdoor toilet. All over in that area was that way. Several years later, the lady who owned the house wanted to sell it and we bought it for six hundred dollars. We had saved the money and I paid cash for it. That was in '37, and it still had that outdoor toilet, but we did have lights and water, and gas for cooking. We lived in that house until 1940.

I had just parked the car and was walking back and forth to work, because gas was eighteen cents a gallon and we were trying to save and get by on less money. Well, eighteen cents a gallon was like paying $1.50 a gallon now. Our son was born in '34 and about the time he was ready to go to school, we wanted to get to a better school district. So, we came to Ensley and rented a duplex on Avenue H for $25 a month, and I sold my house over there for $1,025. In 1941, I bought this lot in Ensley for $500 and we went down to see a builder, got an FHA mortgage, and built a house for $4,500. My monthly payments were $26 with a 4 percent loan.

When I came back to the mill in '33, they said they were going to pay me $119 a month. When I got my first payday, I got only $88. I went to my boss and he told me that they were cutting back and since I was the youngest, I got the cut. Don't worry, he told me, we'll take care of you later on. About six months later, an opening came along for a promotion. I was called in again and was told they couldn't give it to me because that would mean a raise from $88 to $136 a month and that was too much of a raise. They gave me a 10 percent raise instead of the promotion. The man they gave the promotion to was the boss's future son-in-law. I kept my mouth shut and just kept studying at night and took typing and waited my chance.

When World War II came along, I figured I would have to go into service. But then they called me in the office one day and said I would be transferred to the motor transportation division which is where they had all the tires and gasoline and trucks and cars. They were having a lot of trouble with people stealing tires and gasoline, and this was during the war, and I had heard a lot of stuff about all that going on down there. I told the boss that I didn't want to go down there, because I didn't want to get run off. I think it was common knowledge that tires and gas were being siphoned off in wholesale lots. We heard a feller would come in and sign his name to some tickets and people would drop off the goods before they were delivered to where they were supposed to go.

They said they wanted me down there, so I went. I could have pulled some crooks, but that was not the way I did business. After a couple of weeks, they called me back in and the general superintendent and my boss said they wanted to know all about the stealing of the gas and tires. I told them that the superintendent down there was drinking and couldn't get along with his people, and gas and tires were being stolen on a regular basis. The big bosses cleaned house and moved the superintendent out to another job and the ones that had been stealing, they let them go.

When I was at the mill early on, there wasn't any union. In 1951 there was a union, and they decided to strike. The strikers wouldn't stay in the plant and the supervisory people had to go in the plant and do the things that had to be done. I was in the coke plant, and you just couldn't go in and turn off the lights because some of that plant just had to keep going. The supervisory people went in there and they brought food and stuff in there for us. We kept that plant together and kept it going. In the coke plant, if it got cold, it would take several months to build it back up. This was the worst strike we had out at the steel mills, because most of the time they let enough union people in to do the necessary things, but not this time. This strike didn't last but about two weeks, but it was critical because nobody came in. The ones that worked didn't get harassed when we went in because the union men knew some parts of that plant had to keep going. In regular times, we enjoyed going to work because we were family and helped each other, but it's not that way anymore.

During the war, the inexperienced people came into the mills, and I am talking about the women and the colored. They could get by without doing the job. Then, that's when the morale started going down and the production started falling off. Some of those new women in the mills started a little carrying on with the bosses, and a lot of that went on. We had a man right across the street here who was a supervisor at the mill, and he would bring one of his female employees in during the daytime to spend part of the day with him. He worked nights and his wife worked in the daytime, and he had a nice little arrangement there. Naturally, I imagine this woman got by with a lot out at the mill. This man didn't care if everybody knew what he was doing because you had to do something extra bad to get fired back then.

That's when the union came in, too. They started protecting the sorry people as well as the good workers, and a lot of the good workers resented this. The union representative in my office didn't care much about his job and harassed the other workers. They knew he was wrong and that they were being treated fairly by the company, so they didn't pay any attention to him. I heard one time that this union man was out at the gate talking to a bunch of fellows and he told them that he had run off the two supervisors just prior to me—one of them had a heart attack and the other one got sick on the job. He said that Pinson wouldn't be here six months and he would run me off, too. It wasn't a year later that the union man was over at the university hospital on the mental ward.

Drilled by the Mill

E. L. Lovelady, Tallapoosa County

After we moved to Alexander City, my dad got a job in the cotton mill and we lived in a cotton-mill house. At that time, I was about six years old and my dad was making eight dollars a week at the mill, I heard him say. The cotton mill had their own dentist and they came around to check the kids at school, check their teeth out, you know. My brother needed several fillings, so he agreed to get it done, not realizing it was going to hurt. But, he thought, "Well, if I need it done, I'll get it done." Of course, they charged it to your parents that worked at the cotton mill, whatever the bill was. My brother got his teeth filled, and when Daddy got his payday at the end of the week, all he got was a nickel. I mean that was his whole payday because they took out all the dental work on him. My daddy liked to had a fit, you know, but my brother got his teeth fixed.

Two Dollars a Payday

C. E. Bracknell, Jefferson County

One good thing the steel mill provided was real good medical care. They had a dispensary in every camp and every one had a doctor in it. Like if one of the kids stumped their toe or got a boil on their foot or little things like that, they would go down and they would fix them up—no charge. One thing they liked to do was paint your throat. They would paint your throat for just about anything.

The employees had what they called a doctor's fee and they cut it out of his time every month. If you had to go to the hospital up there on the hill—that was the Lloyd Nolan—you had to pay that bill, but it was a good bit off. They just done minor things in the camps, but there was a dispensary in every one—Bayview, Docena,

Edgewater, Ensley, Muscoda, Wenona, and Gobbler's Knob. They had an ambulance in Ensley.

In 1939, my daughter was six years old, about the time to go to school. She had a hurting in her side and the doctor said she had to go to the hospital. That girl stayed up there thirty-one days and had an operation by Dr. Nolan himself, and that operation and the hospital stay didn't cost me but eighty-one dollars. One day at work, the timekeeper came out and told me I had a little hospital bill and asked me how I wanted to pay it. I told him just to cut what he had to cut, and he said, "How about two dollars a payday? How does that sound?" It sounded pretty good, but it took me forever to pay that off.

Book Learning

School in a church, Gee's
Bend, 1937
(Arthur Rothstein/Farm
Security Administration
photo, Library of Congress,
Washington, D.C.)

School room, Skyline
Farms near Scottsboro,
1937
(Arthur Rothstein/Farm
Security Administration
photo, Library of Congress,
Washington, D.C.)

Double Promoted

Olene Latimer, Marshall County

The roads weren't paved up on the mountain when I started school and sometimes the bus would get stuck. They taught through the seventh grade at Mount Shade School. I went through the third grade at Mount Shade and then the schools were consolidated—and that was a big word for me back then. It was really something when I started going to that DAR consolidated school because I was used to going to school in this one-room building with no curtains and there was a lot of noise in that one room with all the kids. And when I got to the DAR school and saw all those rooms and the hallways and the bells ringing for classes and everybody moving down the halls, it was another world.

One day, when I was in the first grade, I must have left my book at home and the teacher told me to go over and sit with my sister in the second grade. I did, and I just stayed in the second grade, and that was the way they did it. It was an embarrassment to my sister because she always had to spend a lot of time explaining how I got in the second grade with her. She thought people would think that she had failed and that was the reason we were both in the same grade together. We had a substitute teacher one day and he really didn't know much. My seatmate and I decided to play a little game with him. We would pick a hard word like hippopotamus and go up and ask him how to pronounce it, and when he would mispronounce it, which he did most of the time, we would go back to our seats and we would punch each other and snigger. I guess it was a mean thing to do, but we thought it was funny at the time.

One of the three disappointments in my life was when I was in the fourth grade, and this was in 1929. The teacher was giving a Valentine party at the school. I was excited because I had never been to a party before. We all helped to make paper ruffles and things that were strung across the top of the room, and we made red valentines and a lot of exciting things for the party. I got a peek at the refreshments which were a bunch of cookies, different cookies, and all of that. The party was going to be on Friday night. Well, my dad had bought an old cream-colored Chevrolet for us to go to school in.

Before that, my brothers had been going to DAR school in a borrowed buggy. I don't know where my daddy got the money to buy that car, but he did. Besides all the kids in our family who rode that old Chevrolet to school, a couple of neighbor kids would ride with us and we would be packed in like sardines. The night of the party, my sister and I got out in the car for my brother to drive us to the party and the car wouldn't start. We pushed it down a little hill hoping to get it started, but it still wouldn't start. Well, I didn't get to go to that party and I still remember how my heart ached that night when I went to bed. When we got back to school on Monday morning after the party, the room was just a mess, but the teacher had saved us some of the cookies. Missing that party was one of my great disappointments.

One day at school, we had a meeting and the officials from the DAR were there. One of our trustees got up to make a welcoming speech and then he called on another trustee to say a few words. This man was real timid and embarrassed and he stood up there and pulled out a long knife and began cleaning his fingernails. He stuttered and stammered and muttered a few words which didn't mean anything, and finally the principal got up and told the man to sit down. My brother happened to be visiting Helen's brother that night, and so, when they got home, they were talking about it and Helen's daddy was listening. When things got quiet, he said, "I declare, that Williams made a bold speech today. I don't believe it would have bothered me to make a speech." And we all got a big kick out of that.

When I graduated from high school, my daddy borrowed enough money for me to go to business school in Birmingham, and this was my first bus trip and the farthest from home that I had ever been. I got on that bus without having a room and not knowing where I was going to stay. That was like somebody getting on an ocean liner and going around the world. The school said they would have somebody meet me and they took me to a boardinghouse. I finished that school, but it was in the depression and there were no jobs. I had a sister who was a schoolteacher who needed to go up to school in Florence to update her teacher's license. She asked me to keep her two girls while she was gone and that's what I did. And at night, I went to business school. I got an offer as a clerk/typist for the department of agriculture through Congressman Joe Starnes. I got that job and I thought I was in high cotton because they paid me seventy-five dollars a month when the girls at the bank were making forty dollars a month. And that was in September of 1939.

Putting on the Dog

Buster Hall, Clarke County

A. L. Payne and I returned to Alabama Polytechnic Institute in September of 1930 for his sophomore and my junior year, and got a room together at the Boy's Dormitory on College Avenue.

About the middle of October, A. L. came dancing in the room one night and said that he had a date to take Doc Benson's niece from New York to the homecoming game the next week. He said that she had never seen a college football game and wanted to sit in the student section with him. Back then, girls were very scarce on the campus and we began to look at A. L. with some envy. Well, A. L. visited every room in the dormitory and all the roominghouses bragging about this beautiful New York girl he was going to take to the game. He really laid it on thick.

The only trouble was, he had already spent his month allowance and had a little case of the shorts, so he called his daddy and told him that he had to have some more money for books and lab fees. He got the money and I went with him down to the store and watched his lab fee money go for a long gray overcoat that reached down to his shoe tops, a scarf, a pair of gloves, and a pair of "Joe College" two-toned shoes. He brought all this stuff home and started practicing by putting on this rig every night and dousing himself with various lotions. You could smell him before you could see him.

He started calling the girl "Miss New York" and said that Mona Lisa would look like a plowgirl by the side of her. He kept on and on about this dream from up North and there was no way to shut him up.

Homecoming day arrived and it was one of those cold, clear days down in Auburn. A. L. shaved twice before noon and used three different lotions. He had told everybody about his grand entrance, just where they would enter the student section, how they would march to their seats on the upper row, and the exact time they would arrive, thirty minutes before kickoff.

It seemed the whole student section was waiting for A. L. and his date when they appeared on the lower aisle. We all craned our necks and saw A. L. in his getup and his famous New York date. We couldn't believe our eyes. That girl was almost a midget, the top of her head coming just above his waist. She had on a fur coat and a fur hat and was leading a fuzzy little dog about the size of a football on a leash made of blue and gold ribbons. She missed being mankind's fairest beauty by a long way. Old A. L. looked up at us with what he thought was a smile on his face, but he looked more like a jackass trying to chew briars.

Then, they started up the steps, and Miss New York handed the dog to A. L. to take up the steps, and he gathered up that fuzzy little dog and they started up. A. L. came up those steps, bowing and smiling to us underprivileged country boys. When they reached the very row I was sitting on, he suddenly held the dog out as far as he could and came to a dead stop. You wouldn't think a dog that little could hold that much water. When it dawned on everybody what was happening, the stadium exploded. We were all rolling in the aisles, dying laughing, and then, Miss New York turned and screamed, "Fido, shame on you!"

They finally got to their seats and A. L. just dumped Fido. For the rest of that year, A. L. was known as "Fido, shame on you!" It didn't take him long to recover, though, and he laughed just as hard as the rest of us.

A Piece of Luck

Houston Cole, DeKalb County

Up on Lookout Mountain, the schools didn't last but four and a half months in the early part of this century. School started in November and got out in April and that was the extent of school. We had a one-room school about a mile from where we lived, but some of the children lived as much as four miles away and they all walked to school. Nobody had a car. I remember after I had a little age on me a car drove up that mountain and you never heard so much discussion of what that thing was. It was just as effective as dropping a bomb. Fellow up at Collinsville had a big store and did a lot of business and he was the first person in this area to buy an automobile.

I finished the sixth grade about the fourth of April. Miss Lura Anderson from Fort Payne was the teacher, and that night they had what they called a school improvement association at the school. The night I graduated, my dad walked down to the school, and on the way he fell in with Miss Anderson. She said, "Mr. Cole, why don't you send Houston to high school next year over at Fort Payne?" My father told her that was impossible—Houston will have to stay home and help gather the crops. Well, I figured that ended it all, even though I had great aspirations to go on to school.

That was about the first of April, and in June, something happened. A man stepped into my life, and if I ever get to heaven, he'll be the first one I look up and thank. The principal of Fort Payne High School, Mr. N. J. Callan, came out to the house and called my dad out about sending me to school. He said he couldn't do that because I had to stay and help on the farm. My father finally compromised and let me go to the second term which was about the first of December. After three months, a typhoid epidemic broke out in Fort Payne and I became a victim and came back home. I was sick for about four weeks and Mr. Callan sent letters out to our house with questions on the subjects I was taking and allowed me to take the examinations.

The second year, I couldn't go back to school because our barn burned down and I had to take out and help build a new one. The only year I went the full nine months was my senior year and that blessed old man allowed me to graduate after attending school only twenty-three weeks out of thirty-six. I would say I was about twenty-one then.

When I was going to school at Fort Payne, you had to pay your own way and travel at your own expense. I would walk over to

Portersville about four miles from home, catch train number 22, which went toward Chattanooga, and get off in time to reach school by eight o'clock. I would stay in Fort Payne all week, and on Friday afternoon I would catch that train back to Portersville and walk up that mountain to our house. One time, I caught the train back to Portersville in midwinter, and when we got there, it was dark. I walked about a mile until I got to Lookout Mountain and I was going to have to walk up that mountain. There came up a terrific electric storm and it scared me to death. They say you don't lie when you get my age. I was walking completely in the dark, and how did I walk? There would come a flash of lightning and I could see a few feet and I could see what was in the road. I would go a few feet and wait for the next flash of lightning. It took me an hour to walk up that mountain and then I had to walk another three miles to get home.

When I went up to Fort Payne to go to high school, I had to stay up there and I had another piece of luck. It cost twenty-five cents on Monday morning to ride the train to Fort Payne and twenty-five cents back on Friday night. Every Monday morning when I left, my dad would give me fifty cents. Fortunately, I had a brother who lived in Fort Payne who worked on the railroad and he left home on Monday morning and returned on Friday. He said, now if you will come and stay with my wife while I'm gone and bring in the coal and the wood and go get the mail, you can stay there free. That was a good arrangement for me.

At home, my dad took the *Chattanooga Times*. Every year, every day, we would get that newspaper and we would get a publication called the *Comfort* and my brothers would come in and bring the *Railroad Man's Magazine* and we always had something to read, and I remember that my dad read it all. He would sit by the light of a pine-knot fire and read to us kids and we were all interested, every single word. He was the best-informed man on Lookout Mountain. About all anybody took up there besides us was the *Collinsville Courier* and it was just published once a week.

There was no thought of going to college after I got out of high school because there was no money. I got a job with my brother-in-law for six weeks, planted the crop, and I got $40 for that summer's work. I got out there and after plowing for two or three weeks, I thought, well, this looks like this is what I will be doing for the rest of my life. After about six weeks, I got a letter from Hugh Edwards who graduated from Fort Payne and was down at Jacksonville at the normal school to get a certificate to teach. You could get a teacher's certificate in just six weeks, first term, five weeks for the second term. He said in the letter that I should come down to Jacksonville the last five weeks and get a teacher's certificate. I knew that my $40 wouldn't be enough because it took $126 for a term. I talked to my dad about it and he put me in a buggy and we drove over to Collinsville and we borrowed $86 from the bank. This gave me $126 and I came down to Jacksonville Normal School and I got the teacher's certificate.

I started looking for a job all over Cherokee County and got a job as principal of a two-teacher school. That's principal and janitor. The term was four and a half months and the salary was $76 a month, a total of about $340 for the year. I saved enough to come back to normal school and finished two years there. My wife and I saved enough money to enroll at The University of Alabama.

Talking about luck, when I finished Alabama in 1921, I was offered the job as principal at Tuscumbia. I was going to write that afternoon and accept the job. Well, I walked into my last class and Dr. Leo King, the teacher, said, "Mr. Cole, I want to see you when this is over," and I had no idea what he wanted. I went up after the class and he asked me how I would like to go to Northport—this is just across the river from Tuscaloosa—and be principal. That suited me fine because it was close to the university and I could continue my education and secure some good contacts there. I went over and talked to the superintendent, presented my credentials, but didn't get the job right away. I told him I was going up to Boaz to my wife's home and asked him to write and let me know if I got the job. When I got to Boaz, there was a telegram waiting for me telling me that I was now the principal of the Northport High School.

Back in 1940, I was appointed director of civilian defense for the state of Alabama. In 1942, I was sitting in my office down there in Montgomery one day and I got a telephone call. All right. I had been flying around the country, New York and Chicago, and that telephone call was from Colonel Ayers here in Anniston. He was chairman of the board of Jacksonville State Teachers College and told me that I had just been elected president. I said to myself, am I really going over there to that place? My wife and I suffered for a week about what to do about the offer, and finally, I said to myself, hey— you had better take that job because this war isn't going to last forever.

I came up to Jacksonville, and for two years I was about as miserable as you could be. I was miserable, my wife was miserable, and my daughter was miserable. I didn't have but 119 students and about half a dozen teachers to start with. When I first got here, there wasn't a soul on this campus but one old lady who was fixing up a room over there in the dormitory for me to stay in. The first day of registration after I got to Jacksonville, another fellow and I walked out on the campus and counted a total of seventeen cars.

Sixty Dollars' Worth

Tera Averett, Coffee County

During my childhood, all of the schools in the country near my home were one-room, one-teacher schools. Only one, Hawridge, six miles away, had three rooms and three teachers. My older sister finished the sixth grade at our one-teacher school and then she went to Ma Waters's house and stayed to be able to go to Hawridge up to the ninth grade. She learned such words as *composition* and *elecution*.

When I finished the seventh grade at Klegg, I couldn't go to Hawridge, but one day while I was picking cotton in the hot field with my back so sore, I stood up straight and said, "I do not intend to do this always. I want to get an education and be a schoolteacher." So, instead of dropping out, I repeated the seventh grade. We had only six students in that class, so I got a good foundation. In fact, I almost memorized the *Modern English*, the huge geography book with the pretty colored maps, and the pictures of the sights and animals of all parts of the world.

One thing that stumped me was the arithmetic problems with "partial payments." I still wonder why I could never come up with the answer correct to the penny. It might have been that I did not drop the one-half cent each time, or that I did drop it each time. One thing I did figure out and that was if I ever had to borrow any money, I would pay it back all at one time so I wouldn't have to figure out the partial payments.

When Papa saw that I was so determined to go on to school, he went to Ozark and asked the superintendent of education to approve the addition of a room and another teacher for Klegg. After that, the new teacher taught the eighth grade. Only one boy, Obie Turner, joined me in that eighth grade class. You talk about individualized instruction! That was it. Obie got one question and I got the next one for every class. After I finished the eighth grade, I entered Coffee County High School in 1922. Papa carried me in his T-Model Ford to Enterprise, got me a place to board with Dudley and Jessie Heath, and headed back to the farm.

I was very happy and not the least bit scared, but I was awed by the huge crowd gathered in the big auditorium for the opening exercises. There was only one person in the auditorium that I knew, a Mrs. Perlman whom I had seen when we went to her store. The principal was Mr. W. E. Snuggs and he seemed so efficient and sure of himself. After he retired, he told me that he was the one that was scared. Before he came to Enterprise, somebody had told him that the big boys, some of whom had already served in World War I, had taken the former principal down to the basement and "whupped him good."

As soon as the opening exercises were over, I rushed to our homeroom to get a front seat. The rooms were so full that the desk I chose touched the teacher's desk. In a few minutes, a tall, husky boy said to me, "You got my desk." I said to him, "I don't know why you think it's yours. I got here first." He said his name was on it, and sure enough, there it was, splashed in big, bold letters—Mack Adams. I gave him the desk, but at our twenty-fifth reunion, I told him I still hated him for that. But, I really didn't. I learned later that his mother was Papa's first cousin.

We were required to take English and history in the ninth grade and could choose two subjects as electives. I chose plane geometry and physics, whatever that was. I dropped physics after a week because when they started talking about "foot-pounds," they lost me. After high school and six years of college, I still cannot tell you about foot-pounds, but so what? I made straight A's and people thought I was smart even if I didn't know about foot-pounds.

After I finished Coffee County High School in 1925, my dad arose before dawn one morning and cranked up the Model T and took me to Ozark where I caught the Atlantic Coast Line train to go up to Troy State Normal College. I went to Troy State and got a teaching certificate and a job with Macedonia School.

At that time, farmers needed their children to help in gathering their crops through September. Schools opened in October. My salary for six months was $60 per month. Can you imagine what that $360 meant to a little farm girl who had never earned a penny— except for one time. Papa gave me a runty pig which the other pigs kept shutting off from the sow's "dinnerpails." I tended that pig carefully, feeding it cornmeal mush made with buttermilk until it could eat corn. Then, Papa said, "If you want me to, I will turn that pig out in the peanut field with the other hogs and fatten it on halves." At two hundred pounds, it was sold at five and one-half cents a pound. I made $5.50, and that was big money for me. So my $360 schoolteaching money went a long way, because Macedonia School was only two miles from home. I could stay at home and pay no board.

My younger sisters drove the Model T to Coffee County High School every day and went right by my school. I got a free ride to work. There were six grades and fifty-two students, but we simply had the basics. We didn't have music or art or physical education. At recess, I played town ball, stealing sticks, and shot marbles with the students.

Somehow, even the twenty-one first graders learned to read very soon. In fact, I do not doubt that much of my success was brought about by the families, because the children were encouraged to carry their books home every night. Back then, the parents bought all the books and they were responsible if the children tore the books or marked on them, or even lost them.

I soon saw what a task it was to get in all of the classes between 8 A.M. and 4 P.M. and went into Ozark to talk to the superintendent of education. He told me, "Miss Byrd, you go on back and when you think you have taught sixty dollars' worth, you go on home."

The next year, the trustees of the school thought I had done a good job and went out in the community and got money for a raise. I got a $12-a-month raise. Even so, I could not satisfy myself with teaching in a school with that many students and that many grades. I went back to Troy and later accepted a job at Atmore for $110 a month.

Knives Were a Problem

Charles Wiggins, Jefferson County

I was in the navy in the South Pacific during the war and got up to acting chief petty officer. After I got out of the navy, well, really in the navy, I saw the necessity of an education. Before I got out of the navy, I made applications for naval schools, but I didn't have the education to get in. A high school education wasn't enough—I saw that—so when I came home, I said the first thing I'm going to do is get a college education. I almost slipped up and used my GI Bill on one of these schools that were popping up all over town. Most of the fellows going to these schools were just going for the money. I remember I talked to my grandfather one night about that and he mentioned to me about being a barber like he was. I said, naw, I wasn't interested in that. He said, "Well, why don't you think about going back to school?" My grandmother was a driving force in my life and she told me that she wanted one member of our family to go to college before she died. Can you believe that?

I finished college and got my first teaching job in a private school, teaching French and social studies. They didn't pay very much. I'm talking about thirty dollars a week and we just got paid every six weeks. Then, I started teaching veterans at night and I never got paid for this teaching. Every time the night school started to pay off, they would say, too bad, but a bunch of thieves broke in and took all the money. I knew better than that and the other teachers were in the same boat. I finally got out of that private school and started teaching in the Birmingham school system, and later on, I became principal in two city schools.

When I started teaching, there was no integration and there were just black teachers and black children. Back then, I don't remember a whole lot of discipline problems. Occasionally, some of the kids would bring wine to school, and if they brought a weapon, it was a knife and they would tell me it was for self-protection. Back then, we didn't have any drug problems, but later on, they started getting involved with pills—yellow jackets and blue jackets and red jackets—barbiturates that would give them a quick high. Sometimes, those knives were a problem, though.

Eight in All

Ben Meriwether, Bullock County

In the spring of 1914, the four families at Mitchell Station that had children decided to have a school. Mr. Pugh donated a lot and the four families got together and built a one-room schoolhouse. The county wouldn't pay a teacher to teach just eight children, but they agreed to pay half if the families would pay the other half. The law said, then, that a child had to be seven before he could start school, so that first year, there were the three Evans boys, one Rutland boy, me, and the three Pugh girls. Eight in all.

The county sent a little redheaded young woman out to teach us, a Miss McCorkle, and when Miss McCorkle said to memorize page 12 for the next day's lesson, we memorized page 12. She stayed there two years and she was a good teacher, but the next one we got, Miss Adams, was not so good. School hours were from eight in the morning until four in the afternoon with fifteen minutes for recess in the afternoon. We had one big bucket of water in the back of the room and one dipper to drink with. Now, I got into a lot of skirmishes with the Evans boys, but if the two oldest Pugh girls were around, it was a free-for-all because they would come to my rescue. Ethel, the oldest, would fight for me, but if I didn't behave, she would fight me.

The Business of Sports

Jeff Coleman, Tuscaloosa County

I first came to The University of Alabama in 1924 as a freshman. I had been up here the summer before as a Boy Scout instructor, so I had seen the campus. There just wasn't much to the university then. We thought it was a big place because I grew up in Livingston. We had a small two-year school in Livingston, Alabama Normal College, they called it. At the university, the Quad was the main thing, and then there was Smith Hall, Woods Hall, Morgan Hall, and Comer Hall, and that was it. All those buildings were built after the Civil War. Student enrollment was about 2,000. I came up on the train from Livingston, but I knew my way around. I lived in Woods Hall and everything was right there in the Quad. I didn't know what I wanted to major in. My father wanted me to be an architect, because he had wanted to be one.

There were all kinds of rules for women students. A boy would go by to pick up a date, sign out, and then you could get on a streetcar and go downtown to a picture show. There were a few rental automobiles, but very few students had automobiles on the campus. Maybe two students owned cars. In the early thirties, the Sunday school endorsed a hall on campus, and I was the superintendent. I would give the students free round-trip tickets to ride the streetcar into town to go to church.

In 1924, we had football, baseball, track, and basketball. We didn't have any women's sports to amount to anything. Women did have physical education. Women had to all wear bloomers, black bloomers, with a white shirt and a navy or black tie. Dr. George Little said in one of his books that the first athletics on campus were mumblety-peg and races on the road in front of the campus. There wasn't any Southeastern Conference then. Alabama belonged to the old Southern Conference. Big football rivals in the twenties were Vanderbilt and Sewanee, along with Mississippi State, but Alabama always beat Mississippi State, so it wasn't much of a rival.

I remember one time in the midforties Alabama was playing Mississippi State, and I think it was Shorty McWilliams's last year over there. I was sitting up in the press box next to Dudy Noble who was Mississippi State's athletic director. Alabama punted and McWilliams caught the punt, right on the goal line. He caught this ball and stepped back into the end zone. The field judge didn't call anything. None of the officials called anything, and I said, "Dudy, did you see what I just saw?" Dudy chuckled and said, yeah. See, Shorty caught that ball, stepped back into the end zone and flipped the ball to the field judge. The field judge took the ball out to the twenty. Shorty got away with it, but then, they were playing over in Starkville. The chief of the Southeastern Conference saw it too, but he didn't overrule the official on the field.

When I graduated from the university back in the twenties, I accepted a job with the National City Bank and I was supposed to go to China for four years. But the university president, Dr. Denny, talked me into staying here and continuing as business manager of athletics. Now, I had that job as a student. So I stayed on as business manager and ran the college store. As a student in 1927, I was made business manager, a new title then. I was Alabama's first athletic business manager. I handled all the gate receipts and tickets and made up the schedules and handled contracts. I used a lot of students to help me. I had a lot of experience handling money working for my daddy's mercantile store back in Livingston. I never really asked for a job in my life, but the president of Livingston wrote a letter to Dr. Denny about me, and I guess that's what got me started.

Dr. Denny told me to study shorthand and typing when I came up here, and that's all he told me. So then, he sent me over to see Coach Wade and said to tell him that he sent me over to work for him. I went out for football but didn't have a chance to make the team, so I went out for manager. Football players didn't have much financial help back in those days. They got their fees and meals, but had to wait on tables when they were freshmen.

Champ Pickens told Coach Wade that he ought to take me to the first Rose Bowl game in 1926 when I was a sophomore. Wade told Champ that he didn't know about that because I was trying to tell everybody how to run the office. I had a relative who was a financial writer for the *New York Times.* He suggested to the sportswriter that I was sports editor for the campus paper and did some other things and that the *Times* take me on as a stringer and report on the trip to the Rose Bowl. The *Times* paid me fifty dollars for each trip the first two times Alabama went to the Rose Bowl.

I filed one report to the *Times* from the north rim of the Grand Canyon. On the trip to California, the team would stop off and practice and I would report on those practices. You didn't have interviews like you do today. You might ask the coach a few questions, but he didn't give out any formal interviews and you didn't interview the players at all. On the second Rose Bowl trip, a man came to see Dr. Denny and got him to advertise a breakfast food. We fed the team Muffets. It was sort of like shredded wheat. We found out later that they were feeding Muffets to the Stanford team as well as Alabama. The Stanford game was a 7 to 7 tie. Maybe the teams were so even because both ate Muffets for breakfast. When we played our last Rose Bowl game in 1946, we had trouble getting transportation due to the aftermath of the war and had to split the team up to get them to California.

Those Rose Bowl trips Alabama made back in the early days just opened up a whole new thing in the South for athletics. A lot of other teams in the South got a chance to go out after we won. We played in six Rose Bowl games. When we played in the Sugar Bowl in '45 you couldn't mail tickets to anybody. I was in charge of the tickets. We had to take all the tickets to New Orleans and people had to come there to pick up their tickets. We had all these tickets put in envelopes with their names on them and everything. We put them in a big box and my wife and I got on the train in Tuscaloosa, got a drawing room, and took those tickets to New Orleans and passed them out at the Sugar Bowl office. Just me and my wife. No guards or anything. We used to play some Alabama games in Montgomery and I would come back from Montgomery to Tuscaloosa with all the gate receipts. Of course, it wasn't a lot of money, but my father didn't think that was a good way to do business.

In Front of Everybody

Burton Troup, Marshall County

Before the DAR school came to Gunters Mountain, we had a schoolhouse built out of a church and it had a little rostrum and grades one through four sat on one side, and five, six, and seven sat on the other side, and there were two teachers. We sat two to the desk and the desks were all carved up with initials and you had a little inkstand there in the center where you could use a pen. When a boy got a whipping, it was right there in front of everybody.

The school was a mile and a half from our house. When I was sitting over there on the first grade side, I spent my time listening to what was going on in the upper grades across the aisle. When I got over to the other side, I had already heard all that stuff. When you got to a word in your book you didn't know, you would put your finger on it and walk up to the teacher. There were people coming and going all the time.

We didn't have any outhouses at all at school. We had the boys' woods across the road and the girls' woods. I wouldn't even look over on the girls' side when the leaves fell. Down the way a piece were several crabapple trees and we passed that way going to our house. I wouldn't go out and get any of those crabapples because they were in the girls' woods.

We had one boy, Stanley Askew, who went home for lunch and he would take his cap off and reach over and get him a little switch, because he wanted to be a horse. He would go down there switching himself and he would get into a run. There was a mud-hole right down there, and you know how horses would shy away from a mud-hole, and Stanley would shy away and switch himself hard to get around that mud-hole.

Love That Dixie

Carolyn Lipscomb, Lee County

We were living in Auburn and really didn't have a lot of money. My mother had to make a living, feed, clothe, and educate six children. She worked as a secretary out at the college, and about the only way I could go to college was to take all the shortcuts I could. Tuition was only forty-two dollars a quarter in 1945, and I had some brothers going to school on the GI Bill taking a lot of math courses. I would put those classes off for a couple of years so that I could follow behind and use their books. Mother was determined that we would have all the opportunities that she didn't have. I remember that Mrs. Caldwell was our piano teacher and my brother, who was two years older than I, was so good that she didn't charge him anything. He was a good advertisement for her. She just charged half-price for my sister and me. Mother bought a piano for five dollars, and we kept it until recently when we gave it to our son in Baltimore.

In Auburn, Mother bought season tickets for all of the six children for every concert at Auburn, and I mean to tell you we went, whether we wanted to or not. We had a good time growing up, but we were one of the poorest families in Auburn. I wouldn't swap the time I grew up with any time since.

After I graduated from Auburn I had a chance to go to New York and teach math in a high school. I really didn't like that high school because discipline was a big problem. I jumped at a chance to transfer to an elementary school nearby. At that time, there was no integration in the lower grades and I had a delightful bunch of little white children. During the course of the year, I taught the kids "Dixie" and we sang this song just about every day. I told them that when we sang the national anthem that everybody was supposed to stand up, and I told them that down in Alabama, we all stood up when we sang "Dixie."

Just about every day, we sang "Dixie" and everybody stood and sang with great gusto. At the end of the year, the sixth grade went through the graduation exercise and we moved all six grades over to the high school auditorium to accommodate the crowd. When all the children were in the auditorium and waiting for things to begin, the principal came over and asked me to get the children to sing something because they were stirring around and getting restless. I walked over to the piano, hit the first few chords, and they jumped to their feet and sang "Dixie" at the top of their voices, totally amazing the rest of the school. Nobody could have sung the song with more enthusiasm and I was proud to be from Alabama.

Looking for a Better Way

Charlie Hill, Walker County

I went to a two-room school for the first six years, about a mile and a half away from our house, and I walked to and from the school. Oak Grove was the name of the school and it had two teachers. There was a folding wall between the classes. One teacher had grades one through three and the other teacher had grades four through six. That last teacher would teach fourth grade for a while and then she would teach fifth grade for a while and then she would teach the sixth grade for awhile. In each of those classes, she would give an assignment to one grade and go back and teach another grade. After I finished sixth grade, I went to Nauvoo Junior High, grades seven through nine. Then, I really went to town when I went to high school in Carbon Hill. I drove the school bus to Carbon Hill, and the way we had to go to pick up the children, it was about thirty miles.

In the little two-room school I started in, we had a young lady who came out to be principal, and she probably influenced my life quite a bit as far as wanting an education. She was a very Christian lady and I felt she had a mission from God to come out and educate the poor people in the country. She did things on her own time, like teaching art and music, and she convinced the PTA to have cake sales to buy a junky old piano. The idea was that she would teach the kids who wanted to learn to play the piano. When my sixth grade class graduated, there was a picture of my graduation class, all six of us. In that class, there were three girls and three boys, and one of those girls got married right out of the sixth grade. She was twelve years old. In those circles, I guess that was accepted.

I had a thirst for knowledge, and I guess it came from my grandfather more than anybody else. He had the equivalent of a second or third grade education. My grandfather always wanted me to be a Baptist preacher, and that's what he wanted. He was a very intelligent man, and he and my mother guided me some. As soon as I was big enough to understand, I knew I didn't want to be a miner and I surely didn't want to be a farmer. I plowed a mule many days as a youngster, but I knew I didn't want to do that the rest of my life. Neither did I want to cut logs and timber and thought there had to be a better way. Looking back, it was funny because we kept a mule to plow the corn, and we raised corn to feed the mule. In Nauvoo, there was nothing to do but be a miner or a farmer or work in timber, and if people talked about getting out and getting a job, they were talking about coming down to Birmingham and that was a long way away.

I didn't have any help when I decided for sure that I wanted to go to college. Summertimes, I always worked at construction jobs, saving my money for college. I worked plenty at home, too. We always had cows and mother milked a cow and I milked a cow every morning and night, and to this day, I don't drink milk because of that. When I drove the school bus, I made $30.00 a month, and after the taxes were taken out, I took home $27.90 and I put that $27.90 in the bank, every penny of it. My father would give me a little money for incidentals, like that Saturday night date, but every dime I made driving that school bus went into the bank for college. I worked while I was in college, too. I was the first person who I knew anything about on either side of my family who graduated from college. Neither one of my sisters went to college, I guess, because in those days it didn't seem too important for a girl to have a college education.

Fresh Meat

Buster Hall, Clarke County

One tradition we had back in Thomasville High School was a little ceremony when a boy came to school for the first time in long pants. Wearing long pants was a sure sign that he had reached manhood and he had to go through a lot of physical and mental pain the first time he showed up at school in his new clothes. Now, the older boys in good old THS had a beautiful paddle whittled from a piece of one-by-four pine, about three feet long and shiny from much use. That old paddle was just used for two things: to introduce newcomers to the ways of life at Thomasville, and the other was to initiate boys into manhood. When I say "older boys" in the school, I mean older boys. Most of them were football players up to twenty-one years old, big fellows, two hundred pounds and more. Back in those days, there were no rules about how old you could be in school or how long you could play football.

Well, I wore those knicker-type pants until I was six feet tall. One day, my mother looked at me and must have reached the breaking point. "Edward," she said, "put on your shoes. We are going into town and buy you some long trousers." Now, these were the words I had been dreading to hear for a long, long time, and I begged my mother to put it off a little longer, but she stood firm. So, off we went to Bedsole's for a pair of long pants, and after some negotiation with the clerk, she paid one dollar and we went home with the long trousers.

The next morning, I put on my new pants and went down to the privy and picked out the thickest *Saturday Evening Post* I would find there in front of the seats. I lowered my pants and stuck the *Post* down in the seat, pulled up my pants, and smoothed out the wrinkles.

The news got to school before I did and all the older boys were lined up, waiting for me with great anticipation. The football players were in front with the small-fry bringing up the rear of the line. When I was in sight, everybody started chanting, "Fresh meat! Fresh meat!" and all the students gathered around to see me suffer.

The first boy in the line was a big football player, about 220 pounds, and he looked at me real mean and said, "Boy, grab your ankles," and I did. He raised the paddle and struck me as hard as he could. That paddle smacking the *Saturday Evening Post* sounded like a shotgun explosion, and I ended up several feet down the road. This big guy looked at me and said, "Boy, what do you have in those pants? Back up here and let me have a look." He found the magazine and made me drop my pants before the whole student body and take it out. After I got my pants buttoned up, I had to grab my ankles and that whole bunch began working on old Buster in earnest.

Certified to Teach

Loyd Berry, Marshall County

I was born April 30, 1906. I started to school when I was seven years old and we had three teachers with about a hundred pupils. Those pupils ranged in age from about seven to twenty-five. Each one of the teachers had about thirty recitations every day and most of the students wore homemade clothes and brogan shoes. Most of the boys chewed tobacco and many's the day I saw the principal subdue a boy by overpowering him. Back in those days when you misbehaved, they took a switch, brought you up in the front of the room, and thrashed you right there in front of the other pupils.

Most of the teachers back then had a certificate. You would have a third grade, second grade, and a first grade certificate. You would get these certificates by taking a state examination. At that time, all you had to do was pass the state exam to get one of these certificates. The teachers had to go to a seminar every summer, and later on, they were required to go three weeks in the summer and they were held in various communities around. This was about in 1912.

Every community had its school. At one time in Marshall County, there were eighty schools. The main reason for so many schools was that the pupils couldn't travel very far due to the roads. These schools had to be in walking distance of the pupils. Each community had to make up money to run the schools because they got very little help from the state. Since the teachers got paid so little, they couldn't afford to have a place of their own so they would go home with the pupils to spend the night. They might stay around with many families during the course of the school year and that was part of their pay.

I started teaching school in 1929 with a year's training and I started out at $85 a month, but when the depression came along, I went down to $50 a month. During the depression, if the community didn't have the money to pay us teachers, they paid us with a due bill. This was kind of a promissory note and I remember I had about $600 in due bills when they passed an income tax in the state to redeem all these warrants. I used some of those warrants to go to school at Auburn in the summer, because Auburn would honor them. I hoed cotton for a man to get enough money to ride the train down to Auburn to go to school. Back then, there were no buses and we would catch the train to Montgomery and another train on over to Auburn. That was the only way to get there.

I taught at my first school in 1929 up on Sand Mountain. I hitched a ride to the school. My equipment for the year was two boxes of crayons and six erasers. The parents had to buy the books if the pupils had any. There were two teachers in this school and I taught the fifth, sixth, seventh, and eighth grades. All these pupils were in the same room. I would take about fifteen minutes with the fifth grade and assign them some work and move on to the sixth grade bunch. Even at that, they were learning something.

Never the Same Again

Buster Hall, Clarke County

When I was going to high school in Thomasville, there were no indoor toilets. The boys had a nice twelve-hole privy that stood under the hill to the northwest of the huge old wooden school building. There was a dandy little one-hole job on the east side of the big outhouse for the professor and the coach. This little building had a big hasp and a huge lock and this particular privy was kept locked at all times.

The professor was a short, dumpy man, nearly as wide as he was tall, easy going, and he really went out of his way to get along with the students. This was his downfall because the boys were quick to take advantage of him.

One morning at recess, a big bunch of boys were standing around the twelve-holer, talking and laughing, when down the hill came the good professor, waddling along in a terrible hurry. He went in, closed the door, and some of the older boys were looking at each other and grinning. One of them casually walked over to the one-holer and dropped the lock in the hasp. After the professor had completed his chores, he tried to open the door, but it would not budge. Now this man did not like close, dark places and he panicked, screaming and threatening and begging someone to open the door. Nobody moved.

The boys let the professor work himself into a frenzy and several took hold of the little privy and turned it over, professor and all. You have never heard such screaming and threatening as that poor man did that morning. He was thrashing around in the little house in a wild sort of way. Russell Stutts was the leader of the gang and he sat up on the door, begging the boys to please let the professor out and all the time doing his best to hold on to the hasp to keep the poor man inside.

The professor finally worked his way around to the hole in the privy where the only light was coming in. He stuck his head through the hole but he couldn't see anything because the boys had moved around to the other side. He tried to get out of the hole, but it was a losing battle because he was about three times as wide as the opening. Finally, all the students left and Russell opened the door, all the while apologizing for the terrible way the boys had acted.

The professor was never the same after this terrible experience and it was not long before he got sick and had to go to the hospital. He never returned to good old Thomasville High.

High on the Hog

*Fishermen with their catch of red
snapper, Mobile, circa 1930
(Erik Overbey Collection, University of
South Alabama Archives, Mobile)*

What a Feast!

Ben Meriwether, Bullock County

Daddy kept a round of hoop cheese in the store with a long-arm cheese cutter. Pull the lever up once, pull the knife down, and you'd cut off a nickel's worth of cheese. The candy we sold was real candy. Some of it came in wooden buckets. We sold salt mackerel packed in little wooden tubs and you would soak the mackerel overnight and fry it for breakfast. When Coca-Cola came in, it would be shipped in by train in cases, forty-eight bottles to the case, and you had to save the empties and ship them back. It was said that Coca-Cola had a little cocaine in them, so children were not allowed to drink any and people began calling it "dope." Then, wagons with four horses began coming around peddling their soda pops, and the wagons would deliver ice, too. Daddy got a big old washtub, put soda pops and ice in it, and we were in the soda pop business. We called them "belly washers," and I remember the first one I had, a big strawberry soda pop, and it was the best one I ever had.

Every Friday afternoon, a basket of sixty loaves of bread would come out from Toole's Bakery in Montgomery on the afternoon train, still warm, and unwrapped and unsliced. It soon got around that we would get this bread on a Friday so people would be waiting for it. We would open the basket and Mother would grab two loaves for us, and a few minutes later, there was no bread left. Cost five cents a loaf.

My grandfather Meriwether lived about a mile from us and he loved cane syrup. He knew how to keep his grandchildren from eating his sugarcane. He raised Japanese cane and it was so hard you couldn't chew it, but it made good syrup. One Sunday, they were going to have some special company and Grandma fixed a special dinner. She told Grandpa, "Ben, this is a special friend coming today and I'm not going to put the syrup out. Don't ask for it." So, she had a nice dinner, and after he finished, Grandpa looked around and said, "Josie, where is the syrup?" If looks could have killed, he would have been a dead man, but she got up and got the syrup for him.

There was a big grove out in front of our house with a barbecue pit in the middle of it. Every summer, the families close around would gather and have their yearly barbecue. They would start the night before cooking, cook Brunswick stew in a big wash pot, cook beef and pork slow all night and the next day. What a feast! I was always glad to see those days because I would have lots of children to play with. I can still smell those odors and remember how good that food was.

We had a black man and his wife living on the place. Early one morning before breakfast, Daddy wanted me to go down and tell the man what he wanted him to do. I went down and the family was about to eat breakfast and they asked me to eat breakfast with them. They had old fatback meat which had been dipped in buttermilk, then in flour, and then fried. They had corn pone and coffee. I thought that looked pretty good, so I sat down and ate, and it was good. That room was spic and span. I drank coffee out of a tin cup, my first taste of coffee. When I got back home, Mother and Daddy had finished eating, but I didn't want anything else. I never drank coffee again until I was grown, but I have had enough Postum to float a battleship.

Getting By on Corn Bread

E. L. Lovelady, Madison County

Before we killed a hog, we waited for a good frost or two. We tried to have a hog up to two to three hundred pounds before we thought he was ready. Usually, a neighbor came in to help and maybe he would bring a boy or two. My daddy would get my brother and me to build a fire under the wash pot early that morning and it would be some frost on the ground and a chill in the air. If you didn't have those cool nights, your meat would spoil, and the only way we had of preserving the meat was to use salt.

So, we'd get there early and get a good fire going under that wash pot and fill it up with water. When the hog was killed, we hung him up and used that boiling water to scald him. We didn't skin that hog, but scalded him with that hot water we put on with two sacks, and after he was steamed real good, we would scrape him good. The men dressed the hog and cut it up into shoulders, middlings, and hams. Most of the time, they would shoot the hog with a rifle to kill it, right between the eyes, and sometimes, they might have to shoot it two or three times. That was a little cruel, but if the one shot didn't do the trick, you had to keep on shooting. Then, they stuck him in the throat with a knife, got him hung up and let him bleed, let him drain. They would cut him open and gut it and just about everything in the hog was used. You've heard of chitlins. Well, some people had them and some didn't. We always had fresh ribs right after a hog killing. Mama would fry them real good, and you talking about some taste, buddy, you had something there.

My brother and I always saved that bladder out of the hog. We took that bladder and we washed it real good and clean. Then, we blew it up and tied it with a string and used it for a ball. You know a hog's bladder is pretty tough. I'm telling you, you are pretty poor when you can't afford a store-bought ball and have to use a pig's bladder.

We would put our meat in the smokehouse, the hams and shoulders and middlings. This was all the meat we had because we didn't have the money to buy any in the first place, then it was a long way to the store, and we didn't have any way to preserve fresh meat anyhow. We just killed hogs, one in the fall, and another one in the spring, because you would be running out of meat by that time. In the summer, we had rabbit many a time for breakfast, and occasionally, a squirrel or two. Back then, you worked so hard, you were happy to have just about anything on the table, whatever, to get by with.

It wasn't that Home Comfort stove that made things so good, it was the work. We were just thankful for what we had, and a lot of time it wasn't a whole lot. For supper lots of times, we would have beans and potatoes and corn bread, and we had worked so hard that there wouldn't be anything left but the corn bread. Mama always had plenty of corn bread for supper. The main meal we had for supper was corn bread and milk, either sweet milk or buttermilk, and that was most of the time. All the good stuff was gone with the noon meal.

Milk was a staple for us and my brother and I did the milking. But when you got to the barn to milk and that old cow had eaten wild onions, you could smell it a hundred feet away. Naturally, we knew that milk was going to taste like wild onions and we knew that's what we were going to have for supper. When the cow was about dry, Mother would pass the milk around and give us about a good half a glass each, but there was a lot of corn bread, but the milk would have to last. What you would do is crumble a bunch of corn bread in that half a glass of milk and go down in there with a fork, raise it up, and the milk would run back down in the glass. You get all the corn bread out and you still had milk left in your glass, see, and then you would put some more corn bread in there. If you don't think that's good, try soaking corn bread in water. That half a glass of milk might last you three or four times, refilling it with corn bread, and still have a swallow or two left to drink.

Many times, we sat there at that supper table and corn bread and milk was all we had and we bowed our heads and gave thanks for what we had. We had corn bread for breakfast when we didn't have any money to buy flour. You can take corn bread and put butter on it and some homemade molasses and you can get by. I know it hurt my daddy an awful lot for us not to have flour and be out, but he just didn't have the money.

Never Heard of Sandwiches

Tera Averett, Coffee County

During my childhood, all eight of us girls would gather around the dining table with Papa and Mama three times a day for a big meal. At breakfast, there were always large, fluffy buttermilk biscuits baked in the large wood-burning stove. There was bacon or juicy homegrown ham that had been smoked and dried by hanging in the smokehouse, plenty of brown-eye gravy, and sometimes sausage patties or stuffed sausage. Then, there was always one of the following: syrup made from sugarcane we grew and made ready for eating at a neighbor's cane mill, jelly made from blackberries we picked from the rail fence on the farm, honey from our beehives which were robbed every May 20 and June 10 by Papa, or fig preserves made by Mama with figs given to us by Grandmother Waters or neighbors.

Occasionally, there was a large bowl of softly scrambled eggs, fresh from the chicken yard. My mother kept a large flock of Rhode Island Red hens and one or two roosters. On special occasions and on Sunday mornings, we had fried chicken or fried steak from our own beef calves.

When we sat down at the table, Papa sat on one side near the middle of the long table with my mother on his left. The oldest daughter sat on his right. One daughter sat at each end, and the other five daughters sat across the table on a long, handmade bench. My father served the plates, and for refills, the children would pass their plates to Papa and say, "Thank you for some more bread" or whatever we wanted. Polite conversation was allowed, but never any loud or boisterous behavior. If we got too tickled about something, we would excuse ourselves and leave the table.

At lunch, or dinner as we called it, my mother served vegetables grown in the garden the year around. We had black-eyed peas, purple-hull peas, snap beans, butterbeans which grew on the wire fence around the garden, collards, cabbage, onions, beets, tomatoes, squash, pepper, cucumbers, English peas, and turnips.

One part of the garden was set apart for strawberries grown in wide beds. The chore I hated worse than any other was pulling weeds from the strawberry patch in the summer. But when my mother cooked one of her delicious two-tiered strawberry short-cakes smothered with those crushed berries, I soon forgot the hot summer job I had getting up all that grass.

In another corner of the garden there were hills of sweet potatoes which were covered with tepees made of cornstalks or boards covered with mounds of garden soil. Inside of the tepees, the potatoes were covered with pine straw. We grew two kinds of pears: Keifer pears were used for pear preserves, and Bartlett pears were good to eat off the tree. We also had peach trees and my mother made peach pickles and also canned some. At one time, Papa built a large canner and canned fruits and vegetables in tin cans for us and for neighbors.

We had several pecan trees and visited hickory trees, chestnut trees, and chinquapin trees for additional treats. We had a large scuppernong vine, also, but nobody was allowed to put a finger on the scuppernongs until they had turned brown.

My father and all his girls had a "sweet tooth" and we always had desserts for both dinner and supper. Dinner was the noon meal. We would have stack cakes filled with caramel or chocolate or coconut or lemon cheese. We had peppermint candy and jelly cakes and pound cakes made from homemade butter. We had fruitcake or sponge cake at Christmastime and Thanksgiving. My mother served peach cobbler, syrup custard, egg custard, and potato custard and potato pudding. Even when we went to school, we carried two lunch buckets. One contained the meat, biscuits, and sweet potatoes, and the other bucket contained the desserts. We had never heard of a sandwich.

For supper, we ate some of the vegetables and meats left over from dinner, but we always had hot corn bread. We called the corn bread "hoe cake" and it was made from cornmeal, salt, and water, baked in a flat bread baker on top of the wood stove.

In the 1920s, we bought a Model T Ford and many times on a Saturday night, we had homemade ice cream. Papa would buy a ten-pound block of ice and bring it home on the running board of that car. When he got home, he would place the ice in the shade on the ground and put a number two washtub over the top until we were ready to crank the hand freezer. Sometimes, the whole community would have an ice cream supper. The ladies would bring home-baked cakes and the men turned the freezers to make the ice cream.

One special food Mama cooked for our family was hominy. She picked the best, firm ears of corn from the corncrib, shelled off the small grains, and put the big grains in the big iron wash pot. In the first boiling, she put lye in the water and boiled the corn until the eye of the grains came off. Then came the many washings of the grains to remove the lye. When she prepared the hominy for serving, she fried it in a little lard with salt and water.

In Alabama back then, dinner time was noon. Mama went to the garden early in the morning and had those vegetables in the iron pots, socked down next to the fire in the wood stove boiling away until about 11:30. Then, she would put on the hoe cake before going out and ringing the big dinner bell hoisted on top of a high pole to call Papa in from the field. Now, Papa took out time at least until one o'clock to eat dinner and to let the mules eat also. As soon as he ate, he got his daily newspaper or his weekly papers—the *Southern Star* or his *Progressive Farmer*—and read awhile before going back to the fields.

Everybody in the family had chores. Mama had eczema on her hands and didn't need to have them in water too much, so the daughters took over. Two daughters washed and dried the dishes, two daughters milked the cows, two more cooked the bread for supper and set the table. In the morning, each of the girls made up beds, swept the floors with the broomstraw brooms, being sure to sweep under the beds. If there was a new baby, one girl rocked the baby in the cradle. That was one chore I really hated. When I had to rock the baby, I would lie down on the floor and rock the cradle with my foot.

Another chore I hated was churning. Papa always kept two or three good milk cows. In the summer, the milk was put into a large container and let down into the open water well to keep it cool. At other times, the milk would be placed into large pans and put into the kitchen safe with screen doors. By noon, the cream would have risen to the top and it was then skimmed off. Mama and Papa drank the skimmed milk. The cream and the remaining milk was mixed with the warm night's milk and placed in the large churn and left overnight to clabber. If it was cold weather, the churn of milk was placed near the fireplace to make the milk sour quicker. The next day, the clabbered milk was churned by a dasher on a churn stick stuck through the hole in the churn lid. My arm would get so tired going up and down, up and down, but the reward was the good buttermilk which we children enjoyed every meal. We mashed up the good yellow butter in syrup to eat with Mama's hot biscuits at breakfast.

One happy day, this churning chore came to an end. One of Papa's cousins from Enterprise came and sold Papa on the idea of buying an electric plant. The plant was a gasoline-operated dynamo which produced electricity. The electricity was stored in large batteries which we kept in a specially built little house in the backyard. Then we had electric lights in every room in the house, one line hanging down from the ceiling with a light bulb turned on and off by hand. But the great news was that Papa bought an electric churn with metal dashers that went up and down.

Papa always had a good supply of corn in the corncrib to be used for food for the family and for the animals. He had a hand corn sheller which was used to shell a large bag of corn to be carried to Thrower's mill for grinding into cornmeal. The mill was operated by water from a mill pond which turned the big rocks that crushed the corn. The miller was never paid with cash but was given a toll of the meal for the grinding.

For cow feed, Papa carried corn, hay, and velvet beans to a crusher and had it ground up together. For the chickens, a bucketful of shelled corn was thrown out and scattered over the chicken yard every morning. For the dogs, Papa made up two thick hoe cakes of corn bread and cooked it on the back burners of the wood stove while Mama cooked breakfast. Then, he broke the bread into pieces and placed them into a large pan of buttermilk. His dogs never, never got a store-bought meal. The cats ate the leftovers from the table.

Three-Hog Family

Tom Roberson, Talladega County

We ate well when I was coming up. The farm we were on was out there at Fayetteville. You could always tell when somebody was a native because if they are, it's always called "Fedville," and we were natives so we called it Fedville. In the summertime, folks out on the farm would put up food for the wintertime, and how much they put up depended on how much the family would need. We had to plan how much we would need so we would have enough. Like we had to have two cans of lard going in, and so many cans of green beans, and so many of tomatoes, and all this was preplanned. We had to have a five-gallon can of butterbeans and a five-gallon can of peas and twenty gallons of syrup.

Now, your basic foods were your meats and your cow for your milk and butter, and your chickens. And all that food was grown on the farm. Your rolling store would come by every once in awhile and the lady of the house would trade eggs and butter and chickens to the rolling store for the salt and pepper and sugar. But we didn't buy all our sugar from the rolling store. We'd let some of that cane syrup go to sugar and use that in pies and cobblers.

We were a three-hog family which means we ate a lot. We would kill those hogs and salt them down, put them up in a meat box, and then hang them up in the smokehouse and smoke them. Rabbits were a part of our diet back in those days. We would have traps for those rabbits and you couldn't say much about sportsmanship as far as hunting went. I'd say along about 1933 or 1934, there was an outbreak of undulant fever and people quit eating rabbits. If you shot something, you were shooting it for the meat. Quail was a Sunday morning breakfast. Breakfast was a big meal in our house because we worked so hard on that farm. An uncle of mine made cane syrup at his mill for the whole community.

The Big War

*Tent camp for war workers at the
DuPont plant, Childersburg, 1941
(Jack Delano/Farm Security
Administration photo, Library of Congress,
Washington, D.C.)*

Guarding the Coast

Joy Buskens, Baldwin County

During World War II, my mother washed uniforms for people who were renting up around the canal when they activated Barin Field, a navy training base for flyers. My dad would always pick up hitch-hikers, soldier boys, during the war. Some of the local girls would marry some of those boys.

The training planes would practice up here on the canal all day long—plenty loud—but we didn't realize they were training for war. Right at the end of the old bridge there at Gulf Shores, mines were loaded on boats there to go on to other places. We had black-outs then, and if you lived within so many miles of the water, you had to have blackout curtains in case the enemy was out there. There were stories that the Germans did come ashore at certain places and people found like little brochures that came from the theaters in Pensacola, thinking maybe the Germans had been into town.

There was a war camp up about halfway to Foley, a prisoner of war camp, and I can remember seeing those boys marching, German soldiers. I had a friend, and her dad would go out to that camp and get the slop for his pigs from that place. She would go out there sometimes with her dad and her little brothers. Those German prisoners couldn't speak English, but they would just hug her little brothers. They would get pictures out of their wallets and show the pictures of their little boys and girls and try to communicate.

When we were growing up during the war, there were these cans of milk that washed up on shore, and instead of spelling "milk," it was "klim," five-gallon cans, and everybody picked them up and had milk for awhile. My dad went out on his fishing boat one time and those boys in the navy planes would shoot at his boat—target prac-tice—and he got hit. I saw his scar where a bullet had grazed his ear. Those boys were just pranking around and using his boat for target practice. He reported it, but nothing was done. It happened to Mrs. Frances Gainer, too. She had a little cabana down at the beach and they came down in their plane and shot at her.

My mother told about the Episcopal preacher in Foley who found one of those targets they towed behind those planes and he had some red pajamas made from the material. Little boys had silk underwear made from those targets, too.

There was an old cannery here that was partitioned off for the military people over at Fort Morgan to live in because there was a real housing shortage on the coast. There was nothing to rent. They had military people who rode on horseback guarding the coast, and my dad said when commercial fishermen fished at night, they had to keep the lights out.

In the forties, we had to catch a school bus and go twelve miles away to Foley to school. I cried every morning when I caught that bus and Mama would tell me that if I went today, I didn't have to go tomorrow. I got a book for perfect attendance that year in the first grade. During the war, we had an elementary school down here at Fort Morgan for the children of the soldiers.

The French Invasion

Mary Frances Tipton, Dallas County

One of the strongest memories I had as a child was World War II. We didn't have much contact with the American soldiers at the base in Selma. It was a pilot training base and there were many French soldiers all during the war who were sent there to train as pilots. Our family befriended these French soldiers and we had them in our house all during the war.

It's interesting how our family became involved with these French boys in the first place. One summer at the beginning of the war, a cousin of mine from Arkansas was visiting us. I was about six years old and she was about sixteen then and we had gone to the picture show and stopped by the drugstore before we went home. The place was just about deserted and the only other customers were these two French soldiers. They were the first ones I had ever seen. Their table was littered with empty Coke glasses and we could tell after a few minutes that they were having trouble being understood by the proprietor who kept bringing them two more Cokes at regular intervals.

My cousin was taking French back at school in Arkansas and she said, "I will go and see what is going on over there." She made herself understood well enough that she realized that they didn't speak any English, and what they were trying to do was get the bill. She was able to get the man in the drugstore to stop bringing them more Cokes and bring them the final bill. She brought them back over to the table where my mother and I were. They could speak enough English to know "What is your name?" and "Where are you from?" and things like that.

My mother invited them to come to our house and they came over a few days later. It turned out that they were only boys, about eighteen, and both had escaped from France when the Germans invaded by going over the Pyrenees Mountains down into Spain. They were kept in prison for awhile, made their way to England, joined de Gaulle's forces, and were sent to America to learn how to fly. They, in turn, gave our name and address to some friends of theirs so we were passed along from group to group.

Most of them came for a supper at night, but sometimes they would come and spend an entire weekend with us, staying at our house overnight. There was only one of those French soldiers that I didn't like. We had a little fox terrier at that time, and obviously the little dog didn't like this boy, either, because whenever Jaque came, the little dog and I both got up under one of those beds out on the sleeping porch. We would hide from Jaque. A lot of families in Selma took in the French boys like we did.

Some of the French boys came up to the girls' school in Montevallo and there would be buses of these cadets coming up for closely supervised dances. This was in the early forties, remember, and the girls were not allowed to go to Selma. My parents were very careful, as most other parents were at that time, about who we went out with, and there was not much dating between the high school town girls and the cadets at Craig Air Force Base. There were a couple of fellows at the base who went to our church and started singing in the choir. I was singing in the choir, too, and I did date one of those fellows.

The Great Escape

Roger Marler, Lee County

Around Opelika, there was a prisoner of war camp during World War II. They had about twenty-eight hundred prisoners in there. My father-in-law was raised up in Pennsylvania but he was down here in the army and he was stationed up at that POW camp as a guard. He said how intelligent those Germans were in that camp. They had an education force in there. The guards got close to a lot of those Germans.

In the evening and in the morning, they had a system where they counted all those prisoners, and one time, they missed one or two. They couldn't find them for awhile and the guards put out the word that a couple of Germans were missing from the camp. All of a sudden, they just turned up. Where they were, they were just sitting up on a hill under a pine tree outside the camp and they were watching what was going on in the camp. They said that they just wanted to see how it was, being outside the camp and looking in.

They had some of those Germans working out on the local farms. Some of them raised bees. My stepfather told me how they would use some of the prisoners working peanuts and cotton. They didn't have any trouble with the Germans, but they kept the SS fellows separate from the rest of them.

The Maxwell Intrigue

Buster Hall, Clarke County

During World War II, Clarke County native A. L. Payne was an officer in the air force stationed at Maxwell Air Force Base in Montgomery. He had invited his cousin, Forest Lee Mathews, and a dear friend, Dr. T. A. Cowan, to come up and visit with him. Before his two friends arrived, A. L. went out to the gate at the entrance of the base and told the MPs to watch out for two suspicious characters who were supposed to stop there and ask for him. He gave the officers an accurate description of both men and asked them to arrest, handcuff, and hold the men until the security forces could pick them up. A. L. then went down to the security office and told them the same story. He told the security officers to question them carefully and to call him when they were through because he had some questions himself.

Forest Lee and Dr. Cowan arrived and were arrested right away, handcuffed, and turned over to security. They were hauled away to the guardhouse and were put through the mill for about an hour. Then, A. L. was called.

When A. L. arrived, Forest Lee was sitting there mad as an old setting hen. Dr. Cowan was all drawn up in a knot and scared to death. The MPs asked A. L. if he knew either one of the suspected spies. A. L. looked them over carefully and said that he had never seen either one of them before. Forest Lee lost his temper and said in a gravelly voice from way down in his throat, "You blankity blank so and so," and when he said this, A. L. broke down and rolled on the floor he was laughing so hard. So much for the spies at Maxwell during World II.

Your Basic Marine

J. Torbett Crocker, Jefferson County

John Schroder was a friend of mine and he belonged to the Alabama Air National Guard back in 1940. John got me interested in the air guard, and one day, he took me out to the Birmingham airport and I signed up. Major Henry Badham, later General Badham, was the commanding officer of the guard. I didn't have any idea what I would do when I signed up, but it looked pretty exciting. There were tests you took that would make you eligible to be a lieutenant. You had to know some math, navigation, some weather, and photography because this was an observation squadron.

I had passed all these tests and was eligible to be an officer. We flew a single-engine plane, the 047, with three people aboard: the pilot, the gunner in the rear, and the photographer in the middle. One day, just about the time the war started, Major Badham told us that our unit was about to be activated and would be sent to England. That didn't excite me very much. He said that anybody who was married or had a defense job should get out. I didn't want to fight the war in the air force, so I got out.

Shortly after, December seven rolled around on a Sunday, and on Monday morning, Lyle Baxter and I went down and signed up for the Marine Corps. Two months went by, and Lyle and I went down and wanted to find out what had happened to our applications. The recruiter looked at Lyle and asked, "Are you the one who wrote Senator Sparkman about getting into the Marine Corps?" Lyle told him, "Certainly." The recruiter said, "Well, you're never going to get in the Marine Corps writing to a damn senator." Lyle didn't get in. I got in. The Marine Corps spent a lot of time telling you how good you are and you believed about half of it.

I went to Quantico in the spring of 1942 for basic. One guy got his hand blown off right in front of everybody while we were in training. It was dangerous. Everybody in that training camp was an officer. With my background, I came in as an officer, but we had to take basic training just like any recruit. We would get in about two o'clock in the morning from some exercise and have to get up at six and go again.

I remember one morning, cold as hell, they got us up and we were issued all kinds of guns, mortar shells, a whole bunch of this stuff, and took us down and piled us on a landing craft. They said we were going to attack a Jap island. This damn thing starts going down the river, very cold and pitch-black dark. Finally, we felt the landing craft go up on the sand, the front gate flopped down, and we jumped off in the water, zero weather. A buddy of mine hit the water carrying about a fifty-pound steel-plate mortar base and I had to tow him to shore. We couldn't get dry and couldn't light a fire, but nobody even caught a cold. We stayed out in that cold and snow with no shelter at all for four or five days and they finally let us go back to the barracks.

They had what they called a casualty outfit, all marine privates, and we would use these guys to practice on, assault exercises, and they used to beat us to death. We finally got smart and we started capturing these guys. We would tie them up to a tree and leave them there, and sometimes they wouldn't find them until the next day. Everybody in my outfit were commissioned officers, lieutenants, captains, and majors. Remember Gladys Swarthout, the famous opera singer? Her husband was a major in there with us. I was twenty-eight years old and the youngest guy in the outfit.

The Pokeberry Connection

Joe Upchurch, Talladega County

During World War II, there was this plant out here on the edge of Talladega where they bagged up gunpowder for artillery. They had this place down there in Childersburg that made the powder and they would put the powder on the train and bring it up here to Talladega. A plant here in town made the bags for the powder, silk, I think it was, and they would take the silk bags over to the big plant and fill them with powder. You've got to remember that this was in the early forties and people were still coming out of the depression and they were all tickled to death to have any kind of job at all. They started paying thirty-two cents an hour down at the powder plant and people were glad to get it. They were plenty glad just to work. See, just about everybody had some kinfolks in the service. They wouldn't mind working two shifts, and sometimes three shifts, in a row for the boys in service. That, and the extra pay.

See, Talladega just about doubled in size when we got into the war, because at one time, there were about five or six thousand people working out there at that plant, but of course, they wouldn't all stay here in town. They came in from Clay County, and Randolph and Tallapoosa and Chilton and Cleburne counties, and they would come in cars, as many as could squeeze in, and old school buses and whatnot, and they would work in the plant as long as the boss would let them. Then they would go back home. Of course, some of them found places in Talladega to stay and they would stay anywhere, and I mean anywhere. Remember that most of these people coming in from the country to work in the plant, most of them would bring their own food, but there was a kind of canteen where they sold sandwiches.

Now, in that plant, they had long lines where they put the powder bag components together. There would be one person who would do one thing to this component and another one would fill that one and there were seven components on this particular line making explosive charges for the 105 howitzer. There was this little lady from up in Clay County, and to her, all the lines looked just alike because the long building was just a series of doors. The reason for all the doors was that if the building caught fire and blew up, the explosion would go out of all the doors rather than imploding, as it were. She had been there a couple of days and I was walking down the line looking things over and she stopped me and said, "Mr. Joe?" I stopped and said, "Yeah?" and she said, "I get lost. I can't find where I'm supposed to go. Can I bring some pokeberries and paint this door just outside of where I work?" Well, she didn't have to stay there but a few days before she found out which door was hers and where she was supposed to go. Thing was, in those first few days, if she had to leave to go to the rest room, she had a small problem getting back to her work station.

That was the type of people we had down there in Talladega at that powder plant. They had never been anywhere and done anything and they were working and making more money than they ever had, working as farmers.

Funny thing about that plant out there. Here we were, sacking up that powder which was manufactured down in Childersburg, in sacks made by a company in Talladega, and the sacking operation was handled by the Coca-Cola Bottling Company. Yeah, that's right, Coca-Cola ran the thing because they had the executive ability to organize a venture like this, although DuPont owned the plant. The plant operated all during the war and closed down after the armistice.

Doing Business

Stone Drug Company, Talladega, 1949
(Heritage Hall, Talladega)

A Lesson in Salesmanship

Bob Hodges, Jackson County

When I was growing up in the forties and fifties, Scottsboro was a sleepy little town of less than 5,000 with a square. My father and his brother operated a drugstore on that square. There was a friendly spirit of competition between the downtown merchants. One day in the 1940s, my father gave me instructions on a tactic directed at his friendly competitor at the other end of the block, Payne's Drugstore. I ambled down the block, all alone in my shorts and sandals, walked into Payne's Drugstore, climbed up on a stool, stood up on the counter, and announced to the customers and employees the specific ingredient that made Payne's lemon ice cream so yellow. Incredibly, I was given a cone of lemon ice cream by the people at Payne's which I happily licked all the way back to my father's drugstore.

In my early teens, I was given a lesson in salesmanship by my father. Back then, Hadacol was a widely heralded and much advertised tonic which supposedly cured almost every ailment known to man, from anemia to sexual old age impotency. On this particular day, there were promotional banners about my father's drugstore touting Hadacol, newspaper ads proclaiming that you could get Hadacol at Hodges' Drugstore if you could get there before they sold out, and rows on rows of the elixir in half-pint, and quart bottles prominently displayed. My father had constructed a large pyramid of bottles in the front windows, the garish yellow labels guaranteed to attract attention. Anna Ruth Campbell, a much-respected teacher, came into the store and curiously inspected the dazzling display of Hadacol. She asked my father if this stuff really worked, and the salesman in him prompted the following: "Anna Ruth, I have a good customer who is a farmer at Aspel, and he has a daughter who is mentally retarded. One month ago, I sold him one of these quart bottles for her, and she is teaching school today."

In Scottsboro, you were expected to exercise good judgment, but practical jokes were an almost everyday occurrence, from the electric shock buzzer in the handshake to Alka Seltzer and other unmentionables rising to the top of your cup of coffee. Walt Hammer was a traveling drug salesman and would come by weekly to take orders in the store and was broken in real good. One time, he was asked by my father to go into the ladies' rest room and check to see if any supplies were needed to be ordered. He was assured that the rest room was empty, but when he cracked the door open, he got a shock. My father had taken a life-size mannequin, dressed it in a swimsuit, and placed it inside the door. He had hooked up an intercom from the soda fountain to the rest room so that when Walt opened the door, he heard a voice say, "Shut that door, you fool. Get out of here before I call the police!" Another time, Walt sent a Christmas card to the Hodges brothers, and two days later, got the same card back with an inscription across the bottom: "Same to you—Charles and R. L."

When Clyde Butler made a trip to the drugstore to take orders for candy and cigarettes, my father told him that the new girl at the front register was hard of hearing and he would have to shout for her to hear him. He then called the girl to the back of the store and told her that Clyde was hard of hearing and that she would have to shout. There was that marvelous moment when Clyde got to the girl's station, and a storeful of customers was treated to this exchange:

"Do you need any cigarettes?" Clyde screamed.

"Two cartons of Camels and two cartons of Luckies!" she screamed back.

"Are you out of Mars Bars?" Clyde yelled.

"No, we have plenty!" she shouted back.

And so went this exchange, much to the delight of the customers and the puzzlement of Clyde and the girl.

Gambling in small doses was tolerated at Hodges' Drugstore, but money had nothing to do with the bet. It was a matter of winning and losing. For over ten years, my father and Paul Conley would bet one dollar on one pro football game each weekend and they kept a running account on who was ahead. The dollar payoff always took place on the following Monday morning at coffee time in front of numerous witnesses. Neither could bear to lose. One Monday morning when my dad had lost, he presented Paul Conley with the dollar bill, tightly rolled up, and deeply embedded in a new jar of vaseline. On the side of the jar was a prescription label which gave Mr. Conley explicit instructions on what to do with his winnings.

Working the Husker

Ulysses Terry, Jefferson County

In 1919, when I was about eight years old, we had moved into Birmingham, and I met a man named A. L. Brewer and he had some husker wagons. You know what I'm talking about—husker wagons—wagons that went around and sold vegetables and bananas and anything you bought at the store. Mr. Brewer owned five wagons himself, his brother operated about three, and a brother-in-law had another three. This was really big business.

I stayed working on those husker wagons with Mr. Brewer every day I wasn't in school and every day after school. I rode with Mr. Brewer on that husker wagon, and as he sold his stuff to people, I would get out and carry the vegetables or fruit or whatnot up to the door. He was about the finest man I ever saw in my life. At one time, he had been a schoolteacher down in south Alabama and I got a second education riding around with him. That husker wagon was just an open wagon and a horse pulled it around. Maybe we would go to Ensley one day and come back to Birmingham and Collegeville and all around. He paid me a quarter a day. Working with Mr. Brewer, I had a chance to go to a lot of places and met many different kinds of people.

Mr. Brewer would leave home at five o'clock in the morning and go down to Morris Avenue where all the wholesale was and I would go down and hitch up the horse and wagon and take it down there to him. I would get down to Morris Avenue about seven o'clock and he would have enough stuff bought for all of his wagons.

Finally, the Italians, seeing what a big business he had, moved in on us and started buying wagons to travel around in the Negro neighborhoods. It wasn't long after that when the Italians began putting up stores all over in the Negro sections. That was in the twenties, now, and every Negro neighborhood in Birmingham had an Italian store on the corner. See, at that time, they wouldn't let Italians put up stores in white neighborhoods. Gradually, the Italians moved out of a lot of the Negro neighborhoods and began setting up stores in the white sections. You look at it now, and the Italians own the grocery business in Birmingham.

An Early Start

Randolph Linn, Marshall County

I got an early start in the business world. My father would go milk about five o'clock in the morning and I knew to be up and dressed when he got back from the barn because I was going to walk with him to Arab. I was going to work in his store until it was time to go to school. My job was to carry out orders for the rolling store. The rolling store was a wagon which would go out in the country to trade and we had about three of these that went out. I would carry out about six cans of salmon and two pounds of coffee and things of this nature. I started doing this about 1921 and I did this job for several years. Every morning, my dad would look at his watch, and about five minutes 'til eight, he would say I could go on up to the school which was just up the hill from the store.

Back in the twenties, not one of the roads was paved around Arab. There was a red hill in front of our house and that was old 231, and I can remember many a night that people would try to get up that hill in a car and they couldn't make it. My dad would go out—he didn't know any strangers—and invite the people in to spend the night so they could go on the next day. He did that a number of times.

My daddy and my uncle had that general mercantile business and they sold everything from fancy groceries and ladies' dresses and cultivators and plows and whatever else people wanted to buy in Arab. This went on until about 1930 or 1931 when the effects of the depression were just getting down to the rural areas at that time. My daddy and uncle furnished quite a few farmers and they paid a little more for the cotton. They bought cotton to make sure that the farmer would come in and pay his bill when the cotton came in.

Furnishing means that the farmer would come in and arrange to buy feed and seeds, a little clothing, and maybe get $500 to carry him through crop-making time.

In the latter part of 1930, there was just no market for cotton. This went on for a little more than a year and cotton just kept going down and the farmers just had to sell it and they didn't get but five and six cents a pound. There were several hundred bales of cotton around town. My dad and uncle had a lawyer from Guntersville who also did some work for the city and he recommended that they go bankrupt. They didn't, though, so they went ahead and finally paid out the debt about ten years later.

In 1931, my father said he wanted to talk to me, so we sat down on the front porch and he told me that he knew I wanted to go to college, but there was no way that he and my mother could send me. The same year, the schools in Marshall County closed in midyear because they couldn't pay the teachers. The county board told the principal that if the senior class could get a qualified teacher to finish out the year, the board would go ahead and issue the degrees. There were about thirty-three students, and there was a coach named Hugh Mooney who told the class if it could get just twenty students to pay five dollars a month, he would come back and teach these classes. We didn't get but eighteen to pay, but he still came back and finished out the year.

I wasn't much of a football player, but Coach Mooney got me a scholarship to play football at Birmingham-Southern College in 1933. I hung on down there and got a part-time job at the A & P and I worked there the whole time I was at Southern. A & P offered me a full-time job, but I wanted to come back to Arab and go in business for myself. I borrowed some money from my brothers and sisters who had a little bit ahead and opened a dime store, right across the street there. I had a fellow working for me one time who came up in the dime store one day and said, "We're selling these lamp wicks for one cent each, and I believe I can sell six for five cents. How about it?" I turned him down, but I knew this man had a future in the promotional end of the business. I kept plugging away and gradually built my stores up to a total of six.

Sometimes, It Was Funny

Carolyn Lipscomb, Lee County

My husband ran a drugstore for years in Auburn. There was another drugstore then, at Toomer's Corner, and his brother ran that drugstore and they were friendly competitors. Back then, Auburn was really a small town and you would know every businessman down the street and everybody else in town. A lot of funny things happened that could only have happened in a place like Auburn. In the thirties and forties, the drugstore did a lot of business on credit.

One day, Lan's daddy was working away in the store and a young boy came in, walked up to the toilet paper rack, picked up a roll, and walked to the door. Lan's daddy looked up and the boy held up the roll of toilet paper and said, "Just charge it to Mama." Lan's daddy scratched his head, and for the life of him, he couldn't place the boy or remember who his mama was. He yelled out across the store, "Son, who is this for?" The boy stopped and yelled back across the store, "It's for all of us."

Across the street there on the main drag, there was a jeweler named Ish Jockisch who was probably the most gullible man on the street, and a person who tended to let everybody know of a major triumph. During World War II, there was some rationing at first, but as the war dragged on, many items got really scarce as the government was pulling away a lot of things that we had always taken for granted. Automobile tires, for instance. Before starting out on even a short car trip, you would check to see how much gas you had, and whether the tires looked pretty good or not.

By some hook or crook, Ish managed to trade for a fairly new tire on the black market and bragged about it with great gusto to his fellow merchants. One of the businessmen down the street talked a stranger, a tobacco agent with a long list of federal credentials, into playing a little trick on Ish. Of course, all the other merchants up and down the street were in on it, too. They were all watching as the tobacco agent went into Ish's shop, flopped out his impressive credentials, and asked Ish to step outside. He said he wanted to inspect the tires on his car.

Ish walked outside with the stranger and the tobacco agent asked Ish to read him the serial numbers off each tire. Ish got down on his hands and knees and read off the numbers of an old tire, then the second one, and then the third one, saving the black market tire until the last. He crawled up to the offending tire, looked at it for a long time, then looked up at the tobacco agent. "I think I'll just give you this tire," he said. The other merchants up and down the street had been hovering in their doorways watching this little action, and when Ish caved in, they fell back into their stores dying laughing. Ish never heard the end of it.

Printer's Ink

Libba George and *Ben George*, Marengo County

Libba: When I was growing up, our family published the newspaper here, the *Demopolis Times*. I didn't work at the newspaper when I was a girl. The only time I visited there was to get a quarter from Daddy. Later on, after Ben and I were married, I started working down at the paper and I was society editor from 1932 to 1987, and that was a few years. The society column is always popular in a small town, because I wrote about the church meetings, club meetings, parties, and who visited who the past week. We had an old country club which had been somebody's house before they lost it. It had a big porch out front and a little ground around it—a cow pasture, really—and people tried to play golf out there. At that old country club, there would be bridge parties. We had chicken salad luncheons at these parties, and regular lunches at the afternoon parties. Actually, we were very social. We would be hot as all get out, and we would play on the front porch. Somebody would have a bridge party and invite everybody in town, then somebody else would have one, and I would write about that because it was news.

Ben: We started the country club when somebody lost his house and a bunch of us boys got together and bought it. Our country club dues were ten dollars a year. That was back in the thirties when times were hard and we had no trouble getting caddies. Colored boys would be out there about half a mile from the club and they would jump over each other to try to get one of those caddy jobs. The caddy job paid fifteen cents for nine holes and twenty-five cents for eighteen holes. There was no organization in the country club. If you could afford that ten dollars a year, you were a member.

Libba: When I was in high school, we had dances at the country club on Tuesday nights and at the Elks Club on Thursday. This was on school nights, now, but we called it the "old folks dance" because everybody went to those things. Anybody who could climb the stairs or who had permission from home could go. The girls would dance with the old men and the boys would dance with the old ladies and it was fun. We had great bands. The Barons were local fellows and they were great musicians and I believe Snooky Barnes who played in that band is still around.

We walked everywhere we went in town in the twenties and thirties. You didn't get in your car on Jackson Street to ride down to the post office. You just didn't do that. You had cars to ride to work in and there would be just one car to a family. Boyfriends would borrow the family car on Sunday afternoons and take us for a ride, but they had to be back by three o'clock because by then, the grown folks would have finished their naps, and they would have to have the car to take a ride.

Taking a ride would mean going just a little way out of town because of the dust or the mud. The roads were built with a hump in the middle so the rain would roll off and you had to drive in the middle of the road so you wouldn't slip off in the ditch and get stuck. When you met somebody you had to decide quickly who was going to give way. The first time Ben came down from Birmingham to see me, he came down the Uniontown road, and he told me one time it wasn't worth it, just kidding, of course. The streets in Demopolis were paved in 1925. There were no sidewalks in town when I was a child, then they put sidewalks in one side of the street so the children could get to school, and they were planks. We didn't have concrete sidewalks until the WPA put them in.

Ben: After Libba and I got married in 1929, we lived in Birmingham for about a year. I had been working at Tennessee Coal and Iron ever since I left Linden. Then, her daddy thought I might like the newspaper business, offered me a job, and we moved back to Demopolis in 1930 and I began my career with the *Times*. Before that, the only time I had been near a newspaper was when I was singing in a quartet in Birmingham. One of the fellows worked in the classified ad department at the *Birmingham News* and we would go by to pick him up to go out and sing. While we waited on him, we would sometimes go down to the press room and watch the presses roll. That was my total exposure to a newspaper operation before I came back and started working for the *Demopolis Times.*

After Libba and I got married, we lived in a very small apartment there in Birmingham. One weekend, her parents came up from Demopolis for a visit. Her daddy looked around and saw how we were cooped up, got back home, and wrote that maybe I might be interested in coming down to Demopolis and working for him. I didn't have much prospects at TCI because it was in the depression and folks were going on part time out there. What that did was cut the payroll about 25 percent. When I got this offer to go in business with Libba's daddy, I jumped at it, even though I had no idea about what I was getting into.

First thing, I went down to New Orleans to the Mergenthaler linotype school and learned how to operate the linotype and how to take care of it. We had a two-week-old baby when I left and I got lonesome. Our next babies were twins and I found out that my trip to New Orleans was probably a pretty good time to be out of the house.

When I got back from that linotype school in 1930, there was just one linotype machine, and I rolled the man for his job. I had that job for a year or two until we could afford to get another linotype man so I could get out and try to sell a little advertising. Selling advertising was few and far between in the early thirties. Our total circulation in 1931 was about 1,200. I was talking to my father-in-law who owned the paper one day, and he let me take over the bookkeeping and circulation and just about everything else in the office. I started looking at the books when I took this over and found that we had folks anywhere up to eleven years behind in paying for their paper. They just couldn't afford to pay that $1.50 a year for the paper. With the publisher's permission, I sat down and typed out a letter to those folks who were behind and I told them that from now on, it would be strictly cash in advance. I told them to respond within a month. I don't guess they believed me and I cut off 500 subscriptions at one time. There was this one fellow who was eleven years behind and I cut him off. He was a lawyer and he came charging into the office after he got my letter one day, just screaming and he said, "I always gave you all my legal advertising. How come you cut me off?" I told him he was eleven years behind in his subscription fees and that was $16.50 and that was big money. I checked back, and this lawyer had given me just three legal advertisements in the last five years. This fellow didn't pay his back dues. He just subscribed for the paper in his wife's name. I sent him his paper. What else could I do?

Libba: We never did all that much bragging about the circulation of the *Demopolis Times.* The *Democrat Reporter* in Linden had a paper, and that was the county seat. The Sutton family ran that paper. Their father and our family were real good friends. They handled all the business below Bogue Creek and we had the business in the northern part of the county, so we felt that we were no competition to each other.

Ben: Just to give you an idea how well we got along with the newspaper down at Linden, in 1941, we had a fire which just gutted our newspaper. I was out of business for seven weeks, or would have been out of business. The Suttons, who owned the newspaper down at Linden, helped me out. I would send my two men down there and they would print their paper on Wednesday, and print the *Demopolis Times* on their press on Thursday and we got by until I could get started again. He didn't charge me a thing except for the newsprint I used. That's the way newspapermen were in those days. The *Selma Times-Journal* offered to let me print my paper down there for free, also. That's typical of newspaper folks, helping each other out.

That fire might have been a blessing in disguise because I needed new equipment and didn't think I could afford it. Of course, when I had that fire, I was forced to buy new equipment, a new linotype machine and type and everything else. I was able to clean up that old flatbed press and we got by on that. I would get up there and feed sheets into the press one at a time and Libba would take the printed pages and fold them when they came out. You just don't find many family-owned newspapers any more. The syndicates are buying them all up and you change publishers just about as often as the Methodists change preachers.

During the depression, we put out one paper a week and we had about four people in total working down there. In 1941 when the war started, we couldn't get help and Libba and I were running the whole newspaper by ourselves. We put out a four-page paper and did a little job printing on the side. Just the two of us handled everything for about a year until we could find some help. We mailed out all our newspapers.

Libba: What saved the newspapers during the depression were the banks, the Coca-Cola Bottling Company, Alabama Power, and a little national advertising, just a handful of people. Most of the local businesses around the square folded, and if it hadn't been for the few advertisers we had, we would have gone under.

The biggest news story that ever happened in Demopolis was the funding of the Rooster Bridge over the Tombigbee River. Before 1925, there was no bridge over the river and this was the only interruption of Highway 80 from east to west. The only way to get across the river was by ferry boats, pulled across the river by cables and pushed by long poles. There was no money to build a bridge so a man named Frank Derby had an idea to raise money. He thought it would be a terrific thing to have important people contribute roosters and auction them off. A big rooster sale was held in Demopolis in 1919 and everybody from President Woodrow Wilson, Fatty Arbuckle (the movie star), and Helen Keller contributed a rooster for the auction. Roosters from out of town were flown in on an aquaplane which landed on the Tombigbee and this was big doings. The big rooster sale was held on Confederate Square and people came from everywhere. Some of the roosters brought as much as $1,000. Stores closed, the legislature shut down, and newspapers from all over sent reporters to cover the event. The money was raised and the bridge was completed in 1925. It was first named Memorial Bridge, but nobody called it that, and the name was officially changed to Rooster Bridge in 1959.

The Doctor's Wife

Joe Upchurch, Talladega County

I've been in the car business here in Talladega since 1945 and one of the most unusual things that happened to me was years ago. I had this customer who had driven down to Miami, Florida. I got a call one day and the operator said would I accept a collect call from Miami, and she told me who it was, and I said I would accept the call. This lady I knew said she was down in Miami and that a man down there told her that she needed a new tire and she asked me what she ought to do. I thought a minute and advised her to go on and get the tire. She trusted me.

One Saturday night about nine o'clock, I answered the phone and there was an old customer on the line and he says, "I'm just over the line up here in Missouri and I want you to come up here and get me." I told him that I wasn't about to drive all the way up there at nine o'clock on a Saturday night and get him and told him to get somebody else to drive him home. He said he couldn't do that. What happened was that his water pump had torn up and ruined his radiator and he was out in a little town with a population of 150 and he was about 150 miles from Memphis and it was a Saturday night. They told him that his car would be ready on Tuesday.

I just told him to stay there until Tuesday, then. He was a doctor and told me that he had an important operation scheduled for the first thing Monday morning and he just had to be back in Talladega for that operation. I said, "Doc, I'm not going to leave now. I'm tired and it's in the middle of the night," and he told me to call his wife and she could come with me. Well, I called his wife, and I got a tow bar and we started out. About 4:30 in the morning, we got to Memphis and I was hungry and tired. I told his wife that I was hungry and I was stopping for a little something to eat. We stopped at this all-night cafe to eat, and when we came out of the cafe next to a motel, there were cars with Talladega tags parked all over that parking lot.

I showed those car tags to the doctor's wife and told her that somebody was going to see us coming out of that motel cafe and we'll be the talk of Talladega when we got back. And she said, "I don't care if you don't care." They were having a bowling tournament up in Memphis and that is the reason all those Talladega cars were there. When I got back home, I kept waiting for some talk about me and that doctor's wife, but never heard a word. Nobody must have seen us coming out of that motel cafe. I was a little disappointed that nobody saw us.

Getting By

Jim Carlson, Marengo County

Back in the early forties, a fellow had to make do with what he had, get by the best he could. On the square in Demopolis, David Junior got in the business of selling newspapers more or less by accident. Mr. and Mrs. Old Man Barger had the *Tuscaloosa Times* paper route, about 400 subscribers in all. Mrs. Old Man Barger had an old, beat-up station wagon she would load up with about 300 papers and make a run, delivering some to individual addresses and she would stick the rest of them in paper-vending machines around town. Old Man Barger had a bicycle with some baskets on it and he would take the rest of the papers and deliver them to his route customers.

David Junior was no relation to Old Man Barger at all, but every day he and a pack of town dogs would trot alongside Old Man Barger's bicycle as the papers were delivered, huffing and puffing and enjoying the exercise. Now, David Junior had very limited smarts, you see, and his IQ was roughly the same as his hat size, but burning back there somewhere was some ambition. He wanted a paper route of his own, but as luck would have it, he failed time after time. He just couldn't remember who got a paper and who didn't.

Then, one day, David Junior got an idea on how to get into this money-making business of selling papers. Every day, he used to hang around the Malone Garage before setting off with Old Man Barger and bum a cigarette off of Malone. This morning, when he got his idea, he bummed his usual cigarette off of Malone and asked him for a dime, to boot. Malone shrugged and handed over a dime. Instead of trotting alongside Old Man Barger on his bicycle, David Junior waited until Mrs. Old Man Barger had loaded up a vending machine on the square there, stuck in his dime, opened the door, and took out all the newspapers. Tucking them under his arm, he started going around to all the downtown businesses, hustling those papers for a nickel apiece. As he sold his papers, he laid on some choice bits of town gossip, most of which he had made up himself. Now, Mrs. Old Man Barger took quick note that all of her papers were gone but only a dime was in the coin box, and it didn't take her too long to figure out what David Junior was up to. Did she put a stop to this? Nah. She just ordered a few extra papers for that machine. Everybody in town knew that this box was David Junior's place of business. David Junior was thirty-five years old at the time.

Back then, there were a number of ways to make a living. Greensboro had his own special way. Greensboro was a short, middle-aged black man and wore a long, oversized overcoat every day of the year, even in the summertime, and most folks figured that he had on something underneath that coat, but none could rightly say.

Greensboro made a living with a bass drum he carried with a string around his neck, and the drum sticking out in front. Just about every night, he would park that drum in Mr. Emmett Clinkscales's store and go back and pick it up the next morning, ready for business. What he would do is take that bass drum and hang around the door of businesses, and when a lady would come up to the door of that place, Greensboro would open the door with a big flourish, give a helluva bang on the drum, and announce the lady's presence to the clerks inside. Well, what could the lady do? Most of the time, she gave Greensboro a tip for all that attention. Sometimes, the store owner gave him a tip, too, but mostly to get Greensboro to move on down the street, maybe to a competitor's front door.

When he was not opening doors and banging on his drum for the ladies, Greensboro would parade up and down the streets yelling out the latest local news and doing free commercials on some good buys he had seen at some store, all the time banging away on that drum. For variety, when the watermelons came in, he would walk around balancing a watermelon on his head. You'll have to give him credit, because he could come up with some pretty good money-making schemes.

One day, people noticed him walking down the street with a sad face, pounding on his drum in a kind of a muffled way, like a funeral beat you might say. He got out in the middle of the street with this announcement: (boom) jes' las' night, (boom) Armie Hay done died down in the Selma hospital, (boom) an' they ain't got no money, (boom) so's he can get buried (boom). Now, a lot of people had known old Armie and they were sad to hear this news and sorry that he didn't have enough money to have a decent funeral. Greensboro knew that folks would want to help out, so he had fixed a sack on the side of his drum, and as he walked down the street, people would come up and put money in that sack for Armie's funeral. Two days later, folks were surprised to see old Armie sitting on a park bench, rested and satisfied after a visit with his sister in Eutaw.

A Mountain Store

Burton Troup, Marshall County

When my granddaddy operated the store up on Gunters Mountain, I would slip off from my mother and go down there and hang around. My granddaddy was the first postmaster in Grant, and he named the place Grant because he was a Republican. Papa had a little farm because Granddaddy put up the money for the farm when Papa and Mama got married.

The old store Granddaddy had was very dark inside because the windows were so high, and I heard it was because those high windows made it harder for burglars to enter. People couldn't see much in there and the only light they had was a coal-oil lamp. Even the clerks had a hard time seeing the goods and people were kind of buying blind, you might say. The walls were filled with cloth and things, and in the back was a display of harness, and then a row of kegs there with horseshoes hung around the rim. Granddaddy had what you call a general store.

Mama would tell me about the drummers who would come in there from Chattanooga. The drummers would come and spend the night because Mama said Granddaddy was good to them. They would stay two nights sometimes to write up the orders. The only way they could get goods up on that mountain was by the Tennessee River and when the goods would come in, Granddaddy would have to go down the mountain and pick up his goods at Laurel Landing there on the river. Up on the mountain, you could hear the boat blowing its whistle to let people know it was coming, and then Granddaddy would send a wagon down for his merchandise. It was about eight miles down to the landing as the crow flies.

Now, my uncle Will was a doctor and he would leave his medical books out on the counter there in the store. I remember my uncle Robert would be down at the store and a bunch of men would be there, just hanging around, and Uncle Robert would say, "Come over here and look at this," and they would all gather 'round that one medical book and just be interested for the longest time. I would wonder what would be so interesting in those books. I found out later that what they were looking at was an anatomy book and they had that page turned back to a picture of a woman, and Uncle Robert would say, "It looks like it's upside down to me."

Sacking 'Em Up

Jeff Coleman, Sumter County

My father had a department store in Livingston and I started in the business early, sweeping the front walk when I was four years old. He had a little of everything in that store, feeds and seeds, laces, plowshares, shoes, and even beds. We tried to stay away from "furnishing" sharecroppers.

Livingston was situated on a square with the courthouse in the middle with stores around the square. We didn't have packaged goods back in those days in the store. Most of the goods came in bulk, and every Friday, we would have to sack up packages of roast coffee, packages of sugar and meal, all the same size packages. Cookies and cakes and all that stuff came in big boxes, almost like the cracker barrel. We didn't have any paved streets in town and Saturday was always the big day. We had that little college there and had some added income that most other little towns in west Alabama didn't have. Most folks don't remember that we had a depression right after World War I, but people in Livingston kept on going.

We didn't have much of a war effort during World War I in Sumter County. We did furnish oak billets for spokes for artillery caissons. A man from Indiana came down and started up a peckerwood sawmill and they would cut that oak up into random-size widths, but the same lengths, and then would load them up on a train. Those billets would be shipped off to another place where they finished making the spokes. Sumter County's material contribution to World War I.

An Eye for Business

Ben Meriwether, Bullock County

We were living in Iuka, Mississippi, about 1909 or 1910 when my daddy got a chance to get this store back in Mitchell Station so we sold everything and went back to Alabama in 1912. The store building was large, with a storeroom and office on the west side, and two large rooms on the east side. Now, all the country stores back then had porches and the store had a porch on the south side that ran all the way across, then went down the east side and ended at the door of the two rooms. A big fireplace was at the back of the store.

We sold everything in that store, from ladies' hats and shoes to cloth, groceries, harness, and most anything you needed. Mitchell Station had only about nine families living there but there were big farms and plantations all around with big families, and the farms were doing good and store business was doing all right, too. On the west side of the store was a huge billboard, and when a circus or some big show was coming to Montgomery, the advance crew would go through the country putting up the advertisements. They always gave us passes and tickets for the shows. So, we saw all the shows and circuses that came to Montgomery.

Since most of the trade in the store was black, they would not buy very much at a time, so we would put up a nickel's worth and a dime's worth of sugar, coffee, rice, and other little things, tie it up in neat little bags, and put the bags up on the shelf for the weekend. Back then, everything came to the store in bulk, big wooden barrels, flour in twenty-four- to forty-eight-pound bags. Coffee came in green and you parched and ground it yourself. Everybody had chicken and eggs but you could still bring in two eggs and get a nickel's worth of anything.

Now, Fitzpatrick was on the Central of Georgia Railroad with a water station, train order station, express office, and a Western Union. Pretty important. There were two passenger trains in the morning and two in the afternoon, both about an hour and a half apart. Now, those two afternoon trains could not go through town unless all the young folks were there, especially on Sunday afternoon. That was our entertainment and there was a pretty good-sized bunch of young people always there, all of us school younguns and the older younguns who were just grown.

A rural mail route ran out of Fitzpatrick and all passenger trains, except the two trains on Sunday afternoon, carried mail. The post office paid the rural carrier nine cents a train to take the mail from the post office to the train and back during the summer. The mail carrier never touched the mail, because that was my job. When the carrier got the check, he endorsed it and gave it to me. Then, the depot agent got me to help him one summer, paying me twenty-five cents a day. I got so I could run that depot about as good as the agent, except for the telegraph instruments, and I was even learning that. Sometimes on Sunday the agent would want to go somewhere, so he would pay me fifty cents to open up from nine to eleven.

Also, there was a man who pumped the water for the train. He had to fire a boiler to run the pumps. His job paid two dollars and thirty-eight cents a day and he didn't have any certain hours because he had to pump that water until the tank was full. Some Sundays, he would want to go somewhere and I did the pumping for a little extra money. So there were a lot of Sundays that I would change the mails (eighteen cents), open the depot (fifty cents), pump water for the rest of the day (two dollars and thirty-eight cents). Boy, oh boy, was I making the money.

One summer, Joe and I decided to make a little extra money by selling ice. The ice house in Union Springs would ship a 300-pound block of ice on the passenger train. We would order the ice and we would start peddling it as soon as it got to the station. This was good business because everybody wanted ice in the summertime, but we didn't figure on how much work it would be. We had no ice hooks, no way of carrying that ice at all. We had to drag that 300-pound block of ice along and cut off just a little piece at each house. It was just too much going house to house, so we worked out a deal with the five stores in town. The owners agreed to pay us twenty-five cents for 100 pounds when they got their freight. We hauled the 100 pounds up to each store and that worked out really good. Lots of days that summer, we would make a dollar and a half apiece.

When Daddy had his store in Fitzpatrick, a young man named Frank Moore bought out the store across the street from ours. Now, Frank's store was just like all the country stores around there with a big front porch all the way across the front with a little window on each side of the front door. Frank's store was about three feet off the ground with steps in front of the door. There were eight or ten older men, I mean from sixty on up, who would come down every day, meet in front of Frank's store, and sit on his steps. If anyone wanted to go in the store, one of the old men had to get up.

Frank asked them several times not to block his steps, but they didn't pay any attention to him. They would not sit on our porch because our porch was only one step off the ground. Finally, Frank got a magneto off an old farm tractor and put a handle on it so he could crank it. Those old magnetos could really give you a shock. Frank mounted that magneto on a shelf inside the store by the front window, ran a small wire from the magneto out the window to the front of the porch and all the way across. If you were not looking for the wire, you wouldn't notice it. I knew he had rigged up that thing and was waiting to see what would happen.

The next morning, Mr. Lum Baker came strolling along from his place about a block away. He went right up to Frank's step and sat down in the middle, right in front of the door. Frank went inside, gave that magneto a few quick turns and Mr. Baker came flying off that step. He looked all around, didn't see anything, brushed off the seat of his pants, and sat down again. This time, Frank really let him have it. Mr. Baker jumped up again and headed for home, running and brushing the seat of his pants. He didn't come back the rest of the day.

A short time after Mr. Baker went home, the rest of the gang came and took their regular seats across the steps. They all got a dose of that magneto, and finally they saw the wire and realized what had happened. They didn't like it too much, but they took the hint and didn't block his steps anymore.

In 1928, I was in Montgomery picking up odd jobs. I worked every Saturday at a grocery store on North Court Street, worked from seven in the morning until eleven at night for two dollars a day. I had been working like that awhile when a friend of mine working at the trolley car barn called home to tell me about a job he had for me if I could get there by six o'clock that afternoon. My mother called me down at the grocery to tell me about it and it was 5 P.M. then.

I told the man I was working for that I was leaving right then for a regular job. He didn't like it but forked over my two dollars. I bought a dime's worth of cheese, a nickel's worth of crackers, and walked all the way to the car barn. I went to work at six o'clock and got off at five the next morning. My job was using a broom and rag cleaning the trolley cars for ninety dollars a month. That was good, but three months later, I got a little promotion, still ninety dollars a month. Two years later, I was night foreman at the shop and still getting ninety dollars a month. That fall, I bought my first car, a 1926 Chevrolet, and was really in high cotton.

Mine Country

*Coal miners leaving their lamps at
shift's end, circa 1960
(Sloss Furnaces National Historic
Landmark, Birmingham)*

Three-Wagon Caravan

Cullman Powell, Walker County

I was born there in Dixie Springs in a mining camp. My father worked in a mine all his life. When the mine got worked out there in Dixie, we moved into Coal Valley. When the mines were worked out, the little community just died. There was nothing in Dixie but a commissary—and that sat on the side of the railroad track—a depot, and a hotel that people would come on weekends just to drink that water. Now, it was nothing but mining water and it would really tear your stomach up, but for some reason, a lot of folks thought it was healthful.

That was the place where I heard my first radio sound. This man got some parts and built this radio and would invite all the neighbors over to hear the radio. They would pass the earphones around from person to person.

Social life consisted of going to church, and they had a little old deal out there that was the school and the church, and everything kind of centered around that. It was a small building with pews in it, and on the back of the pews there was a twelve-inch board that was your desk for school. I started to school in that building. There were six grades in that one room. The grades would be divided, like the first grade on the first row, and right on back. We had one teacher.

I had my first fight in that town. My mother had sent me and my brother to the store one day, and on the way back, a guy whose family ran the hotel came running by us on his Shetland pony. He was running real fast and popped me with his whip. My brother who was just older than I was and who never took anything off of anybody told him, "Buster, if you do that again, I'll make you wish you hadn't." This boy reared the little pony up and come galloping by again. My brother grabbed up a beech limb and hit that boy right on the chin as he galloped by and knocked him off his pony. We turned around and went on home like nothing had happened. The next morning, my mother asked us, "Did you boys hear what happened to Buster, yesterday?" We said, nome, we hadn't heard anything, and she told us that Buster's pony had throwed him in a ditch and broke his jaw all up and they had him in a Birmingham hospital working on it. See, Buster had better sense than to tell his dad what really happened.

To go to the hospital, you got on the train on that little Southern line that went out through there and went to Birmingham. They had a train that went to Birmingham of a morning and another coming back the other way in the afternoon. When I was a baby, my granddaddy, who was a doctor, bundled me up and took me to Birmingham, operated on me, and brought me back home in the afternoon.

We used to go visit people with mules and a wagon. The mines owned the mules but Daddy would get them and we would go down in the country. That's what we called it, "down in the country," which was just down from where we were. We would leave on Friday afternoon and drive that team of mules way into the night getting to wherever we were going and we would leave Sunday after church and drive back.

My oldest brother thought he was a big shot because he got to drive the team. I remember there in Dixie Springs there were just three or four cars for the whole community and one of them was a delivery truck for the grocery store. In those days, you carried a list to the grocery store on a Saturday morning and they would fill up a box with things you had on that list, put your name on it, and deliver it to your house. You couldn't bring a whole week's worth of groceries home walking, you know, and they would deliver it. All the stores delivered back then. That was the time everybody was converting from mules and horses to automobiles.

Well, when the mines played out in Dixie Springs, Daddy got a job over in Coal Valley and we moved down there in a three-wagon caravan. Daddy and Mother were in the number one wagon and us five boys were spread out in the second and third wagons. We were going along and came to a hill just before we got to the town of Coal Valley and Daddy held up his hand for us all to stop. We all pulled over and Daddy got down off his wagon and walked back to where we were stopped. He looked up and said, "All you boys get down here." We all got down and lined up and he looked us up and down. "You boys got to look nice when we go through town," he said, and we all buttoned up our shirts, buttoned our cuffs, and combed our hair with the comb he gave us. Then he told us, "Now get up on those wagons and don't say a word. I don't want to hear a peep out of any one of you because we are fixing to go through town."

My daddy was a real disciplinarian. Like if you said "yeah" to a grown-up, you got a whipping. You said yes, sir, and no, sir, please, ma'am. You got yourself tore up if you showed any disrespect to a grown-up. My daddy wasn't a big man, but you always knew who was in charge. He had a rule and he would say to us five boys, "You be here at this house before dark," and to this day, I still want to be home before dark. None of us boys ever bucked up to my daddy, because if you did, he'd knock you a half a mile. He wouldn't do you any bodily harm, but he wouldn't mind bending you over with that razor strop, and buddy, when he got through, your back end was burning so much that you would remember it. He used that razor strop regular.

When we moved to Coal Valley, I was in the second grade. When we got settled in that new house, the first thing Daddy taught us boys was how to turn on the lights. We had never had electric lights before. He bought my mother an electric iron, too, first one she had ever had. The next thing he did was to walk over to the school with us. We had to walk over a swinging bridge going to the school and we walked through a kind of a wooded area, and all of a sudden, there was the school. The school had a fence all around it but it didn't have any gates to it. It had a stile to go over it and I thought the school was really something, sitting out there all by itself and painted up pretty. There was a drive-in gate around back, but no teachers had cars, so everybody had to go over the stile.

The miners were cut so much out of their pay each month for the school. They called that "stoppages" and a man would say that all these stoppages are eating me up. So much of that stoppage went for the school and so much for doctors and so much for house rent. All the other schools went about six months but Coal Valley went nine months on account of the stoppages.

Coal Valley was about three miles west of Oakman where the railroad was. It was a valley down here with hills all around it and mines going into these hills. All the activity in the community was down in the valley. There was just one road that ran down through there. There was a school and a huge commissary owned by the company, and a time office, a barber shop, a hotel with a poolroom on the side, and a doctor's office and a post office. They had a system at the commissary called doog-a-loo where they issued a coupon book with different amounts on the coupons. You would go to the timekeeper and say you wanted a dollar's worth of coupons. The timekeeper would look in his book to see if your daddy was working that day, and if he was, he would give you the coupons. The system was that they would get these people working in the mines, good people, and they would just keep nicking at him and nicking at him and getting him in debt so he couldn't leave.

In 1935 or 1936, Roosevelt had this law passed what they called bargaining rights. Up until that time, unions were illegal, and when that law passed, the men came out on strike and it was a bloody one. About a year there, it was bad, and they called out the national guard and airplanes were flying over and all. I was a big boy about then. There was this group of miners who would not strike and they kept going in the mines. This group that was striking would always be hassling that bunch that was going in the mines and they would shoot at them of a morning, throw dynamite up on their porches, and dynamite the railroad. They would dynamite the air shafts in the mines where they couldn't get any air.

The company had machine-gun posts up in the hills trying to keep down the fighting. They would put platforms up in the trees at the entrance to the valley for the machine guns and put railroad spikes in the trunk of the tree to climb up on. The company hired guards to keep down the fighting. There was one old guard that sat at the corner of the theater and he was always asleep. There was this one boy who wasn't ascared of anything, and one time he snuck up under the porch there and slipped the guard's pistol out of his holster. That gun stayed in a hollow beech tree over by the cemetery until I went in the navy.

One night a car came down in front of the commissary and dropped enough dynamite to wreck the inside of the building. Everybody was harassing everybody else. The company guards would catch us boys out and run us home and whip us with whips, pop us, really. The company owned the houses, see, and if a man stepped out of line, the company would send the sheriff over to his house with an eviction notice.

Pretty close to where we lived, they sent the law out one day to evict this man. He stepped out on the porch with a shotgun and sat down and told the sheriff, "You step inside that gate, they'll have to drag you out, because I'm going to kill you." The sheriff said, "Well Bill, I got an eviction notice here and I have to serve it." Bill told him he wasn't about to serve nothing. The sheriff said, "Well, I'm just going to leave it on your gate here." The sheriff stuck the eviction notice on the gate and had no more than turned his back when the man let go with the shotgun and shot that eviction notice all to pieces.

About that time, a little old dog went missing and I always wondered what happened to that dog. One day before Uncle Tom died, I was home on leave from the navy and I said, "Uncle Tom, what ever happened to that little old dog that used to hang around?" Uncle Tom was a jolly old fellow, and when I asked about the dog, he just laughed and laughed. He said, "We was out during the strike and we was going around throwing dynamite on people's porches who kept going in the mines. That little old dog had followed us and he had been trained to go get a stick when you threw it. Well, one of us lit the fuse on that stick of dynamite and threw it up on the porch of this house. Before we knew what was happening, that little old dog tore off up there, got that stick of dynamite and started back to where we were standing, lickety-split, the dynamite in his mouth with the fuse lit. Something had to give, and we had to shoot that dog before he could get back to us. It was him or us."

Every Foot of Land

Charlie Hill, Walker County

My father was a coal miner, strip-mined all his life. My grandfather was also a coal miner, uneducated, but the most interesting man I've ever known. In this mining country where I grew up, around Nauvoo, there were three people who were held in high esteem: John L.

Lewis who was the president of the United Mine Workers, Franklin D. Roosevelt who was the president of the United States, and God, in that order. There was a lot of unionism in that part of the country and Lewis was the protector of the miner. People liked Roosevelt because he was bringing the country out of the depression. I can remember going into many houses, and almost without fail, there would be a picture of John L. Lewis and a picture of Roosevelt and a religious picture.

The closest town to where I lived was Nauvoo, but I lived a few miles out in the country. The first house my parents ever owned was built by my father and grandfather. As they were putting on the roof, I was up there with them and I fell off the roof, through the frame of the house, all the way to the ground. That was before I started to school and I was never on top of the house again until we had to put a new roof on the house, and I was sixteen years old then. If you lived in the mining camps, you lived in a company house, a three-room shotgun house with no inside plumbing. They would have a central water faucet in those camps and everybody would take a bucket and go to the water faucet to get water. We were a little bit better off because my parents owned a little bit of property and we built our own house, right in the middle of where all the strip mining was going on.

Many times, when they were blasting—they would blast the rock away so they could strip away the coal—the windows of the house would rattle. We used to say the china would rattle, but we didn't have any china. We used peanut butter jars to drink from. The windows would rattle, though, just like an earthquake. I've been in a small earthquake and the sensation was much the same, and then you would hear the large noise of the blast and then you would see the smoke. We had the strip mining, plus there was also underground mining around there, too. There were two types of underground mining. One was the big company mine, mechanized and all, and then there was the push mine. A push mine was a small operation where one or more men would decide that there was coal in this spot and they would open up a little tunnel and you would start digging back in that tunnel and haul the coal out. The reason it was called "push" is that the cars that you loaded the coal onto were not mechanized and the men actually pushed the cars out to the mouth of the tunnel.

To get the coal out of the ground in a push mine, the men used picks and shovels and augers. The auger was a giant brace and a ten-foot bit, three-fourths inch in diameter, and they would auger a hole in the face of that mine and put the dynamite in the hole to blast the coal and rock. To work that auger, it had a deal that fit on your stomach and you would lie down on your stomach because it was pretty tight in that hole, and you would drill the hole and stick the dynamite in there and then set it off.

The father of a friend of mine and another fellow decided to open up one of those push mines. They started the mine and bought a mule to pull the coal out of the mine. The tradition was that mules were blinded when they started working the coal mines because they just seemed to operate better if they couldn't see. These two men were down in their mine one Saturday morning and they had been into the moonshine whiskey pretty good the night before, as some coal miners were known to do, and one of them got aggravated with the mule. The mule just didn't want to do those things that the man wanted him to do. He carried the mule outside the mine where they dumped the rock, took a stick of dynamite, strapped the dynamite to the mule's head and attached a fuse and then lit the fuse. About that time, the other fellow came out of the mine, saw what was about to happen, and knocked the dynamite from the mule's head.

In the forties, there was a tragedy I remember. There was an independent coal miner who started a strip-mine operation up where my grandparents lived, and he was going to operate the mine with nonunion people, and that was an absolute no-no. The union decided to close that job down and the way they did that was to barricade the roads and harass the people coming in to the job. They didn't have telephones so they couldn't harass them at night, but they would drive by their homes and throw rocks and paint their cars and do these kinds of things. After several of these instances, the union men came out on a Saturday night and dynamited some equipment. That Sunday afternoon, the mine was back in operation and the union came out to stop them. This afternoon, both sides had their guns—rifles and shotguns and pistols—and they actually had a gun battle. During the firing back and forth, one of the union men got killed, and when he fell, the battle abruptly stopped.

At this union man's funeral, and he was a good union man, they had the service at this little country church. When they left the church in a funeral procession for the cemetery, there were four hundred cars in line. I never, up until that time, saw so many cars together in my life. I didn't realize there were that many cars in the world. The reason I knew that there were four hundred cars was because there were so many, I began to count them. Four hundred cars. It was in the afternoon, and four hundred cars on a dirt road out in the country creates a heck of a lot of dust, and that's what I remember, all those cars coming by. It seemed that they would never stop coming, kicking up all that dust. That huge number of cars was a major event because out on that dirt road, traffic was thin, and when any single car came by on an ordinary day, everybody went to the window to see who it was. Airplanes, the same way.

My grandfather lived a few miles away from our house, basically the same type of house that we had, a four-room house, a kitchen and three bedrooms. The bedrooms served many purposes: a bedroom, a sitting room, and whatever other activities the family enjoyed. We were a little more progressive than most folks in that we had coal-burning heaters in our house while my grandparents had coal-burning fireplaces. Houses were built up off the ground, built on rocks because we had plenty of rocks in Walker County. The ground out in front of the house was free of grass, just plain dirt, and was swept regularly with a brush broom. My mother would go into the woods and find dogwood trees about four or five feet tall, kind of bushy in the top, and she would take four or five of these little dogwoods, cut them, tie them together with a string, and use them just like a broom to sweep the yard. My grandparents had an old privet hedge that we see growing wild out in the woods and that was the fence they had. This privet-hedge fence went completely around their house and kept cows and other animals away from the house. That hedge was always kept trimmed and had a gate for entrance.

The coal companies didn't own every foot of land in Walker County, but around the big corporate coal mines, the company owned everything, every foot of land. They owned the houses and the commissary and they had their own money system which was called clacker. My father always worked for independent strippers, but some friends of mine had fathers who worked for the company mines, like the Brookside Pratt Mining Company. The company printed this coin about the size of a silver dollar, or a half-dollar, depending on the denomination. You would go to the commissary to buy something, and say you gave them a five-dollar bill, they would always give your change back in their currency. This meant that you could only spend the change in their store. Pretty good marketing plan. Those stores carried about everything a coal-mining family needed. A miner could go down and charge things from the company store, and rather than getting paid on a Friday afternoon, he would get nothing if he had charged more than what he had earned. The company would continue taking money out of his pay until they got all of what was owed.

The early open-pit mining was done with steam shovels. These big shovels actually burned coal in the boilers and generated steam and the steam operated the equipment. To have steam, the shovels had to have water, and most of the time, the only source of water would be a nearby creek. The operators would find a good-size creek, set up a large gasoline-driven pump, and pump that water from the creek up to where they needed it. They would lay a four-inch water pipe on top of the ground from the creek up to the shovel.

Now, my grandfather had the job of operating the pump, and when they needed water up at the shovel, they had a steam whistle, and they would blow the steam whistle and you could hear that steam whistle for three miles or more. Everybody in the country heard the steam whistle. That's how they signaled my grandfather to start the pump or to stop it, like one short and two longs would tell him what to do. I liked to fish a lot, and since my grandfather was right there at the creek, I could go over when he was at work and we could fish together while he was on the job. While he was at the pump, he would have time to whittle, and he was a good whittler.

When World War II started, out there in the country things got scarce and there was nothing to buy. Besides, a family didn't have much money to buy it anyhow. My grandfather and my father

decided to have their teeth taken out at the same time. My grandfather died in 1981, and those teeth were taken out in 1941, and he
never had a tooth the rest of his life. But he could eat an apple and
corn on the cob. He gummed everything he ate. He could take an
apple and hold it in his hand and I guess his gums had hardened so
that they had shrunk to a tough gristle over the jaw bone, and he
would bite down on that apple and break that apple just like it was
cut with a knife.

I was seven years old when my youngest sister was born, and I can
remember the night she was born, born at home just like all the
babies in the mining country. I remember that night, way in the
night with all the commotion going on during the delivery, and
when my baby sister cried for the first time, I thought it was a
chicken. It sounded to me just like a chicken, and I waked up crying
and calling my mother to get the chicken out of the house. But what
it was was my brand new baby sister, and the doctor came out and
delivered the baby at our house.

The town doctor had an office there and a drugstore combined, a
company-owned doctor. Out of my daddy's paycheck every week,
instead of insurance, they took out some money for the doctor. If
you got sick, everybody went to the same doctor, and that money
paid for your medical. That doctor did everything. He pulled teeth,
delivered babies, and sewed up cuts, and whatever medicines you
got, you got from him.

I remember going to the doctor's office down there in Nauvoo as a
kid and you sit there and there might be thirty people sitting in
there, depending on whatever epidemic was going around, and there
might be thirty people or three people, but you sat there until your
time came. He treated every disease known to man. My grandfather
told me that doctor practiced his entire career in Nauvoo. When he
finished medical school, one of the coal-mining companies brought
him to town. He was a very young man then, and one of the things
he did to try to disguise his youth was to grow a full beard, and he
dyed that beard so that he would have streaks of gray in it to appear
older. He was afraid the people in the community wouldn't accept
him if they thought he was still wet behind the ears. He must have
practiced medicine for over forty years in Nauvoo, and he was the

only doctor in town all that time. He was also the druggist, because if you needed medicine, you got it from him. He had all the bottles and jars and stuff and he would mix up some medicine for you whether you needed it or not.

When I was growing up, Nauvoo had the picture show which was in an old garage building that somebody had built to work on cars, but it had gone out of business and somebody put in the picture show. That picture show just operated on Saturday night. You sat on wooden benches. Then, you had the little building where the doctor was and there were two or three stores that sold feeds and seeds and plow points to the farmers, and they sold mining equipment. We had a post office, too, and a postmistress. For some strange reason, we always had a lady on that job. Then, of course, there was the depot, and all the coal was hauled out of there on rail cars. But we also had a little passenger train that went from Nauvoo to Jasper.

There were no buses out of Nauvoo, and very few automobiles during World War II, so we would ride the train, just like riding the streetcar in Birmingham. That little passenger train was called the Doodlebug, very much like the "Petticoat Junction" train except it didn't have that big blower on it. The Doodlebug stopped at just about every road crossing, and if somebody was standing out by the track and waved it down, the train would stop and pick them up. That was the way to go and do what you wanted to do. Not one of the streets in Nauvoo was paved when I was coming along, just dirt and gravel. The town was much like the towns in the old western movies.

The law in Nauvoo was maybe a constable and an occasional sheriff's deputy, but they never wore uniforms. They would wear their regular overalls and whatever they normally wore, but they would always have that badge on. We had our share of murders. Walker County was dry, supposed to be dry, and you couldn't find alcoholic beverages in stores, but those who would imbibe from time to time usually drank moonshine whiskey. I still don't know what moonshine whiskey tastes like, but I did a lot of hunting up there in the hills and would come across moonshine whiskey stills that had been blown up by the revenuers.

There was this one guy who lived out there close to us and he had never been married, but he was a good old guy and everybody liked him, but he was a drunk. He would get a job and work for two or three weeks for whoever might give him odd work until he had enough to buy some moonshine. My sister and I were out in the front yard playing one day and we saw this guy walking down the dirt road toward our house and he was staggering all over the road. He had on a pair of overalls and had a half-gallon jar of moonshine whiskey stuck under the bib of his overalls, and in his back pocket, he had another quart of moonshine stuck back there. My sister and I ran into the house because we were frightened of the man known to be a drunk. When there was a problem, the sheriff would arrest him and put him in jail for two or three weeks, and then he would get out and start all over again.

Now, the big companies had their own private law, or enforcers, and they took care of the company's business. On Saturday night, it was not unusual for fights to break out between the miners. They would get liquored up and knife each other and shoot each other. This could happen anywhere: out in the dirt road in front of houses or down at the commissary where people usually gathered. Coal miners who worked in that environment were a tough bunch of people because they lived a hard life and their families lived a hard life.

We always had a Christmas tree and all the traditional things that went along with Christmas. We never had a turkey, but we always had a hen. There was a family that was our next-door neighbor, and next door was three quarters of a mile away. There were nine children in that family, and on Christmas morning, they would always come over to our house to see what my sister and I got for Christmas. They never got any toys for Christmas and there is always a sadness in my heart at Christmastime because I guess I remember those kids. I guess I felt guilty a little bit because we had toys and they didn't. Their parents just didn't have any money.

At Christmastime—and I don't know where this tradition came from—a lot of the old people did what they called serenading. They would dress up in sort of a clown type of costume, make a mask with a big nose, and painted up, and eight or ten people would get together and they would go house to house. They would come into a house and sit down and never say a word, and maybe sit there for thirty minutes and not say a word, and then get up and leave. Sometimes they sang and sometimes they wouldn't, depending on their talents. Sometimes they would dance and sometimes somebody would bring a guitar. You could do whatever you wanted to because your face was covered up. When they would leave, the woman in the house would give them fruit or cake, because at Christmastime, everybody had cakes baked. It was a fun time, kind of visiting.

A Ton of Coal

Sue Pickett, Libby Fitts and *William W. Collins, Sr.,* Bibb County

Collins: I've left Alabama four or five times and I didn't stay as much as a year neither time, come right back to Blocton. Pete Thomas organized a company called the Cahaba Coal Company way back yonder. Now, they opened up the number one mine right at the foot of the hill yonder, and pretty soon, people started moving in here to work the mine, but the settlement didn't have no name. They got a block of coal out of the mine and dressed it up and it weighed a ton, and they named the town Blocton, but I don't know what happened to the "k" in the spelling, but they left it out.

I've lived around Blocton here all my life, not right here in Blocton, but about four miles northeast of here in McCulleyhill. I was born in nineteen and five. I worked in the mines for forty-seven years, and in all that time, I never had a lost-time accident. Well, in Bibb County, all the mines was slope mines. The crop of coal would come out and you went down 'til you hit a basin and then it was flat. All around here is setting on a lake of water. Right down the hill here was where the first mine opened up—mine number one—and there's a stream of water coming out of there as square as that table there.

When I first started mining, you had what you called pick mining, then later on, they got machines in there and you didn't use no pick.

But pick mining was just that. You would take a pick and go at that face of coal, and when you got some out, you would take a shovel and load it on the small cars on a track and drag it on out. Yes, sir, when I first started mining in January of 1921, why that was all there was in this country here. Now, number nine was the last mine what was worked here, but it was all machine mining.

I got into the mines, I reckon, because my dad was there and my granddad got killed there in Helena number one, and my dad never saw his dad because my grandpa got killed thirty days before he was born. That was in March of 1881, and my dad was born in April.

I was fifteen years old when I started working in the mines. Fifteen years and four months old. My first paycheck was very small, I guarantee you that. I recall one time when I was in the mines, there was an explosion and that was the only time I remember being scared. The explosion was off another entry from where we was and the air system carried the smoke and fumes away from where we was at. Another time, in number two Piper, I set an eighteen-foot timber and the ladder broke with me and that big timber hit me cross the neck there. I thought it was broke, but it wasn't. I wasn't all the way up the ladder, see. Way we'd do is we'd stand the ladder against the timber that we'd done set, take the hammer and tack a capboard in the top of it, and get on the ladder and pull the timber up. There were a lot of men killed in the mines. My stepdaddy got killed in a mine, and for his life, my mother got $2,500 and that was paid by the union and not by the company. All those years I worked in the mine I never saw nobody get killed, but I've helped get them out who got bad hurt. Usually rock falls.

Pickett: In those days, there was no central heat and no air conditioning and the mines had their own heat and air conditioning. Coal miners loved coal mining and we are not as ignorant as we are supposed to be.

Collins: Back in those days, the company had houses for its miners. Cheap rent. Lights and water went with it. Back when I first started, the mine just paid off once a month, and if you had any money left in there, you got that in cash money. But you had the privilege of going to the office and getting what we called a check, and this could be spent only in the company store. They gave us scrip which was little coupons with various amounts on the coupon, and when you bought something at the company store, why, they just tore off enough scrip to pay for what it was you bought. It was hard to buy anything in Blocton unless you bought it at the company store.

The company had a store here, a big store, and it was complete. They had furniture. They had dry goods. They had, well, they had everything in there in this part of the country then in the way of groceries and meats and medicines. Of course, we always had a doctor. Now, we paid so much a month for the doctor whether we used him or not. If you had to use him, there was no charge.

At the Piper mine, they required you to trade in the store. I had a brother-in-law who moved from Blocton over there when the last mine here before number nine opened up during World War II. Truman Moore married my older sister and he got a job at Piper. Now, they was atrading up at Woodstock with Mr. McElroy, and they would deliver the groceries and everything. The superintendent in the mine, Percy Randall, called him in and told him that he would go to trading in the Piper store or else go to work for Mr. McElroy. Of course, he started trading at the Piper store. Mr. McElroy didn't need him. This was in 1930.

Pickett: We came back from West Virginia in 1932, moved back to Piper, and eggs were ten cents a dozen, pork chops were ten cents a pound. Why, you could take a dollar and buy a week's worth of groceries because everything was so cheap. Bread was a nickel for a small loaf and a dime for a large loaf.

We paid the company a dollar a month for medical care. I had to have surgery and stayed in the hospital for two weeks, and that dollar a month covered it. And that was your doctor bill and everything, and the doctor gave you most of your medicine, too. The company had a contract with, well, most of them down in here had a contract with South Highlands Hospital in Birmingham.

Collins: Around each mine, and there were five or six around in here, there was a settlement of company houses, and must have been 150 houses in each one of the settlements. Well, all of these houses were four-room frame houses with a front porch and the steps come up on the porch. Some of the houses didn't have back doors. When the power came in, all the houses had electricity and running water. We didn't have indoor plumbing 'cause we had a little house out back. The company had what they called ice cream wagons. They had buckets. At the back of the privies was an offset where they set those buckets. And these buckets had about a pint of creosote in it. And the colored people handled that for the company and they would come around every few days with that wagon and a team of mules and furnish you with fresh buckets. The indoor plumbing and all? Why the U.S. Steel was done gone from around here before that ever happened. That's the way it was, and everybody thought that was normal. The streets in front of these houses weren't paved and there were no sidewalks. It was slick and slime. Between the rows of houses, just dirt roads.

Fitts: I lived as close as that road out there from the mouth of the mine at Granddad's and I've seen my grandmother hang out clothes on the clothesline and they wouldn't be out there ten minutes and they would be covered with coal dust, and we didn't think anything about it. We lived right there at the mouth of the mine and we played in all those rock dumps.

Collins: Nobody had any cars. We just walked everywhere. We walked to the mines and in the mines and we walked to McCulley-hill. Now, on a Saturday night, and this was way back before Prohibition, we had what we called dispensers, and what that was was drinking dives. And that's when they done all the killing. Mostly beer joints and whiskey deals. We had open saloons here in Blocton and West Blocton and especially over in what we call Dago Holler now, but back then, they called it Little Italy.

Over in Dago Holler was a big settlement of Italians and Polish and all different kinds of people what was shipped in here by the company to break the strike. They didn't know anything when they shipped them in here. I don't know where they got them, but they came from Italy and France and Macedonia and England. And there were a lot of Polacks in that deal. Lots of them couldn't speak English. My dad started working in the mines in 1896 and he drove a mule and he said those foreigners would save their money. You would see American people lined up being garnished, but you would never see one of them in that line because they would save their money.

Well, they came in and built over there around that holler, and it was real rough over there with hills and rocks and those people made whiskey and they made wine . . . whoooo! Wasn't a house over there that you couldn't buy a drink. And they did that all through Prohibition and you could always get something to drink over there. Well, we got along with those people all right, and later on, they all joined the union and made some of the best union men you ever saw.

Pickett: In the forties here in Blocton it was a very religious town mostly, and when they would have a revival, all the stores would close for two hours so people could go to the revival. Everybody in the coal-mining community were very close. Every Christmas there would be a big community Christmas tree and the company would give money, and every family would give money, and every child in that town got exactly the same thing as far as price range goes. We were isolated out here and we had to stick together. There was a lot of love.

Collins: The man who opened up the bank here in Blocton opened up a picture show, too. This was around World War I and that first picture show was in a tent. The old-timers around here told me about that. Later on, the town burnt up, and this was in 1927, and there was a man, name of Mr. Tuggle, and he was here a lifetime, and he built a building for that picture show.

Fitts: When I was in school, I worked in the office over there at the mine company after school and on Saturdays and I got fifty cents an hour. That was real good back then. Then we moved over to Marvel and I went to work in the mine office over there and I was getting eighty-five cents an hour.

At the mine office at Black Diamond, they would pay every two weeks. They would pay in cash in little envelopes, and the miners would get a statement showing how much they had worked and everything, and how much was deducted. They got all this in those little brown enevelopes with their name on it and they would come by the window and pick them up. If a miner wanted to, he could get a check every day and some of them would come by every day and get a check for what he had made the day before. But then, if he wanted a regular payday, he had to wait two weeks. I wasn't in the union, working in the office, and they didn't have any retirement program for us.

Collins: As long as the company was here in Blocton, and they moved out in September of 1928, any kind of business you wanted to put up here—I don't mind what it was you wanted to sell—you could sell it. When all the mines were running, the most miners working at one time was in 1926 and there were 23,000 working. Now, in the Cahaba field at that time, there were about 2,000 miners working, and that's 2,000 families. Black Diamond come back here during World War II and opened up another mine.

I worked in the mines all the way through World War II. During the war, well, we had newcomers to the mines. They come from out in the country, way out in the country from different places like Johntown and they were farmers and sawmillers and people like that. I was out at the Hill Creek mines at that time.

I'm eighty-six now and been retired for twenty-three years. We had a world of stoppages during my time, a lot of strikes. They quit mining around here, but there's plenty of coal still in the ground, Lord have mercy. We've got one seam close by here that's about fourteen miles square that's never been touched. We got another one under that about the same area. There's a lot of coal in what we call the Cahaba field. There's enough coal right here in Blocton to last three hundred years of minings. We quit mining because the market went out on commercial coal. The railroads went on diesel, coal miners started using natural gas in their houses, so you see, even coal miners quit buying coal. Everybody just quit using coal.

The Straight and Narrow

Convict road gang, Jefferson County, 1935
(Arthur Rothstein/Farm Security Administration
photo, Library of Congress, Washington, D.C.)

Word Games

Tom Ogletree, Talladega County

Highway 280 used to be what was called the Florida short route. All the Yankees, when they were going to Florida, passed through Sylacauga, right through Alexander City and Dadeville. The Tallapoosa River separates Dadeville from Alex City. Now, back in the early fifties, a woman's body comes floating up in the river down there and nobody knew who she was and she couldn't be identified and they put her in the local funeral home for want of a morgue. She stayed there about sixty days because nobody knew who she was.

It developed that she was from New York and had bought a new Cadillac and had employed another lady as a companion. These two ladies headed south toward Florida, and somewhere along the way, the woman companion picked up a man. The two of them killed the old lady and threw her off the bridge there in Dadeville.

After lengthy extradition proceedings, they brought the woman companion back from Florida and put her in the Alex City jail. The jailer there was a little old man, seventy-plus, named Mr. Stowe. This was before implants for eye cataracts, and if you had cataracts, you had glasses about an inch thick, and he had some of those glasses. In the female part of the jail, they had this white companion and a bunch of blacks, and that's all they had in the women's part.

The prisoners then got two hamburgers for breakfast and two hamburgers for supper and that's all they got to eat. One morning, this jailer came in, and from where he stood, you could hear from both the male and female parts of the jail. Now, the woman companion called him over. He went over to where she was and she said, "The next time you go out, would you mind bringing me back a box of Kotex?" The jailer stepped back and said, "Hell, no. You'll eat hamburgers just like the rest of 'em."

Years ago up in Talladega County, there was a black lady up on the stand in court because she had witnessed a cutting out in front of her house in the street, and so the prosecuting attorney had led her through with the questions about how she had seen John Henry when he stabbed James Lewis out there, and she described what she had seen.

On cross-examination, she was asked if there was a streetlight out there. "Nawsuh, there wasn't no streetlight." The attorney asked her, "Well, was your front porch light on?" and she said that she didn't have a front porch light. So he asked her was there any other lights on the street in either direction, and she said, "Nawsuh, not that I remember." And he asked her what kind of light was there, and she said there was a kerosene lamp in the house.

And the lawyer drove home the point in a loud voice, "You mean to tell this court that there, by the light of a kerosene lamp in your house, you saw John Henry stab James Lewis out there in front of your house from twenty-five yards away at night?" And she says, "Yessuh." And the judge breaks in and asks her, "Well, how far can you see at night?" And she looks up and says, "Judge, I can see the moon. How far is that?"

I'll Take Hickory

E. L. Lovelady, Madison County

You know, I was always a mischievous kind of boy. I don't think I was mean, but I was always mischievous. I had to pull pranks on people and I'd get in trouble a whole lot. I'd get a lot of whippings and it seemed like I got one every day. They would cut a peach tree limb to work on me. You know, a peach tree limb hurts. They've got little knots all over them and when they hit those legs, it hurts. Sometimes, they used a limb off a hickory tree, and you know, hickory limbs don't wear out easy.

One time we were sitting at the table and nobody said anything for a good little bit and I crossed my eyes real good and I hollered out, "Oh, I've got my eyes hung and I can't get 'em back." It just liked to scared Mama to death. She jumped up from the table, you know, and I straightened them out. She looked at me and then, man, she liked to have beat me to death.

My brother and I worked together in the fields and the woods and slept together in the same bed. We fought just about every day, but that didn't mean we didn't love each other. When we would go to bed, he would stick a cold foot on me or I would stick one on him and we would get into it. Daddy would have to get up and tear us up good with a belt or a razor strop. He'd get us straightened out, you know.

Sometimes, Daddy would get so aggravated at us for carrying on such foolishness and punching each other he'd make us go out to the barn to the corncrib to shuck corn. Shucking corn would get us out of the house and doing something. Daddy was real scared of gopher rats, and we'd be out there in that crib shucking corn, and it would be real quiet for a while, and I would get an ear of corn and throw it under Daddy's feet and yell, "Look out! There's a rat!" and man, he'd just climb that pile of corn trying to get out of the way from that rat. Then, he would get rough with me.

A Different Set of Values

Bob Hodges, Jackson County

Back then, respect for authority went pretty much unchallenged, whether it was the police or the school principal or the teacher or the mom and dad. I don't remember any lawsuits filed by parents over teachers paddling children, or going to court over whether I had to cut my hair or not, and I can't remember any of us who threatened to take our parents to juvenile court for whipping us. We addressed the town policemen as Mr. Bryant and Mr. Swaim and Mr. Thomas, and we whispered in awe to each other when we happened to glimpse Old Judge Snodgrass on his way to the courtroom, tipping his hat to the ladies. Hellfire and damnation in those days was being told to go to the principal's office.

On the Road

J. L. Lowe, Jefferson County

In the early thirties, the Alabama State band went down to play at a Florida A & M dance after a football game. After the dance was over, we stopped at a restaurant on the highway to get some food. We were used to this, but we were told we couldn't come in, but they could hand it out the window. We accepted that, but then we were standing around out there and still didn't have any food. We couldn't understand it because there were fourteen of us and our money was the same green as anybody's. We waited a long time and decided to go and find another place, but we didn't cancel the order.

We got about fifteen miles away and the bus driver became sleepy and pulled off the side of the road. An open car pulled up with about six white men in there with rifles. They told the driver of the bus that he was parked illegally and they were going to have to arrest him. They took him a little ways from the bus, searched him, and found some bullets in his pocket. They asked him what those bullets were for and he told them he had a gun in the bus. We could hear this and realized it was illegal to have a gun. We knew that if they caught him with a gun, they might just kill him right there.

Somebody at the front of the bus grabbed that gun and started passing it back through the bus, passing it on back until it got to me. I was on the next to last seat and so I passed it on to the last man but he didn't want to take it. I argued with him, said that he was going to have to take it, so he took it. The men came back and said, "Where's that gun?" We pretended we didn't know anything about it. The men said that when they found that gun, they were going to kill all of us. This was when I thought about Scottsboro and those fellows waiting for trial up there. Then, they said, when we find that gun, we're going to get the guy who is sitting in the seat where it was. We got out of the bus, row by row, and we're standing out there with our arms up and I'm thinking about Scottsboro again. I looked at the man who was behind me and asked him, "What did you do with that gun?" He whispered, "I put it under your seat," and I almost had a heart attack.

They didn't find the gun but they took the driver on back to jail. We called the president of Alabama State, he arranged for the bus driver to get out of jail, and we came on home. We almost had another Scottsboro that night in Florida.

Inexorable Justice

William Bibb, Calhoun County

Being in a courtroom is essentially dull, and when something unusual happens, especially something funny, it really breaks up the proceedings. Before I got to be circuit court judge, I was in court one day, sitting there waiting for my case to come up, and Chandler Watson was defending a taxi driver on the charge of raping a high school girl. Her mother and father both worked and they had arranged with a particular taxi driver to go by and pick the girl up after school and bring her home. It was said that the taxi driver and the girl had gotten to prankin' around together.

One day, the taxi driver got too excited, or something, and he supposedly lacerated her. She and her mother and daddy were sitting there at the supper table and the girl seemed blue and dejected, and all of a sudden, she just fainted, fell out of the chair. Her mother picked up the girl, took her upstairs, and when she undressed her, she noticed all this blood. The girl told her mother that this taxi driver had raped her. They had the taxi driver prosecuted and indicted.

Clarence Williams was the district attorney at that time. Well, Chandler brought in about four boys from the high school to testify to the girl's bad reputation around there. There was one little old boy who had kind of short hair, and he kind of kept his head down between his shoulders, sort of like that, and kind of grinned all the time. Chandler asked him if he knew the girl, and the boy said he did, and Chandler asked him how long he had known the girl, and the boy said about four years.

Then Chandler asked him about the girl's reputation, was it good or bad, or what. Chandler said, "Do you know the girl's reputation for chastity and virtue around the school?" and the boy said he did and it was bad. Well the district attorney got up and sort of sneered at the boy through his mustache, you know, and said, "Chastity and virtue. You don't even know what a woman's chastity is, do you?" The boy looked him right in the eye and said, "I saw it!"

Another time, I had a young man over in Cleburne County, I guess he was about twenty-two. When you would call for excuses when a jury was called, it looked like everybody in the county wouldn't want to serve and they would line up quick right there in front of the bench. They all wanted to get off. This young man came up, sort of sandwiched in between two more mature people, and he got up and I said, "Well, what is your excuse?" The boy looked up at me and said that his wife was looking to become pregnant at any time. I sort of leaned back with a puzzled look on my face, and the man behind the boy said, "Your honor, what he means is that his wife is looking to be confined pretty soon." I said, well, in either case, I think he ought to be at home with his wife, and I excused him.

Over here in Calhoun one time, I had a young man, looked like he was about twenty-five, came up and asked to be excused. I said, "All right sir, what is your reason for wanting to be excused from this jury?" The man told me that it was personal. I said maybe it was personal, but I had to know it. The man said, "Judge, it's embarrassing." I told him I would still need to know the reason. "I've got the itch," the man said. Without a bat of an eye, I said, "Scratch that man, Mr. Clerk."

When I started practicing law back in 1937, things were pretty quiet on the crime scene in Anniston—bootlegging and burglary were the most common things that would come up. People knew their neighbors, would stand around and talk to each other. When I would walk down the sidewalk sometimes, going down to meet my father about 5:30 in the afternoon, and we started back home, people would be sitting on their porches, and sometimes neighbors would be sitting on your porch, you see. And, you would see people standing out in the yard, kind of leaning up against the bannister that held up the porch, but they would be talking and getting together.

When I was a young lawyer, the attitude was that the police were the guardians and protectors of property against all those roughnecks. It wasn't a question of upholding the law. It was a question of taking sides, taking sides with the property classes or the propertyless classes. The policemen belonged to the propertyless classes, but they took sides with the property classes. In other words, they looked after the people who furnished the money. Now the policemen back in those days, and I'm talking about in the thirties, were just raw old country boys right off the farm, and some of them were from town but their fathers were pipe-shop workers or cotton mill workers. Why, we had illiterate policemen when I first started practicing law back in the midthirties.

One policeman, I remember, carried a rubber slapjack as they called it, and he would go in those pipe shops looking for uppity black men. The black men had a definite place in the pipe shop and they would clean up. That was the thing they did. And they would pick up the made pipe with a set of tongs, and they would stack the pipe, and knock any drops of metal off the pipe with a sledgehammer. Then they would tar that pipe by dipping it in a vat and it was hot enough to make the tar smoke. Of course, working in there, they would have to inhale all that smoke. That was the place of the black man in the pipe shops back in the thirties, and at one time, we had nine pipe shops in Anniston. A shake-out foreman was about as high as a black man could go in those pipe shops.

This city detective would walk out to the pipe shop and walk up to this black man, and the black man would be working in rags, because the sand and drops of rough cast iron just shredded his clothes. He looked like he was wearing ribbons. His collar would be pretty good, not buttoned, but pretty sound, and his belt would be all right, but from there on down, his pants would be ribbons and his shoes would have holes in them. The detective would walk up to the black man and want to know where such-and-such was, and the black man in the pipe mill would say, "I don't know, boss. I don't know where he is," and the detective would hit him across the face with that slapjack—bam!—"Yes, you do," he would say. There was a white man who used to work in the pipe shop and he told me, "I've seen them hit those boys so hard that those hickeys would pop out on their faces on either side of that slapjack, and the hickeys would bust and blood would run down their cheeks."

That was the police work when I first got out of law school and came back to Anniston. The feeling in the black race, back then, was they would be killed if they objected to this kind of treatment, so they didn't object. A detective would go up to a black man's house and demand to get in, and the man inside would ask if he had a warrant, and the detective would kick in the door—blam!—don't need no warrant. Sort of a mutual fear, really, because the man was just as afraid of the black man as the black man was of him.

At the beginning of World War II, a woman who owned a home about a block away from where we lived had what you called a garage apartment and she rented this apartment to two WACs. One of them was white and one of them black. They moved in and somebody in our neighborhood called the chief of police and said there was a black woman living in our neighborhood, such and such address. The chief told the lady he couldn't do anything about that. It was the law. The woman said she was going to call the sheriff, and the sheriff told the woman he couldn't operate inside the city. She said she was going to call another fellow, who looked upon himself as the guardian of segregation in Calhoun County. That was not an uncommon attitude back in those days, before and during World War II.

A Bad Man

William W. Collins, Sr., Bibb County

When I first started in the mines, there were no unions. The first year the union come into Blocton was 1894 and U.S. Steel had bought up this whole country and they drove the union out. Stayed out until 1908 and then they come back. Well, U.S. Steel shipped a bunch of nonunion people in here, and right up the railroad here, people who live here shot into them and killed a bunch of them.

I been coming to Blocton with my dad since I wasn't quite five years old and there were two lawmen here, Henry Cole and Jack Brown. Henry Cole was the bad man. He killed thirty men here in Blocton. He was a deputy for the company. The last man he killed was a Nix. Now, Nix had been off of a weekend, drinking and gambling, and when he come in on Monday morning, his wife run out the door and come over to the company office. It was right down at the foot of the hill there, and she got Cole and they went back to the house in a horse and buggy. Cole carried a .38 Winchester rifle with him.

When Cole got up there and knocked on the door, Nix was sitting up there in front of the fire. Now, we had grates what held the coal for the fire, and Nix wouldn't get up to answer the door. All Cole did was back up a little and shoot through the door, and when he did, he killed Nix sitting up there in front of the fire.

They drafted Jack Brown into World War I and he made a captain. He lived through World War I and came back. I remember those two company lawmen back to 1910 and they ran the show for many years for the company. Everybody was scared of these two men, especially Cole. The sheriff or nobody else messed with them because they were company men, and the company ran this whole part of the country. The company owned everything and they ran it like they wanted to.

Hoover Days

Making chairs for tourists near
Birmingham, 1937
(Arthur Rothstein/Farm Security
Administration photo, Library of Congress,
Washington, D.C.)

On Being Flexible

Tom Ogletree, Talladega County

There are a million stories about how tough things were in the depression, and nowadays, young people have no idea about what people had to face back then. I was told about a young man who had finished at The University of Alabama and he had a teaching certificate, and needless to say, there were no jobs available and so he put in his application all over everywhere and interviewed across the school systems all over north Alabama. He went around like this for about a year and had absolutely no offers.

He finally heard of an opening down in Coosa County, one of our most rural counties, so he went down and the school board had him in for an interview. They interviewed him at length, and after some thirty minutes, one of the brethren on the school board said, "Well, sir, let me just ask you now, because I really want to know. Do you believe that the earth is round or is the earth flat?" The young man thought about all of those interviews all over north Alabama and all of those many years of schooling behind him and those hungry children at home, and he looked at the men of the board and said, "Gentlemen, I can teach it either way."

As Good as Anybody

Bill Dean, Escambia County

We were just riding down the road the other day from my daughter's graduation from Samford and I was talking about my daddy who ran his own business at Brewton down there in south Alabama. My daddy lost his business during the depression; they lost their home; they lost their automobile. I remember the day they came and pulled the car off our yard. Why they didn't jump it off and drive away, I don't know, but they pulled it off. I was just three years old but I remember that car being towed away.

I must have been about four and I was standing out beside the house one fine spring morning thinking, this is a beautiful day, the birds are singing, and I am going to remember this day even when I am an old man. And I could hear out there on Highway 31, which was a block away, sounds you could not hear today. I could hear a car coming down the highway, an old-model car, running on the rim. And this car was running on the rim off the side of the road, may have been two wheels this way, but one anyway, and as a little boy, I was listening to this sound and I thought I would remember that, too.

When I got through telling about this, I looked back in the rearview mirror to see how the kids were taking it, and they were smiling doubtfully because there was nothing in their experience that could compare with that.

There was the time back then that the big meal of the day was in the middle of the day, and when "dinner" was finished, the food would be left on the table and would be covered with a large cloth, and when you came back to eat supper, you uncovered the remains of the midday dinner. And usually, Mother didn't even warm up anything. You just sat there and ate it. My children asked, "You mean you just sat there and ate cold turnip greens?"

After my father lost his business, he started over again, taking a job with T. R. Miller Lumber Company at ten dollars a week. He fired the boilers and cleaned them out. When I was a little kid, my mother would call me and say, "It's seven o'clock and your daddy is blowing his whistle for you." That was always an intriguing thing because my dad did operate the boilers and the whistle blew at seven for the mill, but mother would say that he was blowing the whistle so we would know it was time to get up and go to school.

When the war years came on, my father still possessed the old Yankee philosophy of industriousness and ingenuity. He worked every day and sometimes would drag himself to work when most people would have stayed home sick. He walked in the house one time in the middle of the day and told my mother he had quit his job. Now, this was in the depression and you just didn't quit a job. My mother just stood there with her mouth open in amazement. He told my mother that there was just no future in what he was doing. He went down to where they were building a new air force base in

Milton, Florida, and they asked what job he was applying for. He told them whatever they were paying the most for. They told him "pipefitting," so he took the test and they employed him.

In 1937, my parents took out the first FHA loan and built a new house, and my father was paying the payments from the ten dollars-a-week salary. He didn't own a car from 1933 until 1941. We walked everywhere we went. We traded with the Cedar Creek Mercantile Store and they sold everything and then delivered it to your house. We walked to church, and if it rained, we either didn't go or broke out our umbrellas. Occasionally, for entertainment, we walked to the picture show to see the old Saturday matinees. For ten cents, the folks had an all-day baby sitter. See the movie a couple of times and the serial a couple of times and several times on the cartoons. I looked forward to the serial at the movies as much as the feature cowboy films.

We thought that poor people were the other folks in town. Having little money had a strong effect on my parents, though. The saving and accumulation of money became their way of life. Having little money had a different effect on me, however. My parents, for example, like in the Sears and Roebuck catalog, they had a good, better, and best, and they always bought the "good." I can concur with that, but I thought that every kid ought to get something every once in a while that doesn't make sense. I didn't feel deprived, really, but there were a few haunting moments. There was a time when I wanted a pair of cap pistols for Christmas and I looked in the Sears and Roebuck catalog, and the ones I really wanted were the Roy Rogers brand. These pistols were the nicest and the fanciest ones and they were the "best" on the page. But I didn't get those. I got the "good."

On Christmas Day, I was out in the yard and I had an English walnut, which was always part of Christmas, and I'm trying to crack that walnut. Now, walnuts were scarce and you hardly saw them except at Christmas. I took the little pistol and used it for a hammer to crack the walnut, and the pistol breaks, right in the bend where it comes up behind the hammer. I cried and cried and my little heart almost broke. I thought that if I had gotten the Roy Rogers model, it wouldn't have broken.

I had two pairs of pants in the first grade. One of them was blue serge and they were made from one of my father's old suits which had come from back in the twenties. My mother had made a pair of trousers and they looked just like factory made. I wore these pants to school in the morning with a white shirt, and when I came home in the afternoon, I had a pair of khakis I changed to.

Now, my mother had come from old Monroeville from a fairly aristocratic family over there. Her father was murdered while running for public office. See, this sounds a little snobbish, but you didn't wear overalls to school. That's what country folks wore and we wanted to look better than that. When I got home from school, I would pull off the serge pants, put on the khakis, and that's what I would play in. Then, my mother would take those blue serge pants and put them on an ironing board. Then she would take a damp cloth and literally wipe the dust and dirt off those pants before pressing them, hanging them up, and I would put them on again the next morning.

When my father died in 1977, we found an old yellow ledger left over from the time when he lost his business back in 1933, and it showed a long list of accounts receivable. This list showed all the money owed to him by people in Brewton who were well-to-do but never paid him. I told my mother to throw the ledger away. It's over and done. When the depression hit, there was just no money. But some of those families recouped swiftly, but they never did pay what they owed before the crash.

When I was growing up in Brewton, there were just about as many millionaires per capita as any place in the country. I played with the millionaires' kids all my growing-up years, but never felt intimidated by them, never felt that their house was more palatial or that they had more than I did, and I guess it was the way I was brought up. My parents would always tell me, "You're just as good as anybody, but you are no better."

A Stop in Big Swamp

Rob Maulsby, Lee County

Opelika was formed by two railroads crossing and became the county seat. To me, Opelika was a beautiful town when I was a boy. Originally, the town grew up on both sides of the track. Before Prohibition, there were saloons on both sides of the track and people would get drunk on Saturday nights and stage small battles across the street. When the train would come through sometimes, people in the coaches would have to hunker down under the windows to keep from getting shot as the train passed through town. The first two streets in town were on either side of the tracks, North Railroad and South Railroad, and then cross streets were added. Around the courthouse there were hardware stores and three hotels, but the old Clement Hotel was the big draw. Opelika means "big swamp" in Indian talk, and if you dig down, you can see evidence of this.

The depression hit Opelika just as bad as anywhere, but as a boy, it didn't affect me too much. We lived a few blocks from the railroad and I can remember hoboes would get off the train there in town and fan out through the neighborhoods looking for handouts. After the train came through, you could just look for them coming down the street and going up to houses looking for something to eat. Sometimes they would offer to work, but mostly they were just looking for a handout.

When they would get a little something to eat from some housewife, they would go off in the woods out behind the house and sometimes they would spend the night out in those woods. The next morning, they would make the rounds again and drift on back to the depot to wait for the next train passing through. They didn't stay too long because there was nothing there to keep them, very little food and no work at all. Put a little food in the belly and keep on moving to the next stop, making the rounds in the next town.

Turn the Bear Aloose

Cullman Powell, Walker County

My daddy was a contract miner back during the tough times and he had this bunch of men working for him. Some of them were Negroes. One day, Daddy was setting on his porch and one of these black men came by, name of Coleman, and walked up to the porch where Daddy was. Coleman said, "Mr. Powell, I'se come over here to see if I can borrow some lard." Daddy told him he didn't have any lard, that he was in as bad a shape as anybody, and didn't have any lard in the house. Coleman said he just had to have some lard, and Daddy asked him why. Said he could get by without lard. Coleman said, "But Mr. Powell, I want some fried taters so bad, I just been wanting some so bad I had my wife fry some taters the other night in water." Daddy asked Coleman how they tasted. "Like biled taters," Coleman said.

We didn't have any store-bought toys except what my granddaddy would give us every once in a while, and me and my brothers, we made all of our own. We would go out in the woods and find a blackgum tree about twelve inches in diameter, real round, and the reason we would get blackgum is because you can't split it, you can't bust a blackgum. We would saw that tree down and saw off sections of the trunk about two inches thick. We would go home and mark off the center of that round section. We didn't have any way to drill holes in the section so we would take a poker and heat it up in the fireplace and run out in the yard and stick it in the center of that section. Then, we would go back and do it again until we had a hole in that wood. We would take a hickory pole about two or three foot long and hew it down to make a spindle and we would fit those wheels on that spindle. We made the bed on there and a way to guide it. When you came down the mountain in that homemade wood wagon, it made a noise like wood against wood, no rattle at all.

We would use those little wagons to go get coal, too. We never bought coal because we couldn't afford it, so we would go up to the mine and pick up the loose coal after the miners had done got it out and load it in those wagons and tug it home. Every afternoon after school, all the boys would go up to the mines and bring coal home. We used coal for everything—cooking and heating, and everybody used it. You could come up around the side of the hill and down in the valley from Oakman and it would be real still and would be like a big cloud covering the whole valley, that smoke cloud just sitting there.

When the polio epidemic hit Coal Valley right there in the middle of the depression, they came out with this solution that was real yellow and you had to buy that with an atomizer. That atomizer was a chromium thing that screwed up under the bulb and you had to squirt yourself every morning. They told you to give a squirt of that yellow stuff in each child's nose every day, and every kid you saw had two little yellow streaks down under his nose. We were forbidden to play with children who didn't have these little yellow streaks, and Mama would say, "Don't you play with no children who don't have no yellow under their nose."

About that time, a carnival had come into the valley, one of these little old street carnivals. They got quarantined on account of the polio epidemic and couldn't leave. They had an old bear in that carnival and they had a ring like a prize-fight ring out there and they advertised that anybody who could stay in the ring with that bear so many minutes could win a quarter. We had this guy, I won't call his name, but he was so ugly—that was the ugliest guy what ever was— he was so ugly, in fact, that he couldn't get in the navy because of that. They put the reason they turned him down on his rejection papers was "extreme ugliness." He was going to fight this old bear for a quarter. Well, they advertised it pretty big, and since nobody could get out of the valley because of the quarantine, everybody gathered up to see this old ugly boy fight the bear.

They got both of them in the ring, and the announcer made a big deal out of introducing the boy and the bear, and this old ugly boy was standing up there in the ring beating on his chest. The crowd was yelling, "Turn the bear aloose! Turn him loose!" The old bear reared up and come over there and grabbed this old ugly boy, got him down, and just wet on him from one end to the other. Boy, that was funny. I mean to tell you it was funny. That might be the same bear that Paul Bryant rassled because it was in the same year.

Back in the depression up there in Coal Valley, people didn't have a lot of spare goods, and sometimes when you went to see somebody and sat down for a meal, a lot of times, you would have some unusual eating equipment. We ate off bucket lids. A lard bucket back then was a nice possession around home and you couldn't get many because people raised their own lard, but when you got a lard bucket, it was guarded. Eating off a lard lid really wasn't a bad idea because it had a little rim around it, just ideal for butterbeans. Our generation of people picked themselves up by their bootstraps after the depression and we never had a bit of government help.

Native Americans

Jeff Coleman, Sumter County

Champ Pickens was a native of Livingston and was the one that started the Blue/Gray football game, you know, and he was a real promoter. The Indians had what they called a stickball game, and back in the thirties during the depression, Champ conceived the idea of taking those Indians to Washington and putting on an exhibition of stickball. He had influence with the railroad, so he got a special Pullman car and took a carload of Indians up to Washington. They had planned to stay just a few days doing exhibitions.

Well, he didn't make much money out of these exhibitions and didn't have enough to get the Indians back to Alabama. The railroad had all those Indians out there in that Pullman car and they were feeding them and they wanted mighty bad to get rid of them. The only trouble was that Champ didn't have enough money to pay their way home. Finally, the railroad figured it would be cheaper to send them home than to keep them up there in Washington and feed them, so that's what they did. They gave them a free ride to Alabama.

Send Us a Man

Denson Franklin, Jefferson County

I entered Birmingham-Southern in 1932. My father was an optimist in that he thought that the depression wouldn't last long. He had accumulated a lot of land which didn't turn out to be worth much and he was in the stock market pretty good, figuring the current problem was just temporary. So, when I went to college, he could help me some, and I helped myself. In 1933, I took a church when I was nineteen years old. This was a little white frame church out toward Bessemer. They couldn't afford a full-time minister so they settled for a student. My salary was $467 a year. That was a pretty good salary because you could buy a lunch at Birmingham-Southern for ten cents—five cents for a hot dog and five cents for a Coca-Cola.

That first Sunday in that little church in November of 1933, a Mr. Martin introduced me and said, "We asked the college to send us a man, but they sent us a boy, but he's going to do, I think." He presented a big railroad watch to me, and said very pointedly, "Nobody has ever been saved after twelve o'clock in this church and we just want you to know that."

That same day, a man came up and said he wanted to talk to me after the service. We went back in a clump of trees by the church and he said, "Now preacher, I was a deputy on the mountain for the steel company, making good money and feeding my family. I haven't worked in two years and I am broke and my family is close to coming apart. My insurance is coming due and I have been thinking about doing something. I have a good gun which I had as a deputy and I've been thinking about putting that gun to my head and killing myself." I asked him about the insurance, and he said that there was no problem with that. Other men had done the same thing to save their families. He said his family could live a long time on the insurance and he didn't feel he could make a living for them any more in this economy. I was young and I didn't have any experience and I told him that, but I understood his problem because my family was having some problems, too. I told him I believed God would do what we asked him to do. I told him that if he was willing, we would just hold hands and pray about it. We prayed and he promised not to do anything until he came back to church the next Sunday.

Next Sunday, he and I went back to that clump of trees after everybody else had gone, and he was smiling. He told me that Mr. Martin had come to him during the week and told him about a store he had. The store had a house beside it with a good well of water, electric lights, a fireplace and a stove, and plenty of food in the kitchen. He said Mr. Martin asked him to run the store and take anything out of it he needed. He told me that he accepted the offer and had put his gun away. I never will forget that incident which happened over forty-five years ago, my first week of preaching.

Those were bad days, back in the depression. As bad as it was, we couldn't believe that people were eating clay until a sociology professor carried a class out to a mountain nearby. We drove out in cars, then walked a short distance and saw people come with those shiny syrup buckets and fill them up with clay. We asked them what they were going to do with the clay and they said they were going to eat it. It came out that they had some food, but the clay would keep the stomach from hurting. The clay had body to it and helped fill them up, they said.

When I finished Birmingham-Southern, there was no money available in the family because the depression was in full swing. I had a double major, history and theology. I loved history and that looked like the direction I was headed. When I graduated, my professor came to me and said that he knew that I had financial problems which I was not used to, and he knew I wanted to go on to school. He told me he had a scholarship available for Vanderbilt. In those days, you could work on your Ph.D. while teaching as a student. At that time, Lottie Mae and I were married, the only married students at Birmingham-Southern, and the professor told me that it would be enough to live on.

It was a big Ph.D. opportunity and I would probably get a job teaching full-time at Vanderbilt later on. I told the professor I would have to think about it, and after talking to my wife, my idea was that I could get my Ph.D. and go right into the conference as a minister.

Lottie Mae told me that if I did go to Vanderbilt, I would never go into the ministry. She suggested that we go ahead and take a little church and sacrifice all we had to. We did take a little church in a mining district that paid eight hundred dollars a year and furnished a parsonage.

They had put in new wallpaper in that little house before we moved in. Just after we had gotten settled, a big rain came. I looked up and saw that wallpaper drop way down from the ceiling and we knew that the roof was leaking and coming down on that wallpaper, making a big bulge, a big water bulge. Lottie Mae told me to run get a tub and punch a hole in the wallpaper so the water would go in one place. All night, I could hear that water dripping into the tub, clink-clink-clink.

I learned more things about people in that Lipscomb camp than any other place I've been. This was still in the thirties and things were very hard and violence was the norm out in the mills. We did find some of the finest people in the world out there, but there were some disturbed people, too, because many of them hadn't worked in a long time.

I had a double-entrance church, and at one entrance, a union man would give out bulletins, and at the other entrance, a nonunion man would pass them out. These two sides just didn't like to associate with each other. One man wanted me to go study in the Holy Land and he raised money for me to go to Jerusalem to study for four months. Lottie Mae kept the church and the baby, and while I was over there, World War II broke out, and sometimes I didn't know if I would get home or not. My tickets were on German ships and I was very concerned, but I finally got back.

After that first postgraduate study after college, I entered Union Theological Seminary in New York and attended that school for the next twenty-three years during the summer. We did without a lot of things for me to do this, but we made it.

It Helps to Smile

C. J. Coley, Tallapoosa County

There were some tough times during the depression, but it was not as bad in Alexander City as it was in some other towns. When I got married in 1932, we went on our honeymoon to Miami, and then went on over to Cuba. In Miami, we stayed at a hotel called the Commodore, and this was at the bottom of the depression. I think we stayed on the seventh floor. We were registered and received and there seemed to be nobody in the hotel but us. I called the bellboy to bring us up some ice water and the person who brought up the ice water was the same clerk who had registered us in. We went on to Cuba and found the same bad economic conditions down there.

There was some humor going around, even during those dark days. One fellow went in to see the doctor with a broken arm. When the doctor asked him how it had happened, the man said it had happened while he was eating breakfast. The doctor was a little skeptical about the man breaking his arm eating breakfast and asked him for the details. The man said, "Well doc, I fell out of a persimmon tree."

During the depression, the WPA was set up to give jobs to the unemployed. One of the projects was a new airport for Alexander City, and the land they picked out for the airport was very hilly and covered with rocks. Somebody asked one of the workers how the work at the airport was coming along. The worker replied, "Well, we just about have the airport in condition for a plane to fly over it."

One day, three unemployed men were sitting on the curb in downtown Alexander City and moaning about the bad economic conditions. Finally, one of the men said, "If things get any worse, I can always go back to preaching. I used to be a preacher, and I am not a damn bit too good to go back to it again."

A Dollar and Beans

Icese Thomas, Jefferson County

When I was a boy back in the thirties, times were bad and segregation was bad, and looking back on it now, my family had a rough time. My daddy was a preacher, see, and a carpenter, but there wasn't any work for a carpenter so he spent his time as a preacher. I remember, he would go around preaching, and sometimes he would be gone a whole week and just come back with maybe three or four dollars. My mama died in 1936 and that left my daddy to try to take care of us children, four boys and a girl. We didn't have any money to pay the rent and had to move around a lot. Back then, people would let you live in a house for nothing to keep it from being burned up. People would see an empty house and strip it for firewood. Why, somebody would move out of a house one day, and by tomorrow, the house would be all burned up. But we still had to move a lot because we couldn't pay the rent.

I remember one time, back in 1936, and I was about six years old and walking home one day out there in Woodlawn. I had on a hat because most people wore hats back then, and I was just walking on that sidewalk minding my business and this white man and his wife were walking toward me. When I got down to where they were at, that man told me, he said, "Nigger, pull that hat off. Don't you see a white man and a white lady walking by here?" And so, I just looked at him, and he said, "Didn't you hear me?" and so I got out in the street. It made me so hot I grabbed a brick and throwed it at him. Boy, I had to pick 'em up and go, then.

My daddy was scared to death most of the time back in those days what with the Ku Klux Klan being so bad. One time, we were living over there just off Georgia Road and I must have been about seven because I was in the first grade. One day, the Ku Klux Klan came up in about four or five of those big black cars, came up there and parked on a kind of a hill across the alley from where we lived. They all got out of those cars and they were all dressed up in those robes and hoods and went up to that house across the alley and knocked on the door.

Now, all us kids were hunkered down, peeking out the windows to see what was going on and my daddy was trying to pull us away from the windows so we couldn't see. All those men went up to this house and knocked on the door. I heard 'em calling out to the man, "Didn't we tell you not to do that again?" and the man was hollering and crying and begging them not to hurt him. They dragged that man out and tied him to an old dead tree right out there in the middle of that alley and they beat him until he died. That man was dead, lying out there tied to that tree, and when they quit beating him, they looked all around and one of the men said, "Do you think anybody's watching us?" and another one looked around and said, "Naw, I think all of 'ems asleep."

They stood around a minute and I heard one of 'em say, "What we goin' to do with this nigger's body?" One of 'em said, "Well, let's take him up to that railroad track there," and that railroad track was pretty close to us. They untied that man from the tree and carried him up and laid him across that railroad track. See, the train would run over him and everybody would say he got run over by a train and that's how he died. My daddy, now, he wasn't going to tell nobody because he was a scaredy type of man. He was scared of white people. He would tell us all the time to be quiet and he put more fear into us than the white people would. He would say, "I didn't get this old by being a fool," so we never did tell anybody what we had seen out there in that alley.

After my mother died, my daddy and my oldest brothers did the cooking. For awhile there, the Red Cross helped us and got us by, but they quit giving us food and about all we had to eat was what daddy grew in the garden—sweet potatoes and corn and stuff like that. To get some extra money, my daddy would work for white people in their yards. Many times, he would go out and work all day and he would come home with a jar of butterbeans left over from the man's dinner, and they would give him a dollar for a day's work. He never could accumulate any money and that was the reason we had to keep moving—couldn't ever pay the rent.

Later on, he married a lady, my stepmother, and she was real good to us. She worked for white people in their houses and she was washing and ironing their clothes at our house. I would hear her talking and she would work for the white people all day, and sometimes into the night, and they would do her the same way, give her a dollar and whatever was left over in the kitchen and sometimes some old clothes. When she came home, she would bring a big bundle of clothes to wash and iron and take back the next day. She had this big old black iron pot out in the back to wash the clothes in and us kids would go up and down the alley picking up wood to bring back to put around that pot for the fire. She would wash those clothes and iron them at night, late at night, and the next day she would take them back. Sometimes she had as many as five bundles of clothes to take back the next day and us kids would have to be late for school to help her. The white people would pay her fifty cents a bundle to wash and iron those clothes, and there were a lot of clothes in each one of those bundles.

The Royster Boy

Bud Dean, Elmore County

I was born in what they call the Friendship community and moved here to the Union community in '28. We moved in a T-model truck with the spoke wheels, of course. It was a one-ton truck—the biggest one they made back then—and it had a twenty-two-horsepower engine, and don't ever let nobody question that. Some call it a Model T, but if you want to know if a man is real in these parts, he'll call it a T-model. It was bought in 1926 for $395, brand spankin' new out of the Ford place in Tallassee. When we moved in this house we had to eat parched peanuts for dinner because we had the wood stove tore down. There were eight of us children and I was sixth in line.

Back in Hoover days, we lived off the land. Even the schoolteachers in these parts were not getting paid. The county had no money, there was no tax base, there were no federal funds; there just wasn't any money. Cotton, you couldn't sell it. You would stand it up on end out there with boards under it and it was going for five cents a pound. We lived off the land and we survived—farming—eight children and Mama and Daddy. My daddy was born in October of 1886, a vintage year because that year there was Sears Roebuck, Coca-Cola, Mercedes Benz, and then there was Papa. The week he was born, the Statue of Liberty was dedicated, so when freedom ended, freedom began, if you can follow that tongue twister. That's a Bud Dean original, as far as I know.

But back to these hills here, this was Indian country, you know that. There were a lot of arrowheads on this place here and I carried many a one to school and give to teachers and this and that. Mama was born in 1892 and it will soon be eighty years since they were married, and that was in 1911, right up here at the old McRae place, and McRae was the justice of peace. House is still standing. All the children were born at home, of course. They had a little infirmary in Tallassee which is a dwelling now, and then they built a wood hospital, then a brick hospital, and now they got a new hospital.

Now, I went to school six years and walked three miles round-trip. We would cut our own wood, and I'm talking about '32, and had no electricity. We got water from Mr. Jack Hale's house across the road. Now, I'm not bragging and my name's not Jeremiah, but on the last day of school, we'd have a spelling bee. So we had to study right up to the last day and then we would have a picnic. Not only did we get the three fundamentals—and you know them—but we got a bonus and that was respect, and a bonus to that—appreciation. We got more in value in virtues out of that depression than all the commodities and food stamps that will ever be printed. We have traded morality for materialism and the churches are following that trend.

My people helped found Bethlehem Baptist Church in July of 1844, right up here, and that was on my daddy's side. My mama's people started the Tallassee Church in 1852. If you know where you've been, you ought to know where you are, and have some idea where you're going. That's history for you.

People believed in discipline back then, at school and at home. My daddy was very low key, quiet, kindly spoken, but firm as Gibraltar, and I've seen Gibraltar, and it doesn't look like the Prudential ads. From the early-on inception, like from the diaper stage, we minded our daddy and we never, never sassed him. That razor strop would come out if you would sneak off and go washing after work or you did something like that, but you never sassed him. I reckon the best day's work he ever did was when he would whup us, he would give us a good one, and he would say "This hurts me more than it hurts you."

Hog-killing time was always a big thing when I was a boy. We would be working up to midnight making sausage in that hand-grinder. We just lived off the land but we wasn't as bad off as some. Old man Bill Reed out here had this big old steer named Tom, and he weighed about sixteen hundred pounds they learned later when they sold him, and old man Reed didn't even have a mailbox. Neither he or his wife could read or write, but there were no finer people who lived on this earth. They lived on a rock pile. It was so rocky they had to strow the cottonseed by hand because it was too rough to use a planter. T-model Fords? They parked 'em all through this country because nobody could afford them. Tags was cheap, and drivers' licenses were fifty cents apiece, and Tallassee didn't have a red light. All the roads were dirt.

We was raised in the church, up here in Bethlehem. When my daddy was a boy, it was a log church with wood-shutter windows and a fireplace. In wintertime, they wouldn't have Sunday school because they would have to close those wood shutters and it would be sort of dark. They had little shelves on each side where they had little brass lanterns, but they didn't give enough light to read by. The first Sunday in May is still the biggest day in the church. That's where we have homecoming and it is one of the biggest ones in Elmore County. Then, when I was coming on, the revival in the summertime was a big time, but it isn't anymore.

In the old days, the church was a social place as well as a worship place. Then, the schools were big social places, too. You would put on all kinds of plays. The grown folks would put on plays and have pound suppers, trying to make up money for the schools. Pound suppers was when a family would fix up a shoe box full of food, and it would be clean and healthy like fried chicken and your fried apple pies and your hot biscuits and whatnot, and then they would have politicians at election time and beauty contests and other little activities. You did all this to try to hustle a little money for the school for stuff like pencil sharpeners or erasers, because the county just didn't have money for extras. Everybody would come to these pound suppers, everybody that could make it, and they would come for miles.

Before I got in service, I had never been nowheres, hardly. Well, I had been to Montgomery once a year. This was part of our social studies at school. This was a big day, the day we went to Montgomery. Coca-Cola would give you all the Coca-Cola you could drink and these old country boys were just like a Sahara camel. It was a wonder some of 'em hadn't got sick they drank so many Coca-Colas. No water that day.

Talking about farming, it was so rocky out here, we'd have to use a big old Scobie hoe. We chopped cotton and then we would hoe it and then we would bunch it. In my daddy's time, he chopped corn. We chopped peanuts, and now there is not a hoe put into a field. A Scobie hoe would have a big homemade handle on it. We would soak it at dinner time so it would swell. Heavy. It took a heavy hoe. Now, using a little light gooseneck hoe in sandy soil would be a pleasure. A mean old country boy around these parts—this is rocky country and a lot of hard clay soil, too—their view of heaven would be working sandy soil with a gooseneck hoe, and that's about the truth. For fertilizer, we used guano. But in 1933, there was no money and there was eight or ten of us at home and we didn't use a dust of fertilizer. We didn't make much, either, but we still survived.

When we did have fertilizer, you put it out with an old distributor. You drilled it in the row. Some did, and some would have a little sack over his shoulder with a funnel with a long extension, and we called that a guano horn, and that was work. Very tedious work, and tough, because that guano was chemical and you would sweat and it would kind of mix up.

To supplement our diet during hard times, and there were some droughts when we didn't make much, we would do a good bit of fishing with hand-knit nets and trotlines. You had to have food. We ate a lot of rabbits and squirrels, but I never would eat possum, but a lot of people would. I tried possum, but the more you chewed it, the bigger it got. Some people would eat coons. You would make hash out of coons. We'd eat birds, too, and we would use traps for the birds. Mama put up a lot of food for the wintertime in mason jars. We would shell peas here until way on in the night.

Mama used that old wood stove. My daddy remembered when they got their first cook stove secondhand from old man Woodall. Grandma Dean cooked on a fireplace. Yeah, we canned everything that would go in a jar and we dried a lot of peaches, figs, apples, and even dried pears. Now, this is interesting. There were ten of us in the family and we all sat down together, all ten of us, three times a day to eat. All the little fellows sat on a long bench on one side, and of course Mama and Papa on the other side. It wasn't like the military, but when the dinner bell rang, you wrenched your hands off, you sat down, and took your dinner, three times a day. Sometimes it wouldn't be much on the table, just corn bread and peas, not any of this seven-course stuff. Even so, my daddy lived to be a hundred on that kind of diet, and the only reason Papa died was the oldest boy had a stroke and died, and Papa just give up. He quit eating is what he done. He remained totally rational until his last breath and blink of an eye. Now, Mama died at eighty-five. She had arthritis and took to the bed, and when you take to the bed, you are gone.

When we were able to have fertilizer, we bought the F. S. Royster, and Mama would make us clothes out of those fertilizer sacks. She would try to dye them, but that black Royster would come through. At school, there were a bunch of kids at school that would make fun of us and they would say, "There's that Royster boy," and I didn't take a fancy to it. There were some other Royster boys, but there were some who wore store-bought or shirts made out of store-bought cloth. I never did fight over being called a Royster boy, but some would fight on principle. There was a man who killed another man for calling him an s.o.b., just that simple. That same man done time, a long time, because the court said that was no reason to kill somebody. He was a real hill man, and he said if anybody ever called him that again, he would do the same, and I think he would have.

Baseball was a big thing in those days. We played in cow pastures. There were a good many ball fields where they played pretty good baseball. During the depression, you would strive to have a glove, but I remember high school football games when the town boys would play a rural school, the players on the rural schools wouldn't even have uniforms. Some of them didn't even have shoes on.

During the depression, there was no money, and the mills all but shut down. My daddy had a sister, Aunt Fanny, and she had five children. Her and Uncle Paul—fine, upright people—they were both working, and the mill just let them go because they didn't have any seniority. They got down to starvation and we shared our rations with them. They moved into a little house that wasn't fit for a hay shed where colored people had lived, seven of them. Aunt Fanny would chew up black-eyed peas and give them to her baby. She would take three fingers from her mouth and put it into his. That was baby food. It didn't look very sanitary.

When I was a boy, we had dug three wells here, but none of 'em was no good, so we toted our water, family of ten. We toted from two springs, one about a good quarter of a mile that way, and the other a good quarter of a mile the other way. We toted every drop of water we used, cooking, canning, bathing, cattle, and everything. Little fellows would tote that water in gallon lard buckets.

One time I had the toothache and Mama said, "Make haste. Run down to the spring and wrench off." My brother Clayton had an old T-model Ford he picked up somewhere, paid nine dollars for it, and it was running but didn't have no tag on it. Mama told me that when I had wrenched off, Clayton would take me to Dr. Lang and he would pull that tooth. Dr. Lang practiced dentistry sixty-something years here, I think. He was just as filthy and dirty as he could be, but I never knew anybody who died of blood poisoning. He snatched that tooth out for fifty cents. I don't know where we got the money.

Mr. Ransome Powell had an old Chevrolet with spoke wheels. He tacked some kind of cattle body on there and called it a school bus. He ran a long route, started up there at Red Hill and picked up all the tenth, eleventh, and twelfth graders. The rest of them walked to school. The bus had a cover on it. Fellow Nichols up at Eclectic built it. Once, a wheel run off that old bus, and another time it wouldn't crank and my daddy took his old truck and hauled the children to school.

During the Hoover days, Papa would get busy and cut up stove wood to take into Tallassee. You could always sell a little firewood or stove wood in town. There were people who worked in the mill that drew next to nothing in money. They lived out of the company store, and if you sold them wood, they would give you a ticket to use at the company store. You bought what they sold—period.

The CCC on Cheaha

Vern Scott, Talladega County

After Herbert Hoover started the Civilian Conservation Corps, Congress provided some pretty good money, and we had two camps in the county, one out between here and Ashland, and one up on Cheaha Mountain. Over the years, the trees had been cut off Cheaha Mountain and never one planted back, and with the trees gone, erosion increased and the topsoil washed away and wildlife on the mountain was about gone: squirrels and rabbits and everything else. I was working for the picture show then and I would go up on Cheaha Mountain taking advertising so I saw what was happening.

One of the first things I noticed was that they were cutting down all the undergrowth, little old bushes and all, and then they went along the side of that mountain, those boys, and chopped up those bushes and made little sticks about that long. Then, some other boys would drive these little sticks in the ground and leave them sticking up about that high, and they would make a line of those stakes all around the side of that mountain, and four feet up from that line, they would make another line of stakes. They didn't know why they were driving those stobs in the ground. Well, after a couple of months, a little pine straw and some leaves would wash down on those stobs, and instead of washing on down the valley, they would stick on those stobs and made little rainbows of trash around there. Within about three months, those rainbows touched and the topsoil began to build up, and when they got all that done, they started planting trees.

In 1936, everybody knew war was coming. Roosevelt wanted a two-ocean navy but Congress wouldn't give him the money, and all of a sudden, the CCC boys started building flat spots on the side of the mountain. Nobody knew why. Then, they started building roads from Fort McClellan down to the airfield at Montgomery. Nobody knew why. Everybody thought they were just giving the boys something to do. That was in '36. The surveyors fell in here and they were surveying all over the place, and people wondered about that. Word got out that they were building a cement plant out at Leeds and they said the surveying was for that. What they were doing was building spots for antiaircraft guns to protect Fort McClellan from air raids because we didn't have a two-ocean navy.

Recreatin'

Wilson's Red Hots, a
Mobile jazz band, 1924
(University of South
Alabama Archives, Mobile)

Auburn Knights play at
the Dallas Street Armory,
Huntsville, circa 1940
(Huntsville Public Library)

Fun on the Mountain

Olene Latimer, Marshall County

Our social life up on the mountain was going to church on Sundays and going to protracted meetings. Many times we would have dinner on the ground at church. We would eat dinner and then we would have preaching, and after that, we would have singing and maybe some more preaching. I would always go to sleep when the preaching started. The dinner was the highlight and I remember that my mama would bring a big trunkful of food. We would load that trunkful of food on the wagon, and there were cakes and pies, peaches, fried chicken, and corn bread, because we didn't think you could eat beans without corn bread. We went to everybody's table to pick out what we thought was the best-looking piece of chocolate pie or cake or coconut pie. I've seen Mama cook when every thread on her dress was wet with perspiration.

We would always go to Decoration on the fourth Sunday in May, and that was a big day. We decorated the graves where everybody was buried, and what we did was put fresh flowers on the graves because we didn't have money to buy artificial flowers. The only artificial flowers I saw were the ones people would make out of crepe paper and sell. That day, we usually had organdy dresses with piqué ruffles, and Mama would send the material to town by Papa, and they would make the piqué for ruffles that would come all the way down and across the shoulders to make a sash. We would have new shoes, white or black patent leather, and we wore that dress regardless of the temperature.

One time, we went to church over at Tin Top in the wagon. That was about five or six miles from our house. On the way back, I was asleep, and my daddy stopped by the side of the road where somebody had made ice cream, knowing that people coming from the church would buy it from them. I slept all through it, and when we got home and they woke me up to take me in the house, my sister told me about the ice cream and how good it was. She said, "Olene, it was in what they called a cone and the cone looked just like a cow's horn." That was a big disappointment in my life. I had never tasted ice cream.

For some reason, we had a phone system up on the mountain before everybody else. And every time that phone rang, everybody on the line listened in. Most of the time, there was so much noise on that line that nobody could hear what each other was saying, and they would say that they guessed that it was Ruth Troup's kids that was making all that noise.

When the crops were pretty well laid by, about the Fourth of July, we would go to singing school, and after school was out, we would have a singing concert on Saturday night. The school was held in the old Mount Shade schoolhouse which was the hub of everything. Mr. Robert McGehee was the teacher and everybody would pay him a little bit. The singing school lasted for about three weeks and we just loved it. After the concert was over, he decided that we would meet up at Mount Shade every Friday night and keep up our singing, so we did.

I visited quite a bit down at Kinnamer's Cove because I had a lot of friends down there. One of them was named Una, and near her was a log cabin Una and I loved to play in. A little boy lived near her who had a horse and a cart and he carried us all over that cove and up in the mountains to a place called Bat Cave. Una's father would kid me and say that this boy was my boyfriend. About a quarter of a mile from Una's house was another friend of mine named Helen. Helen invited me down one weekend to go to the Kinnamer reunion. That cove was just about made up of Kinnamers or folks who were kin to the Kinnamers. Every one of them went to this reunion. I had a couple of sisters who had been before and everybody knew them, but this was my first time to go.

There was a little trickle of a creek that ran through one of their fields. I loved to fish, but I didn't get much of a chance because there was hardly any running water up on the mountain. I bent a pin and I could see these little minnows in that little ditch of water, and I stayed out there all day Saturday and fished for those minnows with that pin. My face was red as a beet the next day. So, that next day which was Sunday, they had the reunion and I was introduced all around. Now, Helen's mother was a very naive person and she said to me, "Somebody told me that you were the ugliest Troup they had ever seen." But she came right along and told me that I was probably

the kind of girl that would get better looking as I got older. That
didn't bother me at all, and when I got home, I told my family about
it and they just laughed. They thought it was funny. I was about
twelve, I guess.

Fishing came from both sides of my family. All of them. That was
about the only recreation we had, going down to the river to fish.
When the crops were caught up, my daddy would say, "Well now, I
want us all to go down to Paint Rock River tomorrow and spend the
day fishing." Mama would cook up a big meal of just about everything, and we would pack it, and the kids would go out and dig
worms and hunt wasp nests for bait. Mama would make up this big
batch of corn mush and that was used as bait for catfish. One of my
brothers found a wasp nest so big that he told us he couldn't even get
it in a gallon bucket. A friend standing nearby said that he had heard
people tell some big lies about fishing, but my brother was the first
one he heard tell a lie about the bait.

Sometimes at night we would go fishing down at Honeycomb
Creek, and that was the place where my daddy grew up, Honeycomb
Valley. One night we were fishing there by the creek bank and I was
sitting there with my legs dangling close to the water. I had caught
this little fish and I pulled up the string to show it around. I pulled
up the string and kept pulling it up and discovered a snake had
swallowed my fish. I threw the whole thing back in the creek and
thought about going home. My parents must have been starved for
entertainment to think about subjecting their children to walking
through a pasture full of growth and sitting on a creek bank which is
a natural habitat for cottonmouth snakes.

When I visited Helen, I thought her daddy was one of the out-
standing characters I've ever met. He drove a school bus and he
would bring all the children living in Kinnamer's Cove up to the
DAR school. He had an exceptional sense of humor and a close,
loving relationship with his children. I envied Helen for having such
a family because my family had a sort of a suspicious nature. They
were always looking for something wrong. One night, Helen and I
had been out with some boyfriends and we came in and it wasn't
late, but for some reason, a rooster crowed. Helen's mother said she
wondered why that rooster crowed that time of night and her daddy

said it was probably crowing for daylight, and we had a big laugh about that.

One morning when Helen and I were getting ready for school, her daddy was out plowing in the garden and she went out and told him that we were going to give our teacher a shower and she wanted some money for a gift. He looked up and saw a big black cloud making up and he said, "She's going to get a shower pretty soon." He was a funny fellow.

The Letter of the Law

Tom Ogletree, Tallapoosa County

If you've ever been around the riverbanks, you've seen those wire baskets made out of chicken wire, kind of traps, that people use to set out and catch catfish. There was an old doctor who was in Alexander City who was the father-in-law of the guy that I worked for in high school. One of my jobs was to take this doctor out on Wednesday when he took his afternoon off to fish his baskets. He liked to set out ten or twelve of these wire baskets that he would set out and pick up. He would already have had a couple of drinks when we got out there, and we would get out there and he would have a few more and we would pull those baskets up.

When you pulled one of those baskets up, you could just feel them shake and vibrate when there was a fish in there and it was just like Christmas for somebody who really enjoyed fishing. After about the fourth or fifth basket and another couple of good drinks, we got to the next basket and I did all the work, of course, and I got the basket up and it didn't have any catfish in it, but it did have about a ten-pound bass in there, one of the prettiest you've ever seen.

I took the net apart and shook that bass out in the bottom of the boat, and this doctor was just so pleased with this fish. The only trouble was that it was against the law to net bass this way. Well, he picked the fish up and he held him in his hands and said, "Now look there, Tom. The Lord really knew what he was doing when he made this fish. Now, look at the scales. That's a protective coating. It would take a real blow to do any serious damage to this fish. Now, look at these fins. They'll guide him through the water, however he wants to go. Now look at this powerful tail. With just a swish of this tail it will take him ten or twelve feet and he'll just glide along."

And he talked about the fins and he talked about the beautiful colors of the fish and he said, "Now look at this mouth." He opened the fish's mouth and said, "He can swallow a fish half his size." And he says, "And it's so unfortunate that we can't keep this fish, because the law says that you have to throw the scaly fish back." So he talked on about the fish for about fifteen minutes and then he said, "I guess, Tom, we will just have to throw the fish back in the lake," and about this time, the fish had been out of the water so long he was just about dead. He eased that fish down in the water for just a second or two, then scooped him back up and brought him back into the boat and shouted, "There you go, Tom, we complied with the letter of the law."

When I was playing football back in the early fifties, guess I was one of the youngest members of the team, like in the ninth grade. I wasn't playing much and we were playing Lanette down in the valley. They had a terrific team that year and they had put two or three of our backs out of the game with injuries. The coach looked down the line and called on a boy who amounted to a third stringer. "Smith," he yelled, "Smith! Smith, get your headgear, Smith." Smith was right over by me and his headgear was right in front of him. He just kicked hell out of it, all the way to the end of the bench. Smith didn't want to go in that game and get killed.

The Night of the Ball

Corner Cafe Gang, Marengo County

Dance clubs were big around Demopolis beginning in the forties. The wives got these clubs up and they had dances, still do. And we had some big bands, you know, twelve-piece bands, and we had some famous bands here, off and on. Jan Garber came down one time. Harry James came down here, too. This was a big society thing in Demopolis. Each member could invite two other couples to a dance, so by the time the dance came around, we had a pretty big crowd.

In these clubs we had bankers, lawyers, and a fellow who ran a service station, millionaires in the same club with fellows making four hundred dollars a month. We certainly didn't have an isolated society when these dance clubs were formed in the late forties and early fifties. When we first started the dance clubs, the men had to wear a tux, and trying to scrape up tuxedos for all the people who didn't have one was a big job. Men had to borrow them and beg them and some of us had gained so much weight since leaving school we had to have that tux pieced in the back to get it on. But now, they go in blue jeans and everything.

Back in those days, we had the dances in a big old wooden community house down by the river, and one end of it was a huge fireplace. We would get a big fire going and you couldn't get within thirty feet of it because you would burn up. The city wouldn't let us have a bar inside, so one night a man backed his trailer right up by the back door and we used his trailer for a bar. Marengo County was dry but the law was looking east, like they usually did. The sheriff never did come up here except at election time.

The Octagon Special

Buster Hall, Clarke County

Years ago, the Gillis Pond was a favorite picnic spot down in Thomasville. The oak trees furnished shade and the pond was a wonderful place to swim. Several times each summer, the ladies of the Missionary Society would sponsor a picnic at the pond and invite all the church members to come.

A. L. Payne's mother was in charge of seeing that the ice cream was made for this particular picnic and she asked her son if he would crank the ice cream freezer. A. L. agreed, and asked his cousin Forest

Lee Mathews to help him. Now, Mrs. Payne should have known that when those two got their heads together it was just trouble waiting to happen. After the two boys talked things over and had made their plans for the picnic, they went to Mrs. Payne and told her how much they enjoyed some sandwiches somebody had served at a recent party, that they had gotten the recipe, and that they would like to make some of these delicious sandwiches for the Missionary Society outing. Mrs. Payne was so proud of her son and her nephew and she told them that she was sure that the picnickers would enjoy them.

A. L. and Forest Lee went down to the store and bought a loaf of thin sandwich bread, a jar of mustard, a jar of mayonnaise, and last but not least, a huge bar of Octagon soap. In those days, Octagon soap was used for washing clothes and they used a scrub board in the tub. They took the clothes, dunked them in the water, applied the Octagon soap generously, and rubbed the clothes up and down on that board until they were clean. That soap was strong, strong.

The boys got all their stuff together and told the ladies that the woman who had given them the recipe had sworn them to secrecy about the ingredients. They trimmed the edges from the bread, then on one slice they spread a generous supply of mustard. On the other slice, they spread mayonnaise. They opened the Octagon soap and noticed that the soap had a fresh look and a beautiful golden color, just like cheese. They sliced the soap and put it between the bread slices. Then, they cut the "sandwiches" in half, making a delicious looking three-cornered little sandwich. These, they carefully wrapped in wax paper.

On the afternoon of the picnic, a large crowd gathered at the pond and A. L. and Forest Lee helped the ladies in every way possible, being just as polite as you please. The two boys were careful to mix their sandwiches with the other food. After all was ready, the hungry group assembled around the table, eyeing all that good food.

There was a minister in Grove Hill at the time by the name of Reverend Truett. The good reverend was called on to bless the food which he did with much enthusiasm, talking long, and at the same time keeping one eye on the table. As soon as his prayer was completed, the good pastor had worked up a great hunger, and he pushed his way to the table, not waiting on the ladies to help themselves. He filled his plate with goodies and stepped back to enjoy the delicious food.

By now, Forest Lee and A. L. had backed off to the edge of the woods where they had a clear path if it became necessary to leave the scene fast. As luck would have it, Reverend Truett happened to draw one of the sandwiches on his first try. He unwrapped the sandwich, admiring the neat trim and its delicious contents, and was heard to say that cheese was one of his favorites. Being very hungry, he bit off about half of the little sandwich and made one or two chomps on the big mouthful. Then, a startled look came over the preacher's face. He hated to spit out the contents of his mouth knowing it would be impolite, so he tried again. By this time, the soap foam was dribbling out of each corner of his mouth, so he backed up to the bushes at the edge of the woods and quickly disposed of the sandwich. The good preacher didn't eat any more of the cheese sandwiches.

The next person to draw one of the Payne-Mathews creations was a very dignified lady of the town. She was also very careful to dispose of her sandwich. By this time, half of the picnickers were foaming at the mouth and all eyes were centered on the two boys, who suddenly decided that they were not hungry and had better make some tracks. For the next few days, A. L. and Forest Lee were what you might call in the doghouse.

The Silver Screen Scene

Cecil Brown, Jefferson County

I really got into the theater business in Selma in 1933 when I was fourteen years old. My first job was in the Academy of Music—that was the name of the picture show—and the first thing I did at that theater was to hold a horse on stage. Tom Mix, the cowboy star, was making a personal appearance in Selma, and my job was to hold his horse Tony up on that stage while Tom Mix did his thing with the audience. All I did was walk out on the stage leading the horse and stand there as long as Mix was on the stage. Back in those days, movie stars did a lot of touring around the country promoting their movies. You had your Tom Mixes, your Lash Larues, your Hoot Gibsons, and your Tim McCoys. It was a lot of fun for me as a young kid to meet all these people.

While I was living in Selma, I thought it was absolutely necessary for me to decide what I was going to do in life since I was an orphan boy. My sister was looking after us then. I looked at several jobs I wanted to get into. One of them was J. C. Penney and the other was the picture shows. I decided to try the theaters first and I hit it right off. I liked the atmosphere of the movie house, and for the rest of my life, working in movie theaters was the only thing I ever did.

My family moved to Montgomery when I was a teenager. I had the movie bug and started right in with theater jobs—the Paramount, the Charles, and the Empire. My first job was at the old Empire Theater and I was an usher. That was back in the days when we had lucky seats. When you went into the theater, you dropped your ticket stub in a big old box and they would take it up on the stage, shake it up, and draw those stubs. People would win prizes or money. Another thing they had to try to draw customers in the theaters when money was so tight was amateur night. We had all kinds of amateurs up there. People would sing and play guitars, maybe tell jokes, and just about anything you can imagine people in Montgomery would do for entertainment. I remember Hank Williams was one of our contestants one time.

Also, down at the Charles, we would book in real live acts there to supplement the movie. We had acts back in the thirties who would go on to great careers, like the Three Stooges, Jim McKinley, Joe Tubbs, and Tex Ritter. Ritter was a heck of a nice guy. The thing I remember about Ritter was that he carried a bunch of silver dollars around in a big old bag, no currency, and everything he bought, he paid for it with silver dollars. Really, what we had was a circuit of these performers, but we didn't press our luck and had these acts in about every two weeks.

I stayed in Montgomery until the war started, went in service, and jumped right back in the theater business after the war as house manager for the Paramount. I started something called "Teen Time at the Paramount" every Saturday morning. We had an emcee there named Bill Bryan, a disc jockey. The way we decided who was going to be the emcee for our shows was this. We monitored the most popular disc jockeys in town, and the one who got the most reaction got the job. There was a popular network show back then called "Monitor," and "Monitor" did a few Teen Time shows from our stage.

We made a deal with Montgomery Aviation to fly the talent into town. Bryan was a hot disc jockey, carried a lot of weight with the record companies, and he would put the pressure to furnish talent for our show. The talent would appear on stage for free and the aviation company would fly them in from Memphis or Atlanta. When the big star would arrive at the airport, we made a deal with the mayor to have police to escort the star to the theater. This was a big production, a big event in Montgomery.

One of the first people who was flown in was Bobby Darin. Darin was a real nice guy and I stayed in contact with him right on up to the time he married Sandra Dee. We had Tommy Sands there. Jerry Lee Lewis was there, and that was what you would call a real swinging Saturday morning show. The morning Tommy Sands was there, the *Montgomery Advertiser* had a big headline: "Sandstorm hits Montgomery." Every Saturday morning, I would stand up on that stage, grab the mike, and say something like this, "This is Cecil Brown speaking to you from the beautiful Paramount Theater in downtown Montgomery, Alabama, the home of Teen Time, USA." Then, we'd raise the applause sign and the kids would just go bananas.

In 1963, I got transferred to Birmingham for Cinerama. We took over the Ritz Theater and converted it to Cinerama. Cinerama really didn't last that long, just ran out of gas. There were really just two pictures that did anything—*The Brothers Grimm* and *How the West Was Won*. The rest of the stuff just didn't make it.

About this time, the blacks in Birmingham were making a real move to integrate the all-white theaters in town. They would come around in bunches and demand tickets, but we couldn't serve them at that time. They would come up to the windows and sing "We

Shall Overcome," and all of that, and really put on a show outside the theaters.

In 1966, I went down to Tuscaloosa and that was the finest experience in my life, I think. Fred Sington, a well-known sports figure in Alabama, called Coach Paul Bryant on my behalf, and the coach was just as nice as he could be to me. I was made an honorary member of the "A" Club and had access to the whole building. If I wanted to eat lunch at Bryant Hall, I just went in and was eating over there about every other day.

One time Coach Wally Butts of Georgia was in town and Butts was drinking like hell in those days. Charlie Thornton who worked with Bryant asked me to look after Butts and try to keep him off the booze. At that luncheon, Bryant's name tag said "Bear Bryant" and I tore that up and wrote "Coach Bryant." The coach never did like to be called "Bear," but later on, he accepted that because he knew that was where the money was.

Up to this point, all the theaters were segregated. The blacks had their own theaters and they never came up to any of our theaters and tried to buy tickets. There was one incident that happened down in Tuscaloosa that was very sad. There was an actor named Jack Palance who was in town. He had married a girl from Tuscaloosa, and he was down there visiting with her family. While he was there, he decided to take in a movie. Something had been said about Palance's association with blacks, and he stood up right in the middle of the picture show and threatened anybody in the building that didn't like what he stood for to come outside. He used a couple of words of profanity and said, "Come on out." Nobody took him up, but somebody called the police because it looked like trouble.

During my forty-seven years in the theater business, I had a chance to meet a lot of movie stars personally. My all-time favorite was Joseph Cotton. I don't know why, but he was just a helluva nice guy. He and Katharine Hepburn came through Montgomery promoting *The Philadelphia Story*. I remember Katharine Hepburn well because she had a bitch of a temper. I think the nastiest woman I ever talked to in my whole life was Tallulah Bankhead. I mean she was nasty talking. She would call you a son of a bitch quicker than she would say your name, and a couple of well-known words before that, even back in those days. Tallulah Bankhead's aunt lived right next door to the Sidney Lanier High School in Montgomery, and it would shock the aunt beyond words the way Tallulah talked.

Joan Crawford was really hard for me to get along with. I had Joan Crawford at the Alabama Theater to promote the Fabulous Flicks and she was married to this guy named Steele who was president of Pepsi-Cola at that time. Jimmy Stewart was a helluva nice guy, but in my opinion, Joseph Cotton was the nicest fellow I ever met in the entertainment business.

One time, there was a movie called *Benji* and this movie was about a little dog of the same name. As a promotional gimmick, I had a luncheon for the dog and got Ken Shorey, movie critic for the *Birmingham News*, to feed Benji steak. We had the luncheon at the Parliament House and I invited the media. Shorey wasn't too popular in Birmingham, especially with some movie houses. One time, Shorey came up and was telling me about a foreign film called *Oil Lamps*, made in Norway or somewhere and it had English subtitles. He said, "Cecil, I want to tell you how great I am. You get your company to book this film and I will put all my effort into making it a success." I told him my company thought I could walk on water and could probably book the film, but I had never heard of a movie called *Oil Lamps*. He said, trust me, so I booked it. We did a helluva business. They tried it in other towns and it bombed out, but in Birmingham, it was the biggest thing since the Last Supper. It proved the point that Shorey had a lot of power.

Without concessions, a movie house just couldn't exist. Actually, popcorn is the big money-maker in any theater. Why, we would make 80 percent profit on popcorn, drinks about 70 percent, and candy is about 40 percent. We would have popcorn equipment down at the Alabama Theater that was as big as a Volkswagen and we would send out the popcorn to our other theaters as well as supplying the Alabama. Back when I first got started, an outside company had the concessions and a smart cookie told my boss he ought to handle the concessions himself. We got into the concession business, way too late, about 1947. We were selling hundreds of pounds of popcorn every week, and then the chain really started making money.

Party Time

Lula Fluellen, Jefferson County

You would think that coming on during the depression that things would be bad, but we had a whole lot of good times. We had some clubs that the young men organized, like the Double E social club. One of the main things these clubs did was save for Christmas. They would put on these little projects, little parties. You could come to their little parties for a dime, and the boys and girls would be dancing and we had good times. The girls paid their own dimes mostly, but some of the girls got lucky and got the boys to pay. At this time, I had a cousin who said she didn't like my writing so she sent me a typewriter. I learned to hunt and peck on that typewriter and I made money typing the invitations for the social clubs.

We had piano music at these parties, sort of like Fats Domino music, boom-boomba-boom, like that. I would play for these parties and would play for dances, too. I got fifty cents for playing at a dance. We had the dances at different houses and only had parties at houses that had a piano. The mothers would chaperon the dances, and you couldn't come in unless you were dressed up—boys wore overalls a lot back then—but you didn't come in with overalls. You had better find you some decent-looking pants and a shirt and a tie. I had a cousin who told me, "Lula, I'm going to come up there and see if I can slip in with some overalls and fool Miss Lina." Well, Miss Lina was my mother and she told him, "Joe, you know better than to try to get in here in those overalls. Go home and get on some decent-looking clothes."

All the clubs had a treasurer, and at Christmastime, all the money we'd saved over the year was divided so we would have money to buy Christmas gifts. To get these dimes, boys would get all those little odd jobs, like one boy's daddy had cows and the boy sold the cow manure, and they would work in folks' gardens and help out on coal and ice wagons. We were brought up to feel that any work you did that was honorable you did it with pride. Those little clubs and the parties gave us a lot of entertainment as we grew up in Birmingham in the thirties.

Good Clean Fun

Tera Averett, Coffee County

Papa always kept several foxhounds. He also kept Henry Stegall's dogs for him while the representative was in Washington. When Congressman Stegall came home to Ozark, he and Papa went fox hunting with other friends. I went with Papa one night to fox hunt, but I could never become excited over hearing the dogs barking out there. One time was enough for me.

Mama enjoyed fishing in the creeks and branches close to our house. She had her own worm bed and she had a catalpa tree which produced nice green fat worms that bream couldn't resist. She made a cushion to sit on at the fishing hole. It was a large croker sack filled with shucks and it served its purpose. It kept her seat dry. You talk about patience! She might sit there waiting for a bite for half a day and come home with three or four little perch or catfish. But it was free and she thought it was good recreation.

Every member of the family had some form of recreation. For the teenagers, we often planned parties either in our house or in homes of our friends. At these parties, we played parlor games like musical chairs. What we would do is line up two rows of chairs back to back and everyone marched around the chairs single file while music was played on the Victrola or the organ. When the music stopped, everyone tried to sit down but there was one who couldn't find a chair and that person was "out." Another chair was removed and this went on until there were only two left and one chair.

Then, we sometimes had a candy drawing. Several boxes of stick candy of different colors were placed into a large box with a hole in the top. A boy and a girl would each put a hand through the hole and draw out a stick of candy. If the two sticks were alike, they could draw again until they drew two sticks of different colors. Then another couple would draw.

During the winter months, we sometimes attended peanut shellings. The farmers had to have their peanuts shelled by hand. Couples would shell peanuts from a large pan which they held together.

After the work was finished, we would have a candy drawing, or cake and ice cream might be served.

Sometimes we played "hide and whoop," a game the city children called "hide and seek." One child was the hunter. The child would close his eyes and wait until a "whoop" was heard. That meant that everyone was hidden. The first one found had to be the hunter the next time.

A New Slab of Cardboard

Cullman Powell, Coffee County

Coal Valley furnished Oakman High School with pretty girls. By the time I started dating, the depression had pretty well ended. I began wearing better-looking clothes and we started listening to the big bands on the radio. Every Friday night, there would be a dance at somebody's house and there would be one of these portable record players and we would dance there. Sometimes boys and girls would just walk up and down the road together, because we surely didn't have any money to spend. Well, we would do what you call smooching a little bit. I would walk three miles in the freezing cold to see a girl, then walk back home later. I could always tell how far it was to a girl's house and I didn't count the miles. My shoes would always have a little hole in the bottom we danced so much and I couldn't afford any new shoes, so I put a piece of cardboard inside that shoe over the hole. When I would leave that girl's house, I would slip a new slab of cardboard in the shoe going home and hope it wouldn't be raining.

High Society

Mary Frances Tipton, Dallas County

The big deal when I was in high school were the social clubs, sort of like sororities, except we had the only social club. This club was started in junior high school by somebody's mother. The ultimate event of this club was the high school senior dance. The school didn't sponsor it, the club did. We would hold smaller dances, like a Christmas dance, but the seniors would have the big graduation dance. It was very exclusive because we held our membership down to about twenty or twenty-five. The only purpose of the club was social. We would have bake sales to raise money that was spent on nothing but having fun.

A couple of us had good friends who were not members of the club. Naively, each year we would nominate these girls for the club and they would routinely get blackballed until our senior year when we needed more money to stage our big senior dance. Everybody in high school was invited. It was a monumental undertaking. The biggest job the president of the club had was getting people to bring stuff to the bake sale.

Selma society divided itself down the middle when I was growing up. You didn't have to belong to the country club, but it helped. There was a distinct set of girls whose people worked in the mill village. There was a cigar factory in Selma, and if you were connected to the cigar factory, you just didn't make it.

Another big form of entertainment back then were the sock hops after football games. You didn't have to have a date to be there. People would just go and the sock hops were well chaperoned. As far as being in the "in group," boys were different from girls. If a boy was a big football star, he could come from the mill section of the town and be a big man on the campus. We had one of the girls in our little sorority dating one of these boys and that took everybody by surprise. Selma was kind of a mean town in that it was somewhat snobbish. I was not entirely comfortable with the town being that way at the time I was going to school.

Real Sports

Ben Meriwether, Bullock County

My uncle Dick—we called him Cousin Dick for some reason—loved to go fishing and he had the best in fishing tackle. Early one morning, Cousin Dick and my cousin Jim hitched up their buggy, and Daddy and I hitched up our buggy, and we left early for Line Creek which had good fishing. When I say early, it was because we got there at daybreak. We found a good place, went to fishing, and had a good mess pretty soon. We stopped awhile to have some breakfast. We made a fire, cleaned as many fish as we wanted, found some big Catawba tree leaves which we wrapped around the fish, and laid all of this on the coals. That was good eating and we still had plenty to bring home with us.

Another time, Cousin Dick and Daddy decided they would go to a little pond not far away and seine it, because they didn't know whether there was a fish in there or not. Jim and I went, too, and we were the ones to go in the water with the seine. We were pulling the seine and bringing the ends together right under a big willow tree. We were about three feet apart when a big old moccasin snake popped his head up right between us. We still don't know if there were any fish there because we left that seine right there and headed for the bank. We would not get back in the water, so Daddy and Cousin Dick had to get it. If there had been any fish there, they were gone by then, and we never went back to that place.

We were fishing one time at Fox Creek which was pretty small. Now, Cousin Dick was a great fellow, had a big stomach, and smoked a pipe. The bank of the creek at that spot was old red clay and was pretty slick. Cousin Dick was standing right on the edge of the bank, an old straw hat on, and he struck a match to light his pipe. About that time, his feet slipped and into that water he went, flat on his back. He went clean out of sight. Then we saw something coming up and it was that big stomach coming up first. We didn't know what to do. Just then, we saw he was not hurt and we started laughing. I mean we laughed! That made him mad, and when he got out, he said, "I'm going home." So, home we went, still laughing, but no fish on that trip.

When we lived at Mitchell Station, there was a little creek back of the pasture, and one day I decided I was going fishing. I got all my stuff ready, but didn't have any lead for a sinker. Now, my mother had a beautiful, green, long silk dress with a flared-out bottom. This was a real special dress for special occasions. Well, sewn in around the bottom of that dress, about every eight inches, was a piece of lead about the size of a pencil and about a half an inch long. I got a pair of scissors, stepped into the closet, and ripped out several pieces of that lead and went on to the creek. It was several weeks later that my mother discovered the missing lead. She called me in the house, and when I saw her holding that dress, I said to myself, "Oh-oh, I'm in trouble. Here we go to that peach tree again." I knew better than try to fool her, so I told her I needed the lead to go fishing. I thought she wanted to laugh about it, but all I got was a good scolding, but that was better than going to the peach tree. I never saw that dress again, but I did learn that the lead was to hold the bottom of the skirt down . . . for the sake of modesty.

The old swimming hole was usually pretty busy during the summer months. There was a high, red-clay bank on one side of the creek that we would use as a slide. We would splash water up on it, and when it got wet, it was slick as glass. We would slide down that bank and really hit the water with a splash. We were always in our birthday suits and it's a wonder we didn't hurt ourselves. There was a large clump of blackberry bushes close to the creek, and when they were ripe, we would go swimming, come out, and eat blackberries. On the other side of the road was a big muscadine vine growing up a tree, and when they were ripe, we were into muscadines.

One time, it rained for about two weeks. The creek was way out of its banks and the road was underwater and there was no place to go swimming. We had to go somewhere, so we went down to the railroad trestle to swim and that was really dangerous, but we didn't think about that at the time. Water was at least thirty feet deep and very swift. I got out on the end of one of the sills which was covered with tin and began kicking on the tin. Before I knew it, I was covered with wasps and they got me good. I slid off in the water and stayed under as long as I could. When I came up downstream a little ways, that gang of wasps was circling right over the spot where I had gone under.

One thing we did back then scares me now when I think about it. The big water tank that watered the trains sat on pillars higher than the trains. The tank was twenty-six feet high and twenty-five feet in diameter. Lots of times during the summer when the tank was full, we would wait until dark and go down there, pull our clothes off, climb the ladder up to the top, and go swimming. The water was cold and deep with nothing to hold on to but the top rim. We could have drowned, but we didn't think of it then.

When I was about fourteen years old there in Fitzpatrick, we played a lot of baseball. One summer, the Methodist Church was going to have a meeting and the grown-ups decided to bring picnic baskets and make a day of it. When the boys heard about it, we challenged the older men to a ball game because we just knew that we could take care of them. When the day came, all the stores closed, we all gathered, and it was time for the game. We got to playing and the old guys who we thought were going to be so easy weren't going to be easy at all. At the end of the sixth inning, the score was 6 to 5 in our favor when Mr. Jesse Pugh came to bat. He owned one of the stores there and was about thirty-five years old, much too old to play with us boys. Well, our pitcher threw the ball to him and he hit it, and when I say hit, I mean he hit it! He knocked the cover off that ball and the cord started unraveling and the ball started getting smaller and smaller as it sailed through the air. I was playing right field and it was coming right to me. I went back as far as I could go, but there wasn't a ball to catch by the time it got to me, just a long piece of cord. Of course, Mr. Pugh got a home run and the game ended 6 to 6. We had to quit on account of we didn't have another ball. We didn't ever challenge the old folks again.

Just up the road from our house was a little hill, not too steep, but steep enough for a little ride down. So, on lots of Sunday afternoons, my buddies would come over for a little fun. We would pull our old buggy out, pull it up to the top of that hill, take the shafts off, tie a rope on each side of the front axle close to the wheel so we could guide it. We would get it right on the edge of that hill and everybody would get in except the one who would give us a push over. The last one would give it a push and then jump on the back, and down that hill we'd go. When the buggy finally stopped, we would pull it back up again and do it all over. That would go on sometimes for several hours, and it seemed like a lot of fun to us back then.

Every morning at seven o'clock, a fast freight going to Montgomery stopped to get water. Hilton Baker and Bennie Frank Tamplin decided they would hop this train and take a ride to a long hill about a mile and a half from the depot. This hill caused the freights to slow down enough so you could jump off, but this Sunday morning the train was real short. Bennie Frank and Hilton got on it anyway. When the train got to this hill, it didn't slow down a bit and the boys were afraid to get off. That train went fifteen miles down the road before it had to stop and go into a siding to meet the passenger train coming out of Montgomery. Bennie Frank and Hilton slipped off the freight, fifteen miles from home, and neither one of them had a nickel in his pocket. Bennie Frank had a brother working in Montgomery and they looked up in the passenger train and there was the brother. They hopped on the train and Bennie Frank's brother had to pay their way back home.

Making Music

J. L. Lowe, Jefferson County

When I went to Alabama State in the early thirties, they had a dance band there but we started a second band. In that second band was Erskine Hawkins and Dud Bascomb. Nobody heard of Dud much, but some say he was a better trumpet player than Hawkins. Of course, Hawkins was in a class by himself as far as high notes were concerned. He was playing notes then that nobody else was playing. They counted fifty C-notes on Louis Armstrong's record of "Shine" and Erskine was playing one hundred. After the hundred, he went on up to F. Later came Avery Parrish, the greatest jazz pianist Birmingham has ever produced. Parrish wrote "After Hours" and his brother is still getting royalties from that piece. I spent three years at Alabama State, rushing through, and sometimes regret not spending more time down there. Our band was playing just about every night, as much as twenty nights a month, all over the state. When the band played, the money would go to the school, and if this money hadn't come in, they would have had to close the dormitories. The students were getting part of their tuition and their expenses and that was all.

Before World War II, there were more musicians in Birmingham than Atlanta, or even in Nashville. We went to these places to play many of the dances—Chattanooga, Atlanta, and Jackson, Mississippi. We traveled with a big band back in those days, twelve to fifteen musicians. Say, in 1936, this big band traveled to Jackson, Mississippi, we went in two cars. Fess Whatley had a seven-passenger Cadillac and he had another car and the Cadillac pulled a trailer for the instruments.

During the war, I was at the Tuskegee Army Airfield. This airfield was opened just to train black pilots. The bandmaster at Tuskegee was trying to organize an air force band. His company clerk had played with Fess Whatley and kept up with musicians as they were drafted into the army. He got them from all over the country, including me. Being the only black air force band, we were able to get the best black musicians in the country because they had been rejected by the white bands. This band gave concerts and marched in parades all over Georgia, Mississippi, Alabama, Tennessee, and Washington, D.C. We never experienced much racism in bands since I started playing in the thirties. It seems that musicians, baseball players, and other athletes are treated in a different fashion and a different category as far as racism is concerned. Some of the best treatment I have ever received as a musician is from the white race rather than the black race.

The whites have been protective of us even though they didn't accept us on a social level, but so far as man to man, they accepted us. For example, we played for many homes over in Mountain Brook and in the country clubs and have always been well received. They would come up and offer us all types of alcohol, but that's the end of it. They would say something like, "You boys being taken care of?" and they didn't have any idea that "boy" was a resentful word to us. They thought they were being kind, but they would never think of calling us a man. We accepted that because we were employees.

One of the experiences I'll always remember was the time our band had an engagement up in Cullman. In 1933, Cullman had no Negro residents and had a reputation that if you were a Negro, and through mistake you got to Cullman, then you had until sundown to get out of town. Fess Whatley talked to the band about whether it would be safe for us to go up there. The people in Cullman insisted that we come, so Fess told them that we wanted police protection. We got to Cullman and had a police escort into the city and we played for a dance at the high school. Even with the police, we were all waiting for some kind of disturbance to show that this was really Cullman. We had heard that a lot of Germans had come to Cullman after the First World War and thought maybe that they were the cause of the ethnic feeling. But the whole area had that reputation. We were really surprised on this date though. Cullman was Roosevelt country. I remember the man speaking during intermission, a political speech really, and talking about Roosevelt being the best president we'd ever had. Of course, Alabama in the thirties was heavily democratic. The attitude these Cullman people had that night was very good, orderly and courteous. While we were up on the stage, one of our trumpet players dropped his mute and one of the white girls ran up and handed it up to him. That was quite unexpected. After the dance was over, the people went out of their way to see that we were treated well. We really didn't need it, but the police escorted us back out to the city limits after the dance was over. They were receptive to the band and were really nicer to us than the people here in Birmingham. This showed me that a town could get a reputation it didn't deserve.

We Made Our Own

Libby Fitts, Bibb County

Back before television, we had our radios and one or two kids even had record players. Every Saturday night out there we would have a party at somebody's house and we would gather up and listen to the music and most of the time we would have some refreshments, too. On Saturday afternoons, a bunch of us would just walk from Piper over to Coleanor to have something to do. There was this swinging bridge that went across this creek between the towns and we would have a lot of fun playing on that swinging bridge. Then we would go meet the train and that was always exciting. Out there, there was not much to do and we just made our own entertainment.

Churches were a great part of our lives back then, too. Well, the missionary societies met on a regular basis and they used to have these Christmas parties. And there was always something going on at the school. They had Halloween carnivals and all this stuff just like they do now. Then, every town around here had their baseball club, and that was a big thing on Saturday afternoons. Towns all around here would play baseball and they had a nice baseball field. Baseball was a big thing here all summer and all the towns—Piper, Coleanor, Marvel, Dogwood, Blocton, and Siluria—had teams and everybody would just pile into cars and go to wherever the game was that day.

Close Kin

*Picnic at Macedonia Methodist
Church, Dogwood, Alabama
(near Alabaster), in the early 1920s
(Albert Lebourg photo, Frank Lebourg
Collection, Gadsden)*

Sugar, Eggs, and Snakebite

Burton Troup, Marshall County

One time, we were over at Aunt Dicey's and she told us about how the great ship, the *Titanic*, had gone down, and later on, a song came out about it, "The Wreck of the Titanic," like it was sad when that great ship went down. Aunt Dicey was about the best woman I ever saw, but she wasn't a "yes" person. One time, Mama sent me and my brother over to Aunt Dicey's to get some sugar. She was going to make some strawberry jam and she had sent Papa to the store to get some sugar, but she didn't know how soon he would get back, so she sent us over to Aunt Dicey's to get some just in case. On the way back, me and my brother got into that sugar. It was down in that bucket. When we got home, Papa had just walked in with some sugar so Mama just turned us around and told us just to take that sugar back to Aunt Dicey. Aunt Dicey looked down in that bucket and called Mama and said, "Nannie, you didn't send back as much sugar as I sent you," and we were just caught red-handed. I ate so much candy down at that store that Mama had to hide the sugar from me. I was always like that, craving something sweet.

Now, my uncle Robert lived with Grandma and Uncle Bud down at what they called Flat Rock, and it was out sort of in the pasture. The circus came out there one time and I thought we were a long way from home when we were down there at that tent. They had a clown and he was swinging real high, and they had a bear on a chain and two monkeys, and I think a zebra. Now, that was some circus, and how they ever got out on that mountain, I don't know.

I had a cousin, Carter, and he later became postmaster at Grant, but he had a long road getting there. I learned to cuss from Carter. One day, Carter was reaching up in the closet for a carder, one of those things you card wool with, and I could just still see him when he knocked that thing off on his bare foot, and he said, "Goddd-dam." I went running to Aunt Dicey and I pulled on her dress. You know back then, it wasn't easy for kids to talk to adults, and Mama and Aunt Dicey and two or three others were talking. I kept pulling on Aunt Dicey's dress, and finally, she turned around and said,

"What is it?" and I said that Carter had said "goddam." Boy, she took him out, and I mean to tell you she really hurt him.

So, Carter and I had been building hog pens, we called them, out of wood, like you built a rail fence, but in a circle, and we called them hog pens. You would have thought I would have known to have been on the lookout for Carter after I had told on him. He was about two years older than I was and was a lot bigger than I was. Well, I was out there building my hog pen and he came sneaking up on me and he knocked me and that hog pen over with the same lick. He jumped up on me and shook me and said, "Now, goddam you."

A little later, Carter came by one day—we lived between them and the store—and he asked my mama to let me go to the store with him. She said yeah, and she gathered up some eggs to go with what she already had and me and Carter started up the road to the store. Papa had got me some new shoes and I had scuffed the toe of one of them, knocked a little piece out of the toe, and I was real concerned with that scuff mark. I was walking along with that gallon bucket nearly full of eggs with Mama's little note sitting on top about what she wanted from the store. I stopped and pulled my foot up to about my knees, looking at that scuffed place on my shoe. Carter saw me in that position, standing up there on one leg looking at that shoe, and he came over real quick and just shoved me backwards. I can just see Mama's little note floating around the yellows of those eggs after they all got busted up. Carter had a long memory.

Carter and Aunt Dicey and them moved down there to Cameron Cove, they called it. One day, somebody came over with the bad news that Carter had been snakebit and he was real bad sick. Me and Gracey went out in the orchard and climbed up in a Juneapple tree, and Gracey said, "Well, there is one thing about it. Carter is just ten, and if you die before you are twelve, you'll go to heaven." I thought that well might be, but I didn't believe Carter would ever make it.

One of a Kind

J. Torbett Crocker, Jefferson County

Back about 1910, a boy going to Auburn didn't have much to do in the way of entertainment, because in the first place, the school was so small that outside activities were at a minimum, and the little town was just about the same size as the school. Anything out of the ordinary would get a whole lot of attention. I had an uncle down there then, Charlton Torbett, and Charlton was somewhat of a character but very inventive in the ways to get in trouble. Really, he was a mean son of a bitch, burning down houses and things like that. Then, on the other hand, he would do something nice every once in a while.

For instance, there was a little circus that came through town and they would always have a parade. Charlton would get a roll of brown wrapping paper and draw every one of the wagons and animals on this roll of paper and take it down to the kids in the orphanage.

While he was at Auburn, a tent meeting was set up down by the railroad tracks and was well attended. Studying the situation one day, Uncle Charlton noted the big tent was backed up to the railroad tracks. He enlisted some help, and that night as the tent meeting was getting into full swing, Charlton sneaked around the back, tied one end of a strong rope to the tent and the other to the rear of a freight train that had stopped briefly on the track. Inside the tent, the preacher was getting up a good head of steam and there was lusty singing and a lot of "amens." At the height of the activity inside, the freight train got to rolling down that track pulling the tent with it, uncovering the people in the meeting and dragging chairs and a few folks along with it. The train kept on going down the tracks and pulled that tent halfway to Montgomery.

When Charlton was initiated into a fraternity, the fraternity brothers took this big bowl, put it on the floor, and emptied a bunch of inkwells in there. They made Charlton drop his pants and sat him down inside the bowl and spun him around. His fanny stayed blue for a long, long time.

Buying Cheap Birds

Carolyn Lipscomb, Lee County

I loved my mother-in-law, Miss Freddie. She was so cute. She sang and played the harp and entertained the soldiers during World War I. We got along fine, but she was a worrier. We used to get together for Thanksgiving, the whole family, and usually there would be more than twenty people over to Miss Freddie's house for the big dinner. Every year she would always worry that she wouldn't have enough turkey to feed everybody. We went through this routine for years, and no amount of reassurance could calm her doubts about having enough food for that big crowd. Of course, she used the same great blue speckled roaster to do the turkey in.

One year, my husband, Lan, and I decided to play a trick on Miss Freddie on Thanksgiving Day. We got a big blue speckled roaster like Lan's mother used, found a little Cornish hen, cooked it in the roaster, and carried it over to Miss Freddie's house that Thanksgiving morning. We snuck it in the kitchen door and told the cook what we were up to and how we were going to work this thing. She thought it was a great idea.

All morning, Miss Freddie would break off visiting with the family and hurry back to check on her big turkey cooking nicely in the roaster, and satisfied, she would go back and visit some more. Just before the big dinner was announced, Lan and I swapped the big turkey for the Cornish hen just as Miss Freddie made a final check. She raised the lid, looked in, and almost had a spasm. As she gaped down at the tiny hen in the big roaster, Letty was standing by watching and enjoying the scene, and then got off the best line of the day. "Miss Freddie," she observed, "I done tole you 'bout buying them cheap birds."

There was this little black woman, Louise Works, and she had nursed my husband when he was a baby and we had known her for what seemed like forever. She was a favorite of Miss Freddie and we all visited back and forth, getting to know Louise almost like one of the family. And in a way, she was. One day, somebody called me and told me that Louise had died, and when the funeral was going to be and all. At that time, my mother-in-law was getting on in years and she had some good days and some of the other kind, but I thought I would call her and tell her about Louise.

I called Miss Freddie and told her that Louise had died and that I was thinking about going to the funeral and wondered if she wanted to go. She thought that was a good idea, so on the day of the funeral, I went by and picked up Miss Freddie and we went down to the church. As we drove down, I remembered Louise Works, how she used to be as long as I had known her, a little woman who didn't weigh more than seventy-five pounds. She had a small, narrow face and tiny hands and feet. The most remarkable thing about her was that I had never seen her hair in all the years I had known her. She always used to wear a bandana or some kind of cloth hair cover and she wore that cloth real tight on her head so that if you kind of closed your eyes, you would think Louise had nothing on her head at all, just scalp on her skull.

Miss Freddie and I got to the church and we were the only white people there, but we were treated with courtesy and were ushered down to a good seat for the funeral. They had a little program which was passed out to everybody, and the program gave all of Louise's vital statistics about when she was born and who her family was and everything, and then there was the preaching and singing, and finally, the preacher said that now we were going to view the remains.

Now, I was not sure that Miss Freddie wanted to go up and view the remains, but she said she did. The family went up first and they stood around and there was a lot of crying, naturally, and grieving, and when they got through looking down where Louise was laid out, the ushers started a line of everybody else to go up and pay their last respects to the departed and get one last look.

When our turn came, Miss Freddie and I filed by, and when I looked down, Louise was wearing this huge, curly red wig. Why, that wig was so big that it dominated the casket. And there was poor little Louise's thin face framed in that big, curly red wig, and it just didn't look like Louise at all, certainly not the way I remembered her down all those years. When Miss Freddie gazed down, she squeezed my arm real tight and we filed back to our seats. We sat down and

Miss Freddie leaned over to me and said in a very loud whisper, "Carolyn, I have never seen that woman before in my life."

My husband's great aunt, Nettie Ross, was also very cute. She was a little bitty lady and she wore great big hats with birds and flowers and all sorts of things decorating those hats. She went to a funeral one time and took her hat off. She was sitting there when the pallbearers closed the lid and started moving the casket out of the room. Sitting right on top of the coffin along with the rest of the flowers was Nettie's hat. She thought it blended in real nice with the rest of the flowers.

Another unusual thing she did one time was when Lan's grandparents on his mother's side were talking to Miss Nettie one day and they were telling her that they couldn't decide just where they wanted to be buried. Miss Nettie gave them two cemetery lots for a Christmas present. Strangest Christmas present anyone ever got, I guess.

A Smart Lady

Lula Fluellen, Jefferson County

When my brother died in 1932, there wasn't a man in the house, but I didn't feel afraid or threatened. My mother was fiery. Somebody would come up and she was fat and fine, and she would put her hand on her hip and they would back off. She scared off a lot of my boyfriends. If she didn't like them, she would send them sailing. If she did like one of these boys, she wanted me to like him too, so I didn't like him. I sort of resented the fact that she wanted to boss me, and I didn't want her to boss me. I wanted to be independent.

My mother should have been a psychiatrist because she knew how to get things out of you and wiggle you around. When I was about sixteen, they were having a party in the neighborhood, and I knew this was going to be like a big folks' party because two married couples were giving it. They were going to have some drinks and I had never had any drinks and stuff. I was going to this party with my boyfriend and I was going to sample the drinks that night. When they brought the drinks out, I guess it was corn liquor because it was as clear as water. I looked at that corn liquor and I said, u-mmmm, I don't want that. They said, that's not good for you anyway, you supposed to drink that other kind, what's colored. I guess they went in there and mixed it with some tea or something, because when they brought it back, it was colored. Boy, I don't know how much I had, but it burned going down and it was enough to make me high. So, coming on back home, we were walking along with a bunch of people and I was telling them all about how pretty the stars were. Oh, those stars were so pretty that night.

When I got home, my mother was sleeping because she was sleepy headed. I told Robert Mama was asleep and he said he was going on home because he didn't want Mama mad at him. He told me I shouldn't have had that drink, and I said, "Well, you're the one that went back and got it for me." I went in the house and shook Mama. Woke her up. She said, "What time is it?" I told her it was eleven o'clock and I had been drinking whiskey. I told her she ought to try it because it burns all the way down. Then I told her that she ought to go out and look at the stars because they were so pretty. The next morning, she said, "I understand you woke me up last night. You acted like you were drunk or something." I said, "Oh, Mama. That stuff just burns down in your stomach, but it makes you feel good afterwards." She asked me if I wanted to do that, and I said I did. Then, she told me about this man in the neighborhood who was a drunk and asked me if I wanted to be like him. I said I didn't, and she told me that was how he started. We got through that hurdle.

She could wiggle me around before I knew it. My sixteenth birthday was coming up and she asked me what I wanted for a present. I said, "Mama, I want a pack of cigarettes. That's all I want," and she said, "Cigarettes?" and I said, "Uh huh." I just knew she was going to buy me a dress or something nice, but on my birthday, she gave me a pack of cigarettes and that's all I got. I pulled one out right there in front of her and lit that thing up and I liked to have strangled to death. She just didn't oppose me, and that took all the joy out of it, and I didn't smoke any more.

When I wanted to court, I came home one day and told Mama I

was in love with Puddin' and she said, "You in love with Puddin'?" I said I was in love with Puddin', and she said if I was in love with Puddin', let him come to the house. Don't be dodging, going around in the street, she would say. When she said that, I found out I wasn't in love with Puddin' anymore. Besides that, he was an ugly little old boy, and if he suited Mama, he didn't suit me anymore. Well, Puddin' went off to Chicago. He came back one time and he had gotten uglier and uglier. I looked at him and I thought, how in the world did I ever think I was in love with him. He had two teeth out in the front and he was about the ugliest man I ever saw.

Another time, I told Mama I wanted a pair of shoes, and you know, they weren't paying but about a dollar and a half for shoes back in the thirties. She told me she had just bought me a pair of shoes and how hard times were and where she had to put her money. I told her that I had just given her all the money I got for playing at the church. She said she couldn't get them. I told her that I would just kill myself, you know, commit suicide. She said, "Well, that's a pretty good idea. Mama's dead and John is dead and I just bought a new bottle of iodine. Tell you what, you drink half of that iodine and I'll drink the other half." I told her, "Mama, you must be crazy, telling me to drink that stuff." She just came back at me from all angles. She was a smart lady. She knew if she told me not to do something, I would try it.

When I got out of high school in 1932, Mama said I could go two years to teacher's training. The house was in bad shape and the roof wasn't just leaking, it would be raining inside. I said we needed to do something for the house, but she said we could tough it out for a little while longer. But I thought I would be out there at Miles College and people would be coming to the house and I would be ashamed, so I got a job down at Britlings. Sometimes, when you were waiting tables, people would leave a nickel tip, and when they would tip a dime, man that was high, boy.

I got married while I was at Britlings because I wanted a husband so Mama couldn't boss me anymore. Besides that, she was still getting my money like she always had. I told Robert we were going to be married secretly. Robert had a friend who worked at a newspaper and he met Robert coming out of the courthouse after buying our marriage license. Robert showed him the license and the man put it in the paper that same week. One of Mama's friends saw the announcement and came struggling up to our house and said to Mama, "You didn't tell me Lula and Robert was married!" Mama said we weren't married, and her friend said, "It's right here in the paper." When that happened, I told Robert I didn't want to get married then, and he said yes, we were. What he did was go down to Sears, buy a new bedroom suite and a radio, and had it delivered to our house. When Mama saw that radio and bedroom suite, she didn't want it to go back. In 1933, we got married. Me, mainly to get out from under Mama. What happened was, Robert just moved in with us. I found out pretty quick that Robert was just like Mama. He could get me to do just what he wanted me to do.

Mama didn't want me to marry Robert at first. She thought this other man would make a better husband, but then, she liked Robert fine. She turned around and loved him better than me. After she had had her second stroke, Mama was completely confined to bed. The last thing every night, I would go in to see what else I could do for her. One night, she told me to pull the chair up by the bed because she wanted to talk to me. She said, "I want you to promise me that no matter what Robert does, I want you to promise me that Robert will always have a home here until he dies." Well, I had put Robert's clothes out on the porch a lot of times when he didn't do like I wanted him to. I would put his clothes out on the porch and Mama would hippity-hop out there on that stick and say, "Bring 'em back in here. That gal ain't got no sense." I could never depend on Robert financially and hated to promise what she wanted. Mama wouldn't stop until I promised her that Robert could always stay. That was the last time I ever spoke to Mama. The next morning, she was lying in that bed, just staring up, and never did talk again.

Granddaddy Was a Doctor

Cullman Powell, Walker County

My doctor granddaddy had an office over there in Cordova. My mother would take us kids on a train over to visit my granddaddy of a morning, have dinner with my grandmother, and ride the train back in the afternoon while my daddy was working in the mine. It hardly didn't cost anything to ride the train to Cordova, and if we didn't have the money, my grandmother would pay for it. I really liked going over to my granddaddy's house because he had a car and he would let us go with him on calls. Mama would take the whole flock of us and there would be a lot of cousins, too. My grandmother would give us money to go to the picture show and usually she would hand us a nickel to buy some popcorn. I remember that these were silent movies then. There was no sound, but they had this playola piano run by electricity sitting up on the edge there. I don't remember if the playolas came with the film, but it seemed like when a chase was going on, the music would be faster.

My grandmother's house wasn't all that big, but it had a full basement. Grandmother had a vineyard out back and she made wine. One wall of that basement had concrete shelves and it was always full, completely full of quarts of wine with rubber stoppers on them. You could push off those rubber stoppers like you do champagne now. One rainy day, she sent all us kids down to the basement and told us to stay down there. They had a toilet in the basement and that's where I was introduced to an indoor john, because we surely didn't have one back home. We lived in a company house, and if you looked at that house today, you would say we were on poverty. Anyhow, that rainy day, we got to popping off those rubber stoppers on those wine jars, shooting them off like guns, you know, and Grandmother came down there and beat us half to death.

That wine had a lot of alcohol in it and you could get woozy on it. My granddaddy would even give it to us kids at mealtimes. They had a great big dining room table, and a huge lazy susan sat in the middle. All the way around that table was a place for you to sit and each place had a spot for our plate and one for your glass and one for your silverware. You just turned that lazy susan to get the food you wanted. Granddaddy always had a bucket of ice on the table and a jug of wine in it and he would always give us some. We got the ice from the ice house there and the iceman delivered ice every morning. We would follow that ice truck around and get the shavings off the truck to make snowballs, but it tasted just like burlap.

My granddaddy started out practicing medicine down at the edge of Tuscaloosa County, but he got in a little trouble and was sent to prison. Then, they had a flu epidemic around 1918 or 1919 and they pardoned him to come to Cordova to fight the flu. He contended all along that he was innocent. My mother never did talk about it, but my aunts told me that he was framed. What it was, they were building Lock 17 down on the Warrior River then and my granddaddy was the doctor for that government crew down there working. They would bring the payroll down there from Birmingham on one of those little putt-putt cars they had on the railroad. The little putt-putt was robbed and a couple of guards were killed. They said my granddaddy was involved and he went to prison for it. He never was locked up while he was down at that prison. He kept on practicing medicine in there and he came home every weekend. The only thing was that he wasn't making any money. Some of the old people around there gave him credit and said that if it hadn't been for my granddaddy doctoring, there wouldn't be any Cordova, wouldn't have been anybody left.

They had a big old mill there in Cordova, Indianhead Mills, and a lot of coal mines and there were a lot of people there. My granddaddy had a big practice there. Riding the train was the only way to get to Cordova because the cars—Model T's and Model A's—were just coming out, but the roads were so rough that in the winter you wouldn't dare get on the roads with a car.

A Nice Homeplace

Tera Averett, Coffee County

Mama was a charter member of the Mount Liberty Missionary Baptist Church. It was three miles away, but it was only a quarter of a mile from Grandma Waters's house. Church services were held only once a month, on the second Sunday. On Saturday before that Sunday, Papa hitched up old Laura and Dock to the two-horse wagon, loaded up Mama and all us children, and we drove off to Grandma Waters's house to spend the night. I can just smell that good old ham Grandma cooked for supper, served with big biscuits and juicy fig preserves. I can almost feel the pressure of the rough hand-hewn half-log bench against my knees as I sat there to eat. Ma Waters had a large room that sufficed for a living room, a den, and a bedroom. There were two smaller rooms with one bed in each, but that was not enough for so many of us to sleep. The rememdy was to put mattresses on the floor for the smaller children. These mattresses were made from cotton grown on the farm. The cover was quilts, hand-pieced and hand-quilted and padded with homegrown cotton that had been hand-carded. Of course, there were no store-bought blankets and we had never heard of a sleeping bag.

Uncle Walt, Mama's brother, and Aunt Cora, Papa's sister, lived next door to Ma and Pa Waters with their six children. We all raced back and forth from one house to the other as the notion struck us. Mama's sister, Aunt Ellen, was a young woman who must have had strong nerves and great self-control. She never scolded us or seemed like she wanted to scream when we played "hail over." She would keep her yard swept with her gallberry broom. The early pioneers started that practice every weekend to prevent fire from creeping up to the house. Our running feet left dents in the yard and erased the broom marks that let any passerby know that this was a well-respected family who maintained a nice homeplace.

Just Humming Along

E. L. *Lovelady*, Madison County

Daddy's brother lived up the road about a mile or two. We would go up there sometimes to spend the night. They had about a five- or six-room house that never got finished on the inside. The walls weren't sealed on most of the house, and overhead, there were a few planks and they weren't sealed, either. Of course, they had a fireplace—that's what everybody heated with—and there were cracks in the floor. You could look through those cracks and see chickens walking around under there, and pigs, and their old hound dog who would go under there for the shade. We would spend the night with them, me and my brothers, and their four or five kids plus the mamas and daddies.

My uncle was just about blind, had cataracts, and didn't work. When we all went to that old homemade eating table, the flies would be going in and out because they just had shutters at the windows, no windowpanes, and those shutters would stay open in the summertime. We would sit down at the table on benches and a few straight chairs and nail kegs. I would always eat out of a bucket lid because there weren't enough plates to go around. But the food was good and it didn't make any difference to me. Back then, when you broke some dishes, you just did without.

Now, one of these cousins, I guess he was about five or six years older than I was, he hummed in his sleep. When he went to sleep, he set in humming, and when he got his breath, he'd set in again. When we spent the night with them, it was real important to get to sleep before he did or you would have to listen to that humming all night. He wasn't a good singer, but he was a good hummer, and I found out later that he hummed in his sleep the rest of his life.

Important People

Railway engineer, Mobile, late 1930s
(S. Blake McNeely Collection, University of South
Alabama Archives, Mobile)

A Good Friend

Roger Marler, Lee County

I worked on that farm when I was coming on. Man, I hoed cotton and peanuts and corn, but I never did get to drive a tractor much. We had this old fellow, he was really part of the family, and he was a hired hand on the farm. He was the tallest man I had ever seen, had a long face, and always had on a pair of brogan shoes and overalls and kept that pipe in his mouth. For some reason, he always carried a pencil in his pocket even though he couldn't write a word. My mom finally taught him how to make his name—Willie.

He started working on the farm when I was just a little bitty boy, and he stayed with us for a long time, moving with us every time we moved. Daddy bought him a little trailer after awhile and Willie would fix his own food. About the only thing I ever saw him cook was sausage, and he would eat this with light bread and coffee. He loved coffee better than anything in the world. The old fellow didn't have any social life. Our family would go into town on a Saturday and there was a little seafood place there and he might drink a beer and eat some oysters, and that was about it for his social life.

Willie's wife had died pretty soon after they married, and he kind of took up with us and my daddy looked after him. He told me when he was younger, he made his living going around the country and sweeping off people's houses. When he was going around, he had a little Brownie camera and he would take pictures of people. He was one of the few people then who had a camera. I spent a lot of time listening to his stories.

We were already bad out in the country, but this one time, we moved really out in the sticks, way down below Andalusia somewhere. It was getting to be around Christmastime and we didn't have a Christmas tree. We had just about quit farming and things weren't too hot. My mother asked Willie and me to go out and get a Christmas tree and Willie and I started out. I tried to keep up with him going across those cold fields, but those old long legs were pumping and those brogans were popping that frozen dirt, and pretty soon, he stopped and said, "This is it." I looked at that tree he was pointing at and told him that this was a holly tree and not a

Christmas tree, but he cut it down anyhow and we started back toward the house. I fussed at him all the way back. We put that holly Christmas tree up and I didn't have anything to do with it at first, but it got to be pretty, and that's the only Christmas tree I can remember when I was growing up.

I got up old enough to leave home and Willie lived with my brother for awhile, then moved into a boardinghouse. They found him dead in that boardinghouse one day, but I remember him as the best friend I had when I was a boy.

Tall Tales and Commentary

Denson Franklin, Coosa County

I enjoyed my childhood in the little town of Goodwater, Alabama. We had a man in the town that everybody knew, but nobody knew well. His name was Haig Boyd and he had stories to tell. As a boy, I enjoyed his stories. My father had a country store and Haig Boyd would come and sit in a chair in front of the store and people would come and listen to his stories. I sat there on the pavement, and not only listened to his stories, but believed every one of them. One time, my father threatened to whip me if I didn't stop slipping out of the store to listen to Haig, because my father said that Haig was the greatest liar that ever existed in the world. His stories sounded so good to me that I still slipped out to listen.

Haig said that in World War I, he captured a whole regiment of Germans, but my daddy said he had never been to the seashore, much less overseas. Haig said he got tired of being in France and decided to go home. He went down to the troop ship, but it was loaded up full, so he just slipped down in the water and held on to the bottom of the ship all the way across the Atlantic. He said he got very tired before he got to New York, but he saw a lot of interesting things while he was down under the ship. He said that he saw a fish that nobody had ever seen as far as he knew. He said that the fish had a mouth like an RJR tobacco sack and when he would swallow those other fish he would hold up his fins and pull the strings together. He said this fish had one eye on a pivot and this eye would roll around all the way from the left to the right, and he said he was the only one that had ever seen this fish.

We started a picture show in Goodwater and Haig Boyd had invented an electric piano, a big box with batteries in it, and nobody knew what was inside. The first night the picture show opened, I went to the movie, and that piano was turned on and it just played one song, "Micky, Pretty Micky," and that's all it ever played during the whole evening. They soon got that piano out and moved it on.

Back in the thirties, after I had gone to college, my mother wrote and said that Haig had a strange bird in his backyard which he said had come from Brazil. He said that this rare bird was being flown from Brazil to New York, and when the plane got over Goodwater, the bird fell out and he captured it and put it in his garden. When I got home from college, I went down to see it, even though I knew it was a fake. Haig called that bird the Shy Gooster. There must have been a hundred people standing there looking at it the day I went to see it. I found out that Haig had taken an old rooster, pulled all the feathers out of it, painted it with oxblood shoe polish, then sewed some rattlesnake rattles on it with invisible thread. When the rooster walked, he rattled just like a snake. People enjoyed Haig's fake.

Haig's house was full of sabers and helmets from World War I and he had a story to tell about each one of them. He said he went to Florida one time on vacation and had a Negro man to go along to drive him. He said that he ran out of money and stopped by the first country church he came to and picked out the name of a famous evangelist. Back then, about 1920 or 1921, people didn't get to see the faces of famous preachers. He rang the church bell, and when the preacher came to the door, Haig said he was that famous preacher and he had been called to hold a revival in this church. He told the preacher that he would start the revival the next morning at ten o'clock. He said he preached for four days, and when he got enough money, he closed the revival and came back to Goodwater.

We had another famous man in Goodwater who was chief of police at one time, Uncle Jack Bice. He had whiskers way down on his chest and we thought he was a very wise man because he had the answer to everything. The train stopped twice a day there in town and everybody went down to the depot to see it. Stores would either close or just one clerk would be left on duty. You could see up to 150 people standing around there at the depot to see who would get off the train and who would get on. That was a big event in town. The trainmen would throw out the *Birmingham Age Herald* and Uncle Jack would pick one up and read the headlines to all of us as we stood around, and after he would read what the paper said, he would comment on it. About half of those 150 people would go over and listen to his comments.

He would take his knife and cut the string on that *Age Herald*, take the top copy, and read something like, "Floyd Collins dies in Kentucky cave," and then he would say something like, "I don't know anything about these spelunkers or whatever you call it, but those people don't have any business going in the ground and staying a long time. They ought to die. Every man deserves six feet down and he's a lot further down than that. Just let him stay down there." Another headline he read out one day was, "A-rabs revolt in Arabia." Uncle Jack said that what we ought to do was take a machine gun and go over there and mow all those A-rabs down and come on home for breakfast. He had simple solutions for all world problems.

Presidential Privilege

Jerry Oldshue, Tuscaloosa County

Dr. Frank Rose was president of The University of Alabama during the integration process. He knew the Kennedys and they were on the phone to each other regularly. Now, Dr. Rose was from Meridian, Mississippi, and was a preacher and dressed in dark blue suits, white shirts, and dark ties. Every day at noon, he would come out of the administration building, go home, eat lunch, then lay down to take an hour's nap. After the nap, he put his white shirt on and came back to his office. In those days, he had a butler.

One day while Dr. Rose was taking his nap, the phone rang. The butler answered the phone and it was the White House asking to talk to President Rose. The conversation went something like this. "This is the White House calling for President Rose." And, "Well, you can't talk to him right now, he's taking his nap. And, "Well, this is John Kennedy, president of the United States. I need to speak to President Rose." The butler replied, "I don't care who you are. Don't nobody wake up Dr. Rose in the middle of his nap." Kennedy got a great charge out of that.

Radiating Power

C. J. Coley, Tallapoosa County

Benjamin Russell was born down on the Tallapoosa River, but later his family moved into town and his father started a little store. Russell went to the University of Virginia and graduated in law. He came to Birmingham and established a law practice, but he didn't stay there but six months. He moved to Alexander City and started a bank, but two years later, he began to think about a textile factory. He bought a little mill over in Georgia, moved it to Alexander City, and set it up in 1902. He began to build on that little factory. I believe Benjamin Russell was the smartest man I ever knew. He had a photographic mind and was a tireless worker. He brought the telephone system to town, bought up a lot of land, and established a bakery and creamery. He hardly ever fired anybody, working on the basis of finding the employee's problem and correcting it.

When Mr. Russell died, I told his son, Tom, that I had written a letter to him about his daddy's passing. I told Tom in that letter that I could have killed Benjamin Russell many times but that this letter was wet with tears when I had finished. Russell was that kind of man. He radiated power and his voice carried conviction and purpose.

Another hero of mine was Dr. George Hutcheson Denny, the former president of The University of Alabama. Back in the depression, Dr. Denny felt the need for a new library and saw no reason why he didn't get some of that federal money being spread around. He asked his friend, Senator Claude Pepper, to get him an appointment with President Roosevelt. Senator Pepper accompanied Dr. Denny into the president's office and Dr. Denny launched into a plea for funds for his new library. The president replied that there was no money except for emergencies like a cyclone, flood, or fire. Dr. Denny exclaimed, "That is my case, Mr. President. Fire! Fire!" The president replied that he had heard nothing about a fire at The University of Alabama. Dr. Denny shot back, "The Yankees burned our library in 1865." The president roared with laughter . . . and Dr. Denny got his library.

Speaking about Fess

J. L. Lowe, Jefferson County

Fess Whatley was a great influence in my life. He is not a household name now, but back in the twenties and thirties, he was known as a maker of musicians, not only in Birmingham, but all over the country. "Fess" was short for professor and nobody else has that name around here. Musicians from coast to coast recognized that name. You could walk into any black band in the country and say you studied with Fess Whatley—didn't even have to audition—and you had a job. He was not a person who was identified with improvisation in music. He taught his students to play the music just how it was written.

He was never the bandmaster in the Industrial High School as far as contract was concerned but was hired to be a printing instructor. Nobody was hired to teach music and he took the slot as printing instructor to fulfill the board of education requirements for an industrial school. I was one of his students. He would have me to come down to the printing shop, and there would be a lot of girls down there, and sometimes it would be embarrassing. His manner of teaching was crude, not polished at all, and he would hit you any time. That was his technique, and if you made a mistake on the horn, he would hit you. I learned Fess's way of doing things and got to be a disciplined musician. I was under his influence all during high school before entering Alabama State. Fess saw that I was studious and he got me to be his proofreader for printing jobs. All his important printing jobs, like for the Masons and Elks, would have to be reviewed by me before he would let them go.

When I came back to Birmingham in the thirties, Fess wanted me to play a saxophone in his big band, but I didn't have a saxophone. Fess said he would get one for me, and when it came to uniforms, the band was wearing tuxedos. Fess gave me one of his tuxedos and my mother altered it for me. I played for him when I got back from the army, too. I think Fess Whatley had the best band in the state during the twenties, thirties, and forties. A lot of the members of the band were playing with bands up north, playing with Louis Armstrong, Duke Ellington, Cab Calloway, Claude Hopkins, and they were coming in and out of Birmingham. They played with Fess when they came back, because Fess was the master. I played for Fess longer than anybody, eight years, before I went in service during the Second World War.

During Fess's last years, he left his scrapbook with me and told me that on his death, he wanted me to finish it. Out of that came my desire to establish a jazz hall of fame here in Birmingham. He was somebody special in my life.

Taps

Oak Hill Cemetery, Talladega, 1992 (Michael Thomason photo)

Jemison family cemetery, Sunnyside plantation, near Talladega, 1992 (Michael Thomason photo)

But for the Grace

Houston Cole, DeKalb County

Two weeks before I would have to register for the draft back in 1918, it happened that the war was over and they didn't take me. But a couple of my friends were just a few weeks older and they had to register and go into the army. They were just kids, never been any farther away from home than the barn, and they went to New York and to France and two of them were killed over there. One I remember especially, name of Herbert Hill, because Herbert saved my life one time when I was four years old. Pulled me out of the creek when I was about to drown. He was the Methodist preacher's son.

They brought Grady Cannon back and he's buried out there at Mount Vernon, and the other one is buried over there in Flanders. I remember when they brought Grady back. I went to the funeral there at Mount Vernon. He was supposed to get in at one o'clock, but he didn't arrive until three o'clock and the auditorium was crowded to capacity. They brought him in and it was the saddest thing you ever saw. When the service was over, we walked about a block where they were going to bury him in that little country cemetery. And as I was standing there and they were letting him down into that hole, I said to myself, "There but for the grace of God, that could have been me." Old Grady Cannon.

The Luxury Tax

Joy Buskens, Baldwin County

My grandmother told me about the 1906 hurricane. Her daddy had a boat, the *Mary Gray*, and they would get what they called seed oysters to plant. They would go over to Dauphin Island to Cedar Point to get them. He had gone over there to get a load of seed oysters and this big storm came up and he spent the night with relatives. This storm came in, and the next morning, the boat was gone. His brother had spent the whole summer building a boat with his two boys and they had decided to stay on the boat. The boat disappeared and they never found my great uncle or either of the two little boys.

Back in the thirties when my grandmother was three days old, her mother died, and her father put her body on a sailboat and was going to take her to Mobile where her family lived. They were Smiths and they were going to meet him at the dock. He got started across the bay and his mast on the boat broke. He had to come back, unload the body, and start again. When they got to Mobile, they transported her body to the Magnolia graveyard. A little later, I got to see her grave. Back then, they decorated graves with seashells. You can't find seashells on the beach anymore.

When people died in my grandmother's day, they laid them out on what they called cooling boards after the body was prepared. The coffins were handmade and my grandfather paid eighty dollars for my grandmother's coffin. This was the first store-bought coffin in the community. My grandfather was upset because he had to pay a luxury tax on it.

Decoration Day

Charlie Hill, Walker County

Every year in the springtime, we had Decoration Day at the cemetery, a big thing in the community, a kind of Memorial Day. There was no regular maintenance at these cemeteries and grass and weeds would grow up during the year. Everybody would come and clean the graves, get the grass out, and cut bushes and this sort of thing. There were places where roads had been cut through the sides of hills and mountains and there would be white sandstone there. When the sand was dug out, it would be just as white as the sand at the beach and people would dig that sand out of the sandstone, pulverize it, and put it on the graves. All the graves on that Sunday would be covered with this white sand.

Everybody in the community did this thing, and the graves would be just like if you went down to the beach and got this white sand.

The women made these paper flowers to go on the graves, made them out of crepe paper, and they would start two or three months in advance making flowers. Each of the ladies would take great pride in the flowers and everybody would stroll through the entire cemetery, visiting every grave, admiring the flowers. We had dinner on the ground and preaching and singing, and the first time I ever saw my father singing was at Decoration Day.

All the ladies bought a new dress and a hat, even though they never wore a hat except maybe a sunbonnet. They would dress up like Easter. The big thing after lunch was the singing. Decoration Day was . . . THE . . . big . . . day.

A New White Shirt

Bud Dean, Elmore County

We walked to church, but a lot of people went in wagons with straight-back chairs in there, and you know what a straight-back chair is. The churches then were fundamental, and now, you know, they have gone citified and that speaks for itself. When folks would die, my daddy would help lay them out at home. When old man Mr. Bloof Hornsby died in '31, that was the first dead man I ever saw. I was six years old. Mr. Bloof had seven sons and they were hardworking, good people, the Hornsbys. He was the patriarch of what became a large clan, and when he died, my daddy helped lay him out on the dining room table. They would lay them out on the dining room table and sort of clean them to start with, and then they would dress them.

My dad said when they went to put a shirt on Mr. Bloof laying there, Miss Bessie Hornsby—that was Mr. Bloof's daughter-in-law—she said, "Oh, that shirt won't do." It was white and clean, but it was old. Some of them thought that it would do for an old, old man, so it wouldn't matter that much. Miss Bessie was pretty emotional about it because the old man died at her and her husband's house.

They did buy a store-bought casket. I never laid anybody out but I've been called out a lot at night for death and sickness. Back then, there wasn't such a thing as leaving a corpse at a funeral home. Unheard of, almost sacrilegious. They always brought them home and people sat up, and that almost belongs in the archives now.

A Proper Burial

Mary Frances Tipton, Dallas County

We had a dog named Calvin in the house when I was a girl, a dachshund, not a big dog, but extremely tough on other animals. Now, he liked people, but he just didn't like other animals, and it didn't make any difference what the species. He would see a cat, a squirrel, a chicken, a snake, or even another dog and he would go into a frenzy and attack without fear or reason. It was such an issue that we kept him in the house, and when we did go out for a walk, some member of the family kept him on a stout rope so he couldn't get away. Now, a dachshund is a small dog, but he would jump on a German shepherd without any fear at all. Everybody in the family loved that dog and he stayed with us for a long time.

After I left home, I was up at the University of Montevallo and got a call one day from one of my aunts who lived in the house with my father. She was utterly distraught. She said, "Calvin is sick, Mary Frances, and I don't know what we're going to do. We've had him at the vet's and he said that there was nothing more he could do. You've got to come home right now." I was very upset about Calvin because we all loved him and I jumped in my car and headed for Selma lickety-split.

Somewhere on the road, my car started to hiccup and founder and I made it to one of those little crossroad stores with the gas pumps and all. Now, I knew that those fellows at this little station wouldn't be impressed if I told them that I was hurrying home to see about my dog, so I told them that they had to help me because I was going home to see my sick daddy. There's not a southern man anywhere who could refuse a young lady rushing home to see about a sick daddy, so they got the car going enough to get me to Selma. I rushed in the house, and there was Calvin lying there on the floor and I could tell right away he was in bad shape.

My two aunts and my daddy were grieving and I knew something had to be done. "We're going to take him to Auburn," I said. "They've got a vet school down there, and if anybody can help him, they can." So, we took poor Calvin down to Auburn and left him to the tender mercies of the vet school, and waited. A couple of days later, we got a call, and were informed that Calvin had gone on to the great barnyard in the sky. "We can dispose of him here," the man said. I was horrified and told him that we would come and pick him up. We drove down to Auburn and the man handed Calvin to me, all wrapped up in a plastic bag.

We had a good-sized farm out in the country and one of my aunts called the black man who ran the place and told him to build a wooden box to bury Calvin in and to dig a neat hole for the box. We got back to Selma and drove out to the place for the funeral. The man out there ushered us to the spot where Calvin was to be interred, and we saw a huge hole in the ground, meticulously faced with brick all around. We could have buried a good-sized farm tractor down there.

"Okay," my aunt said, "where's the casket?" Well, the man had forgotten to make the casket and my aunt was furious. Out of the corner of my eye, I could see a large group of children watching us, but they were respectful and didn't intrude. With no casket, we looked around for something to put him in and finally found a brand new zinc garbage can. "That will do," my aunt said, and we placed Calvin carefully in the can. "Now, I want his little face to be looking toward the house," she told the farm manager. How he knew where Calvin's face was, swathed as he was in the plastic packaging, I'll never know, but we made our way back to the huge hole in the ground.

As we placed the can in the hole, the children gathered around, and when the can was in place, everybody just stood there, and I knew that the assemblage was waiting for somebody to say something. My aunt must have sensed the same thing, because she cast her eyes toward the sky and said, "Calvin was a good dog. We all loved him and we will miss him very much." We turned and walked away, heartbroken for our lost friend. Satisfied that we were really leaving, the man began throwing dirt on Calvin.